SHIRIN DEVRIM was born in 1926 in Istanbul, Turkey, of an illustrious family. Her early education was in Berlin and Baghdad. Later she attended the American Girls College in Istanbul, Barnard College in New York, and graduated from the Yale Drama School. She became one of the leading actresses and directors of the Turkish theatre and has also performed widely in the US. She was a professor of drama at Stanford University, Carnegie-Mellon and the University of Wisconsin. She now lives with her husband Robert Trainer in Princeton and New York City. *A Turkish Tapestry* is her first book.

A TURKISH
TAPESTRY

SHIRIN DEVRIM

QUARTET BOOKS

First published in paperback by Quartet Books in 1996

A member of the Namara Group
27 Goodge Street, London W1P 2LD

First published by Quartet Books in 1994

A catalogue record for this book is available from the British Library

ISBN 0 7043 8035 8

Photypeset by Intype, London
Printed and bound in Great Britain by BPC Paperbacks Ltd

Contents

One must still have chaos in oneself to be able to give birth to a dancing star.

Nietzsche, *Thus Spoke Zarathustra*

To my husband Robert Trainer without whose assistance, forbearance and support I never could have written this book.

Glossary

Abayeh	Ankle-length cape-like covering with hood
Abla	Older sister
Ağabey	Older brother
Baklava	A sweet Turkish dessert prepared with crisp dough and walnuts
Besleme	Adopted girl brought up in the household
Bey	The way a gentleman is addressed, like the words 'Sir' or 'Mister'
Börek	Crisp dough filled with feta cheese or ground meat
Brevet Superior	High-school degree
Çarşaf	A full-length black garment with a scarf tightly covering hair and forehead and a separate veil covering the lower part of the face so that only eyes and nose are visible
Chevalière	Ring worn on the little finger
Defterdar	Ottoman fiscal authority, a provincial minister of finance, second only to the governor in rank
Dolma	Vine leaves or vegetables stuffed with rice, raisins and pine nuts
Dondurma	Ice-cream
Emir	Arabic for 'prince', also spelled 'Amir'
Fakir	Beggar
Ferman	An imperial decree
Fez	Dark red, bucket-like, brimless hat for men, with a black tassel
Grand Vizier	Prime minister appointed by the Ottoman sultans, highest administrator of the empire
Halvah	A sweet Turkish dessert

Hamam	A Turkish bath
Hanım	The way a lady is addressed, like the word 'madam'
Harem	Women's and children's quarters
Hoja	Teacher of the Qur'an, the Islamic holy book
Houri	An angel
Imam	Muslim prayer leader
Kabul	Open house
Kadı	Muslim judge
Kalfa	Senior or elderly servant
Kalpak	Cossack hat
Kaymak	Clotted cream
Kayık	A double-ended rowing boat
Kefflyeh	Arab man's headdress
Köfte	Turkish meatballs
Mehmetcik	Turkish foot-soldier
Merhaba	Hail! Greetings!
Meze	Turkish hors d'oeuvres
Millet	Ethnic or religious group in the Ottoman Empire
Mousakka	Eggplant dish with ground beef and tomatoes
Pasha or Paşa	Title of a general or bestowed on a high-ranking civilian by the Ottoman sultans
Peçe	Veil worn under the *abayeh*, covering the face
Pera	A main section of Istanbul, now called Beyoğlu
Rakı	Distilled anise-flavoured alcholic drink called ouzo by the Greeks and arak by the Arabs
Ramadan	The ninth month of the Muslim year, when the faithful fast from sunrise to sunset
Sancak	Administrative division of the Ottoman Empire, smaller than a province
Selamlık	Men's quarters and reception rooms
Schwerster	German for 'nurse'
Şalvar	Loose, baggy pantaloons worn by peasants
Sharia	Islamic law
Şeker Bayram	Muslim holiday which follows Ramadan
Sherif	Title given to descendants of the Prophet
Şiş kebab	Cubes of lamb grilled on a skewer
Sitti	Arabic for 'My lady'
Souk	Arab bazaar

Taka	Small one-cylinder wooden boat used for freight
Tekke	The meeting place of a religious sect
Uzun	Turkish for 'tall'
Yalı	A wooden Turkish house directly on the Bosphorous

Note:

In Turkish the letter

C sound like J, as in John

Ç sounds like Ch, as in church

Ş sounds like Sh, as in ship

Ü sounds like the French Tu

In most instances I have used the Turkish 'Ş', but in some, like Shirin, Shakir, Sherif and Pasha and Sharia, I have used the English 'Sh'

Foreword

The stories in this book, including large portions of Turkish and Middle Eastern history as it is intermingled with my family history, come out of tales that I was either told or overheard as a young child. Rather than try to overlay them with a later acquired factual authenticity, I have chosen to reproduce them as they came down to me, with all of their possible distortions or tonal inconsistencies, to keep, as it were, the tone of the memory rather than that of an external reality. Therefore I ask the reader please to forgive any factual errors incurred in such telling and to look, for the straight history, to other sources.

A great deal of the material came from my mother's diaries and interviews and from my cousins Fureya Koral and Erdem Erner, to whom I am beholden.

My gratitude to Professors Talat Halman, Şükrü Hanıoğlu, Halit Inalcık, Bernard Lewis, and to Mr Cecil Hourani for their advice and encouragement, and my thanks to Erika Duncan and her workshop for their comments and suggestions, and to Mairi MacInnes, Doris Kuller and Alev Courtier for their help.

The Shakir Pasha Family

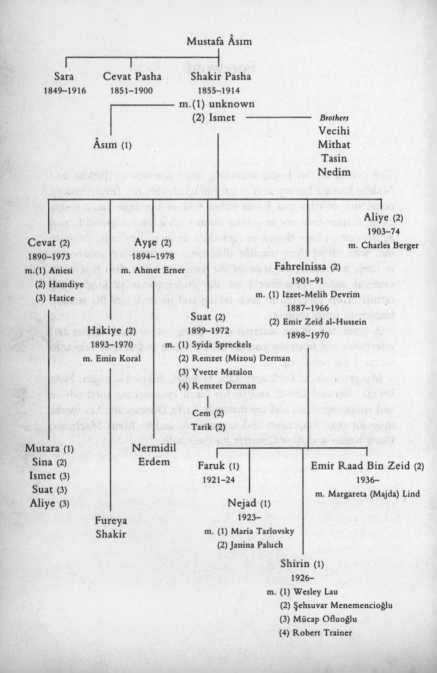

Prologue

A Night in Vienna – 1985

It was past midnight, and the whole household was asleep. I was sitting at the marquetry desk writing New Year's cards in the upstairs salon of the 103-room Italian High Renaissance palace, now the Turkish Embassy in Vienna, when I heard a loud moan coming from the guest room where my mother lay very ill.

When I ran to open the door, I was stunned to see her seated in an armchair opposite a five-foot-high unfinished portrait of my cousin Erdem. She was shivering, groaning, and painting. My first impulse was to help her back to bed where she belonged. However, as I knew that nothing short of total exhaustion could deter her from painting once she had started, I went instead to the gold and white lacquered armoire and removed her ankle-length mink coat. Slipping it over her, I carefully rolled up the wide cuffs so that they would not dip into the mounds of paint on her palette. For added protection, I threw a blanket over her knees.

'Thank you, Shirin, thank you. I am glad you came. Your pink presence will help me live through the night,' she said tenderly, if a bit dramatically, surveying me in my pink robe and slippers.

As Mother suffered from cataracts, she was straining to see the colours in the dimly lit room. 'Which is black and which is navy?' she asked. Since she had removed her hearing aid, I had to make myself understood by gesturing. Noticing her big black alligator bag on the floor next to her bed, I pointed first at the bag, then at the mound of black paint on her palette. She picked up a clean, thin-bristled brush and dipped it in the black paint.

'*Il faut aller contre le mal avec le mal*,' she muttered, as if to explain her torment, and lurched forward with a groan to add a touch of black to the pupil of Erdem's eye.

My favourite cousin, Erdem, was the Turkish ambassador to

Austria, and Mother and I had come to visit over the holidays from our respective homes – she from Amman, Jordan, with my half-brother Prince Raad and his family, and I from my home in New York City with my husband, Robert Trainer. The visit was to have been a family reunion in this historic city that our Ottoman forebears had twice surrounded but never captured. Unfortunately, the journey had been too much for my eighty-four-year-old mother, who, upon her arrival, had fallen very ill with a severe lung embolism.

On Christmas Day, so as not to disappoint her Episcopalian son-in-law, Bob, she had risen from her bed with great effort and put on the long-skirted brocade evening suit her dressmaker in Amman had made especially for her Vienna visit, and all the jewels she had brought with her. To the 12-carat diamond ring (which to me has always looked like an automobile headlight) and the enormous emerald cabochon which she never took off, she had added diamond, gold and pearl chains and ropes and bracelets. From her ears hung long pearl earrings, and she had decorated her lapel with a pearl pin in the shape of a cluster of grapes with a diamond stem. (That pin had been her gift to me on my eighteenth birthday, but at her request I had returned it to her a few years before. This was not unusual in our family, where jewels constantly made the rounds.) The maid had curled her hair, and to cover her pale, sickly complexion she had used quantities of foundation, powder and rouge; but the heavy make-up lay on her skin like a mask.

In spite of the fatigue from the long preparation, she managed to preside at the table gracefully and to stay up until the last package under the tree had been opened.

Erdem's attractive wife, Gökçen, had trimmed a Christmas tree for the first time in her life and, in Bob's honour, had asked the Turkish chef to prepare a traditional turkey dinner with all the trimmings, as well as a plum pudding (which he had badly botched: he would much rather have prepared *baklava*). Bob appreciated the efforts of this Muslim family and staff to create a real Christmas for him. When he thanked Gökçen and complimented her on the tree, she replied, 'Oh, it was so much fun to do. I wish we had Christmas, too. All those colourful packages and gifts. How festive it is! We are happy that, thanks to you, we had occasion to celebrate.'

However, the Christmas effort had been too much for Mother, and she once more collapsed into bed, where she was ordered to remain by the attentive, hand-kissing Viennese doctor. Her evening gown and furs hung in the armoire, unused.

After Christmas my brother, his family and my husband had gone to Lech to ski and to meet His Royal Highness Prince Hassan, the crown prince of Jordan, while I had remained in Vienna to tend to my mother. I was hoping to go to Lech myself for New Year's Eve, if Mother was well enough.

'Here,' Mother said abruptly, handing me a thick brush. 'Please help me. Fill in the background with vermilion red. If I try, it will exhaust me, and I so want to finish the portrait tonight.'

To please her, as I have tried to do all my life, I pulled up a stool and started to cover the white canvas with thick strokes of red paint. For several hours we sat side by side painting, my enfeebled mother's groans breaking the silence. As I watched her struggling to paint, I knew this was her way of enduring the agony of this long, cold, painful night in Vienna, and my heart filled with admiration for her determination and with compassion for her suffering; yet at the same time I felt irritated and frustrated.

'Why does she have to paint now? Why doesn't she just stay in bed?' I thought. 'She is doing everything to worsen her condition. All of us have tended to her, hovering constantly around her bed. Erdem and Gökçen have hardly left the embassy. I have seen to it that the doctor calls on her every day. The staff has stood to attention. She could at least do her share.'

However, as there was no way to dissuade her without an argument, I continued to paint, my strokes getting quicker and choppier as I worked my frustration into the canvas. Then, as the early morning light slipped into the room, suddenly the whole scene struck me as absurd. I began to giggle nervously, then to laugh uncontrollably. After a few moments, my mink-clad mother noticed and began to laugh also.

'You are laughing at us, and you are right,' she declared. 'We are a sight!'

Finally exhausted, her face ashen, she sat back, unthinkingly dropping her paintbrush on the oriental rug. 'I cannot paint any more. Help me. But first clean the brushes – I don't want them to dry. I'll sleep a little and continue later.'

In the bathroom, I poured turpentine over the bristles and watched the red paint run like blood down the white marble basin. That done, I helped Mother into the oversized Empire bed. She fell back on the pillows, gasping for air. Her face, ravaged by age and twisted with pain, was like a magnificent rock against which oceans had beaten for aeons. It still held traces of her past beauty and reflected her strength of character.

'Allah,' I thought, 'please, please don't make her suffer. If you are going to take her, do it gently. Please, Allah, please! She has had her share of suffering, spare her more.'

Choking back my tears, I covered her shivering body with all the blankets and quilts at hand, kissed her burning cheek, and left. As I crossed the hall on the way to my room, I saw the butler setting the breakfast table in the upstairs dining room. While undressing, I thought to myself, 'How will I cope if she leaves me? How will I live in a world without her?'

Once in my cold bed, I wrapped myself around my pillow for warmth and comfort and dozed off. I dreamed of Mother, young and beautiful, sitting with her three sisters, my 'other mothers', by the jasmine bushes in the garden of the house on the island of Büyükada.

Introduction

Ancestors

This is the story of my family during the last years of the crumbling 500-year-old Ottoman Empire and their tumultuous lives in the seventy years of the new Turkey which rose like a phoenix from its ashes. During the Empire my ancestors were scholars, soldiers and administrators. My parents' and my generations were artistic – writers, painters, etchers, musicians, ceramists and actors.

We were Muslim Turks, members of the privileged class of a privileged city, Istanbul, which until 1923 was the capital of empires. In Istanbul, the only city in the world which straddles two continents, the extraordinary complexity of the past can be seen everywhere. It is a wondrous combination of ancient history, art and architecture and a mixture of East and West. Byzantine monuments, Ottoman palaces, towers, domes, minarets, church steeples, old wooden houses, modern apartments, all buildings speak of this or that part of history.

The record first establishes my mother's family, the Shakirs, in the early part of the eleventh century, in the little town of Elmalı, near Antalya on the Mediterranean Sea, renowned for its scenic beauty, its Seljuk monuments and its Graeco-Roman ruins. Later, according to family lore, they travelled by oxcart to the village of Kabaağaç (hard tree) in central Anatolia, where they decided to settle. The local population urged them to move on. 'This land is rocky, impossible to farm. You'll be better off further on,' they advised. And my ancestors replied, 'Even if we have to spend a dozen oxen to make this land tillable, this is where we are staying.' Thus they settled in Kabaağaç and farmed the land. To this day, when a member of the family is being strong-willed or stubborn, the others say, 'Remember the dozen oxen. Nothing will deter him!'

Later, the Kabaağaçlı clan, as they were by then called, moved to the nearby town of Afyon Karahisar, where over several centuries they founded and ran *medresas* (theological schools). Many of them were scholars and teachers. One was a mystic who spent years in his cell-like room. After that, no family history has come down to me until the nineteenth century when my great-great-grandfather decided there had been too many scholars in the family and that it was time for a change. Knowing his wife would disapprove, he hid his son Âsım in a cart covered with vegetables, took him to Istanbul, the capital city, and enrolled him in military school.

After graduating from the Staff College, my great-grandfather Âsım rose to the rank of colonel and was appointed to the Military Council, a prestigious advisory body to the sultan and the grand vizier. I remember a portrait of him in uniform wearing his dark red *fez*, a fair man with a trim blond moustache and tranquil, liquid eyes. While on duty in Damascus, he married the homely daughter of the Hattatzades, a prominent Syrian family of calligraphers, and had two children, Sara in 1849 and Cevat in 1851. Later, in 1855, when Âsım was stationed in Bursa, the first capital of the Ottoman Turks, my grandfather Shakir was born.

In Bursa, my great-grandmother developed tuberculosis and became bedridden. One day the invalid, from a seat on her balcony, saw her husband in the courtyard kissing and fondling a *besleme* girl (a dependant brought up in the household). Although she immediately retired discreetly, Âsım had glimpsed her. Seized with remorse and guilt, he leapt on his horse and went galloping off so hard that he developed a perforated hernia; peritonitis set in, and he quickly died. His sickly wife died three days later.

Left behind were three orphans, thirteen-year-old Sara and her two brothers, Cevat and Shakir, aged eleven and eight, respectively. As young as she was, Sara had the wit, determination and courage to obtain permission to go to Istanbul (at that time, one needed a form of visa in order to enter the sultan's city) where she placed herself and her charges under the protection of Âsım's old friend Atifzade Hüsamettin Effendi, who later became Sheikh-ul-Islam (head of the Ottoman religious and judiciary establishment). This tremendously powerful man took Sara and the brothers under his wing. Eventually, he married Sara off to a wealthy landowner who was so fat he had to make his way about in a wheelchair; when he died, they say, she was still a virgin. The two boys were enrolled in military school, and both graduated from the Staff College with honours.

After graduating at the astoundingly young age of twenty, first in his class, Great-Uncle Cevat married the daughter of a very wealthy *pasha* and moved in with his wife. It was customary for bridegrooms to live with their fathers-in-law until they could afford to set up their own households. When presently Cevat was posted to Constanza in Romania, his spoiled young wife chose to stay with her prominent father in the capital instead of following her husband to an obscure town in the Balkans; they were divorced shortly afterward.

Shakir, on the other hand, married a lady of Hungarian origin, about whom no one in the family seems to know anything. She died shortly after giving Shakir a son, named Âsım after his grandfather.

When war with Russia broke out in 1877 and Russian troops poured into Bulgaria, Cevat was sent to the front and promoted to the rank of major. In 1878 he came to the sultan's attention when he wrote a comprehensive history of the Ottoman Empire (*Ma'lumat al-Kafiye fi mamalik al-Osmaniye*). A year later he became a colonel while serving as a delegate at the Congress of Berlin, convened to draw up a peace treaty. There he met the reigning Kaiser's grandson, then a young man of twenty, who later became Kaiser Wilhelm II.

In 1881 Cevat wrote *The Military History of the Ottoman Empire*, which was translated into French and published in Paris the following year. The history included the story of the Janissaries from their creation to their suppression. Subsequently Cevat served at the embassy in Çetine, the capital of Montenegro, while my grandfather Shakir was appointed military attaché in Rome and Montenegro and, like his brother, was made a member of the Military Council.

In 1889, both Cevat and Shakir were posted to Crete, the former as acting military governor and commandant with absolute power, and the latter, by then a brigadier-general, as Cevat's aide-de-camp and commandant of Resmo (now called Rethymnon). The island was a hotbed of unrest, troubled by constant feuding between the Greek and Turkish populations.

In Crete, Shakir married my grandmother, Ismet. My grandfather had caught sight of her while presenting diplomas to the graduates at her school, for she was a remarkably pretty girl with wavy blonde hair to her waist, a skin so fair it seemed translucent, and honey-coloured eyes. On Shakir's behalf, my ubiquitous Great-Aunt Sara sought out Ismet's family, islanders of humble origin. Grandmother was only fourteen when she was married and in 1890, in Crete, gave birth to her first child, whom they named Cevat after his illustrious uncle.

As acting governor of Crete, Cevat Pasha was fair and just and succeeded temporarily in calming the feuding factions. His successful handling of the situation won him promotion to field marshal at the age of thirty-seven. On his return to Istanbul in 1891, he was amazed when his ship entered the harbour to be met by a twenty-one-gun salute and a messenger who arrived by launch bearing a *ferman* (imperial decree) from the sultan that appointed him grand vizier.

My grandmother loved to tell the story of how, a few days after Cevat became grand vizier, his divorced wife was held up by a procession of horses and carriages while walking across the Galata Bridge over the Golden Horn. She asked who the dignitary was. 'It's Cevat Pasha, the new grand vizier,' she was told. 'And,' said Grandmother with satisfaction, 'she was so piqued that she fainted.'

Cevat had become the most important administrator in the empire at the age of forty. His rapid rise to power indicates how easy it was for an unknown to come up through the ranks in the Ottoman administration, provided that he had intelligence, ability, talent and dedication.

Ogilier de Busbecq, the Holy Roman Empire's ambassador to Istanbul in the mid-sixteenth century, in his letters to his superior at the court of Emperor Charles V in Vienna, expressed his admiration of the Ottoman system of merit: 'At the Sultan's court there is not a single man who does not owe his position to his valour and merit,' he wrote. 'It is by merit that men rise in the service . . . This is the reason that they are so successful in their undertakings . . . These are not our ideas, with us there is no opening left for merit; birth is the standard for everything.'

The grand vizier was the sultan's chief minister and head of the administrative service. He appointed men to major posts in the army and the central and provincial administrations, as well as to the Interior and Finance ministries.

During his ministry, Cevat appointed his brother Shakir ambassador to Greece. One of the earliest memories of my Uncle Cevat, Shakir's second son, was of playing hide-and-seek in the Acropolis with his child mother.

Meanwhile Sara, Cevat's indefatigable elder sister, busied herself finding him a new wife. She bought a beautiful Circassian slave, trained her in Ottoman protocol and manners, had her take French and piano lessons, taught her how to dress, and presented the finished product to her brother.

The Circassians, a Muslim tribe from the Caucasus, had been invited by the sultan to settle in eastern Anatolia, for they were excellent soldiers and farmers and their women were highly prized for their beauty. The Circassians raised children for the slave trade and sold the girls in the Istanbul market. Many Circassian girls of noble birth and wealthy families voluntarily auctioned themselves into Ottoman slavery in order to enter the imperial palace or some princely house.

I have in my possession a photograph of my Circassian great-aunt and my grandmother, both young, willowy women wearing court dresses of pale, heavy satin, close-waisted and ankle-length, draped over bosom and hips. Both wear ropes of pearls and on their heads the charming, cushiony little silk toques called *hotoz*. My grandmother, an ostrich-feather fan in her hand, smiles, aware of her loveliness; the other, taller and even more beautiful, looks abashed.

As grand vizier, Cevat Pasha lived in a magnificent town house, now a school in Nişantaş, filled with exquisite treasures. Among them was a large Aubusson tapestry given him by Edmond de Rothschild on the occasion of Herzl's visit to the sultan to try to purchase Palestine, then an Ottoman *sancak* (smaller than a province), as a Jewish homeland. In addition there were a set of six screens sent by the Japanese emperor and two huge Ming vases, a gift of the emperor of China. The house also contained two large, throne-like, gilded armchairs made in Paris especially for the Ottoman court and an immense crystal chandelier.

Cevat Pasha and my grandfather were both Renaissance men – skilled militarists, authors and historians with a command of six languages, Turkish, Arabic, Persian, Greek, Italian and French, and both amateur photographers with their own darkrooms. In 1903 Shakir won second prize in a photography contest in Paris. Cevat assembled one of the largest private libraries in Turkey. (Its 5000 volumes were later donated to the Istanbul Archaeological Museum.) Shakir, interested in the exquisite tiles and ceramics of the sixteenth century, worked in clay and experimented with different methods of glazing pottery. He also kept a greenhouse where he raised orchids and experimented with cross-pollination.

In time, Sultan Abdulhamid grew to resent Cevat's policy of building up the *Porte* (Government) at the expense of the Palace;

neither could he tolerate Cevat's sharp criticism of areas of misman-agement in the empire. Twice Cevat tried to resign his office. At last, in early 1895, Abdulhamid accepted his resignation and, just to show who was in charge, put Cevat under house arrest. Two years later, in 1897, when civil war erupted in Crete, he once more sent Cevat to the island as commandant. This time, the Concert of Europe intervened; both Greek and Turkish troops were withdrawn, and Crete became semi-autonomous.

In 1898, Kaiser Wilhelm II made his second visit to Turkey to negotiate a new stretch of the German-built railway from Konya in central Anatolia to Baghdad. On his first visit, in 1889, a year after his accession, the kaiser had renewed his acquaintance with Cevat, begun twelve years earlier at the Congress of Berlin. When he requested Cevat's services this time as a liaison officer, however, the sultan, ostensibly acquiescing but inwardly suspicious of the request, sent Cevat from Crete to Beirut to prepare for the royal tour. Then, just before the kaiser reached Beirut, he sent Cevat ahead to Damas-cus, then to Jerusalem, and then to the kaiser's next destination, repeating this procedure again and again. Thus the sultan made sure that Cevat and the kaiser never met. The very thought that a Turkish subject should make a private friend of a foreigner, particularly one as important as the kaiser, excited all of Abdulhamid's fears of betrayal. The sultan's animosity was entirely impersonal. He was a man who wore a suit of mail under his clothes, installed steel doors throughout his palace at Yildiz, hung cages of parrots everywhere because they shrieked at strangers, and constructed miles of tunnels and secret passages as bolt-holes in the event of a surprise attack. He was so paranoid that he had mirrors installed over his desks so that he could always see behind him.

When at last the kaiser's visit was over, Cevat asked for permission to return to the capital. Denying his request, the sultan instead kept him at a good distance by appointing him commander-in-chief of the Fifth Army in Damascus. Tubercular like his mother, Cevat Pasha soon fell ill in the hot, humid climate of Damascus, but Abdulhamid ignored his frequent pleas to be allowed to return to Istanbul. At last Great-Aunt Sara, braving a confrontation few others would dare, went to the palace and told the sultan, 'If you don't allow my brother to return home, he will die, and blood will be on your hands.' Finally permission was granted, but it was too late. Arriving home on a stretcher, Cevat died soon afterwards in July 1900, at the age of forty-nine.

My grandfather, Shakir Pasha, was devastated by his brother's untimely death. He bitterly resented Abdulhamid's shabby treatment of Cevat, and when the sultan offered him the town house that Cevat Pasha had enjoyed as grand vizier, he refused it, vowing to live only in a place where his beloved brother had never set foot and where there was no reminder of him. He chose to settle on the island of Büyükada. By then he and Grandmother had four children, Cevat, Hakiye, Ayşe and Suat, and in 1901 on this enchanted island my mother Fahrelnissa was born, followed two years later by her sister Aliye.

It is in the house on the island that my story begins.

1

The Prince Arrives — 1934

Büyükada, Turkish for 'big island', formerly known as Prinkipo, is situated about ten miles from Istanbul. It is the largest of nine islands in the Sea of Marmara, which the Byzantines called the Princes' Isles.

At the time my mother Nissa (a diminutive of Fahrelnissa) was born, the local population of the island consisted of Greek fishermen, modest shopkeepers, and a few Turkish families who lived there year-round in semi-retirement. Every summer this population expanded with the arrival of many wealthy townspeople – Greeks, Levantines, Armenians and Jews, as well as Turkish, French, Italian and English families. They owned lovely, turn-of-the-century houses, set in gardens full of almond, acacia and Judas trees, bougainvillaea, oleander and rose bushes, all the flowers of the Mediterranean glowing in a thousand colours.

I was at home there as I have been nowhere else on earth. I loved my grandfather's rambling old wooden house with its gingerbread ornamentation, its three storeys of spacious rooms, its traditional *hamam*, and its stately, outmoded European comfort. I loved the overgrown lavender-and-honeysuckle-scented garden, the narrow cobblestone lanes outside the house that connected us with the village, the turquoise coves and pine groves of the island. But, more than anything, I loved my mother's family, charmers all, with their warmth, their passion, their creativity, their exuberance.

My most vivid memory of the Büyükada house is the day Mother arrived with her prince from Athens where, six months earlier, away from the wagging tongues of Istanbul, they had been married. I was eight years old. All the Shakir family was present, ready to greet Emir Zeid and welcome him into the clan.

A corner bedroom with a view of the Sea of Marmara over the

red-tiled rooftops had been selected for the newly-weds. The big brass bed had been taken apart, and the gardener had attacked its legs with a blowtorch to burn off the bedbugs (the curse of all those old wooden houses). The floor had been polished, the pale oriental rug thwacked. The bed was made up with my grandmother's fine embroidered linen sheets, and, after having been laundered and starched, the mosquito netting was draped from a suspended crown so that it hung in graceful folds on both sides. On the bedside table sat a jar of rose-petal jam with a silver spoon in a glass of water. Flowers picked by my youngest aunt Aliye from every corner of the garden filled the room, mingling their scent with the smell of lavender wafting from the sheets.

For this special occasion, the table in the formal dining room, reflected in the floor-to-ceiling gilt-framed mirrors which were relics of Cevat Pasha's town house, was also dressed in full regalia for the evening meal. I watched Uncle Suat's half-French wife Mizou make an elaborate centrepiece, her graceful white hands with their long, bright nails fluttering like doves over her creation.

Their preparations complete, the family gathered for lunch at the long table under the ivy-covered arbour in the garden. As usual, they were seated according to age and rank, a protocol that was always honoured. At the head sat my portly grandmother Ismet, surrounded by her children, their husbands and wives, and at the foot of the table we grandchildren with our governesses. Grandfather was not there. He had long been dead, felled by a bullet. I knew him only from a large portrait, in full uniform with a chestful of medals, which dominated the formal living room.

My two older uncles were also absent. Uncle Âsım, the elder, from my grandfather's first wife, stayed away from the family. He lived in town in one of the flats of the Shakir Pasha apartment building with his much younger wife, a bank-teller. I only saw him in the halls of the apartment, a tall, thin, wiry man with a haggard and slightly mad expression. Even as a child, I found it shocking that Uncle Âsım worked as a ticket taker in a cinema. For a boy who had been bounced on a grand vizier's lap and played at the palace at the feet of the sultan, who had gone to the prestigious St Cyr Military Academy in France, to have to eke out a living in such a lowly manner!

Uncle Cevat, my second-oldest uncle, Grandmother's eldest son, I had never seen. All I knew about him was that he lived in a fishing village on the Aegean Sea called Bodrum and wrote under the pseudonym 'Fisherman of Halicarnassus' (Halicarnassus being the ancient name of Bodrum) and that we were not allowed to ask questions about him. We children called him the 'mysterious uncle'.

For days I had been wondering what Mother's new husband would be like and how he would treat me and my older brother Nejad. I knew that stepfathers could be mean. What if he beat us? At lunch that day my apprehension proved too much for me. The sight of the eggplant *moussakka* on my plate made me turn pale and start to shiver.

'Too many green plums from the garden, I expect,' said my governess Miss Tina kindly as she excused herself and me from the table.

'A little rest and she will be all right,' said Hakiye, my austere oldest aunt.

'Some dry toast and tea with lemon,' suggested little Aunt Aliye.

'The poor child is over-excited at her mother's arrival,' commented my favourite aunt, Ayşe, the pianist of the family.

'Shangrila, Shangrila!' sang my gallant, debonair Uncle Suat, calling me by my pet name as he rose to help. But he was forestalled by Lala, who swept me into his arms, carried me upstairs, and laid me on my bed. Miss Tina, following, closed the dark green shutters. The quiet of the room, disturbed only by the far-off talk and laughter from the lunch table below and the whisper of the pines beyond the windows, was soothing.

Lala was a Sudanese black eunuch, an ex-slave. At the turn of the century, many prominent Ottoman families still owned black slaves who were employed only as household servants. The men often rose to high positions; the highest were even called 'Lala Pasha'. Purchased as a young boy in Mecca, Lala had risen in my grandfather's service to the position of majordomo and, on his retirement, had married a white woman and, with the family's help, bought a grocery shop in Istanbul. Lala called regularly at weekends and never failed to be present at special occasions and family crises. Whenever he appeared, always carrying chocolates, we children ran to him, kissed his hand, and placed it on our foreheads in a gesture of respect. Everyone loved Lala, and his devotion to the family was absolute.

On that particular day he and his wife had come from town to help with the preparations. After lunch Lala sat beside Grandmother and over Turkish coffee they discussed Nissa's luggage. Since she travelled with many trunks and bags, and since motor vehicles were not allowed on the island, Lala decided that four porters would be needed and that he would go down to the ferry landing to supervise them.

'I shall go down to the ferry to meet them myself,' announced my pious grandmother. As she rarely met anyone because of her age and status, this was a significant gesture. She was going to the dock to honour Emir Zeid because he was a direct descendant of the Prophet Mohammed. Such lineage permitted him the title of sherif. Based in the Hijaz in Arabia, the Emir Zeid was a sherif of the Hashemite dynasty, hereditary keepers of the holy cities of Mecca and Medina; and for Grandmother, a devout Muslim who prayed five times a day, that was reason enough to meet the boat.

The other members of the family were less overcome by the glory with which Nissa had allied herself; after all, the Ottoman Turks had ruled the Arabs for four centuries in the days of the empire. However, having heard the praises of the prince sung by Grandmother, who had accompanied Nissa to Athens to attend her wedding, they looked forward to meeting him. Moreover, for the Shakirs, meeting the boat from the city was a demonstration of feeling, and they all intended to be at the landing to greet the newly-weds.

When I awoke, still feverish, everyone had gone to the pier. Persuaded by my urgent pleas, Miss Tina let me get up and put on my party dress. With a pink bow on the crown of my head signalling a special occasion, I stood nervously at the corner window, looking down the steep road that led up from the boat landing.

Suddenly they all appeared: in the lead, Grandmother and Mother, with my chubby brother Nejad holding her hand, followed by my three aunts. Then came the men, Aunt Hakiye's husband Uncle Emin, a retired four-star general, stiff as a pole thanks to an old spinal injury, labouring up the hill on his cane, next to Aunt Ayşe's husband Ahmet, a dour, stern man, a former governor of the Ottoman Empire. Between my uncles Suat and Ahmet a shorter man in a crumpled white linen suit was lurching from side to side like a sailor. I knew it was Emir Zeid, for I had seen many photographs of him, but I had not realized he was so short. Behind them walked Lala, my cousins and, at the very end, four porters bent low under piles of luggage.

When the procession reached the red iron gate, the bell tinkled as it swung open; then they passed out of my sight. Soon I heard hurried footsteps on the stairs, and like a ray of sunshine my mother burst into the room, looking slim and beautiful in a dark blue and white silk print dress with matching coat. Tossing her white Panama hat on the bed, she hugged me so hard I nearly suffocated and kissed me as if she were biting into a juicy peach.

'Shirinaki, Shirinaki, my darling child, what happened to you?' she asked, full of concern. (Shirinaki is a diminutive of my name.)

As I was about to explain, the Emir Zeid came slowly into the room and stood by the door, perfectly calm. When he came closer I could see he was a kind-looking man with a precisely oval face, a shiny bald head fringed with tiny black curls, huge black eyes, and a moustache. Without uttering a word, he pulled something from his pocket, then reached for my hand and released it into my palm. It was a gold ring with a sizeable diamond.

'Here, it is made for your little finger! They call the style *chevalière*,' said Mother, taking my hand and slipping on the ring. 'Zeid had it made especially for you.'

It was obviously a gift only my mother could have devised. From my early years I had become accustomed to Mother's extravagant and sometimes inappropriate gifts, and therefore accepted the ring with pleasure but no surprise. When I thanked Emir Zeid politely, he bent his head and indicated that I was to kiss him somewhere on the top of it. As I kissed his pate, giggling, I noticed a faint aroma of cologne and tobacco, which lingered in the room until I went to bed that night after my convalescent's supper of toast and boiled rice. I couldn't help thinking how different in looks and behaviour the prince was from my father. The latter was a handsome, elegant dandy who would have strode into the room in his immaculate blue blazer, bow tie and wing-tipped shoes and presented the ring in a beautifully wrapped box with a perfectly tied satin ribbon, instead of slipping it to me as the prince had done. Different as he was from my father, however, I liked the prince instinctively. It looked as if all would work out in the end.

The Emir Zeid was a hit with everyone. He charmed because he did not appear to try. At tea-time, when the samovar was lit, the Shakirs would gather in the bright upstairs living room having tea, embroidering, sketching or just conversing. Grandmother, like most Cretans, had a mania for cleanliness. Storeroom keys at her belt, she would bustle about the house all day dispensing provisions to the cooks and cleaning after the maids. Only at tea-time would she change her plain house dress and relax with her family. As Emir Zeid discovered that one of her few pleasures – except for reading the Qur'an – was playing backgammon, he would pull up a chair in front of her and challenge her to a game. Out would come the beautiful mother-of-pearl inlaid backgammon set which her brother-in-law, Cevat Pasha, had sent her from Damascus. Soon she and Emir Zeid would be deeply absorbed in the game, Grandmother glancing up from time to time like a happy girl.

Although Emir Zeid, always cordial, was willing to listen to the ladies' endless conversations, he preferred the company of men. He enjoyed sitting for hours under a big pine tree in the garden smoking his pipe and talking about past campaigns, war and politics with his new brothers-in-law, Emin and Ahmet. During the Great War the brothers-in-law had fought on opposite sides, Emin and Ahmet both in the Ottoman Army, while Zeid and his older brothers Faisal and Abdullah, with Lawrence of Arabia, had led an Arab army up the Arabian peninsula from Mecca to Damascus, in revolt against the Ottomans.

We children took to Emir Zeid immediately because he was not only gentle but extremely generous. To the servants he was undemanding. No one really knew him, nor were we ever to know him totally. Mother called him 'my sealed box'. Yet everyone liked him. That was his mystery and his charm.

The Shakirs approved of the marriage wholeheartedly and, to justify Mother's action, except for Grandmother, became highly critical of my father.

'Imagine your father married to one of the most beautiful women in Turkey, a woman whom Edouard de Rothschild said has "the most perfect head in Europe", and he has to go running after every skirt!' Aunt Hakiye commented.

'Your father has always kept your poor mother short of money, but he's never been slow in spending it on himself,' said Uncle Suat.

Even little Aunt Aliye could not avoid throwing a barb at my father. 'Never mind about the divorce, Shirin. You've got us, and now you have Emir Zeid. He is a good, kind man. See how he treats your mother! He has handed over his purse to her to spend as she wishes. No more counting pennies and entering them in his ledgers every evening! Now I don't want to say nasty things about your father, Shirin, but . . .'

Turkish children are not permitted to argue or contradict their elders. Respect for age is paramount in every social context. So I could say nothing to defend my father, especially to those I loved most, those uncles and aunts whose freely expressed love had carried my brother Nejad and me like a great buoyant current through the threatening narrows of our parents' separation and divorce.

A few days after Emir Zeid's arrival, in his honour, Grandmother ordered six horse-drawn carriages for a day's outing.

All the Shakirs loved picnics. The day began like other days, with a burst of Chopin downstairs as Aunt Ayşe's hands floated and plunged over the keys of the grand piano in the gloomy formal salon. Her children, Nermidil and Erdem, who were our playmates, and our two governesses helped the servants carry into the garden hampers of food, baskets of fruit, bundles of cushions and rolls of oriental carpets that would be spread over the pine needles in our favourite grove overlooking the sea.

When the first carriages drew up at the red gate, they were loaded up and, with the servants squeezed into the remaining space, dispatched. The next carriage took more hampers and a contingent of children. We began a gentle clip-clopping along the red dirt road that skirted the sea for some three miles and gave us enchanting vistas through the dancing tassels of the carriage awning. By the time we arrived at the picnic ground, the servants had already spread out two beautiful oriental carpets and piled cushions around them and were unpacking the hampers. In the mysterious quiet of the pine grove muffled by pine needles, we began to play, but, as the other carriages came one by one, the placid grove quickly became a nomads' village. All it needed was a few tents and several yoke of oxen.

Without waiting for assistance, Aunt Aliye jumped spryly down from a carriage and caught her petticoats on the wheel. With her tousled hair, big lavender eyes heavily lined with kohl, and her torn petticoats, she looked like a doll a child had played with for years and cast aside.

Uncle Suat, resplendent in white flannels, adjusted the silk cravat at the open neck of his shirt and turned to help his wife, graceful, swan-like Mizou, down from the carriage. They made a striking couple. Though Suat had indulged in several amorous escapades, he always returned to Mizou in the end.

And then Aunt Ayşe climbed down and smoothed her pink linen skirt over her wide hips. With a pink ribbon holding her blonde hair in order, she looked completely feminine beside her sturdy husband Ahmet, dressed in a plain threadbare suit.

Grandmother stepped out of her carriage and, with Emir Zeid holding her by the arm, huffing and puffing, walked up to the picnic grove. Mother, in a white linen halter-neck dress that showed off her deep tan, followed, humming the Toreador Song from *Carmen* while she kept time with a pine branch.

Grandmother's brother Mithat, a retired officer who lived all year round at the Büyükada house as a caretaker, arrived with his much younger second wife and their five-year-old daughter, whom we called 'Japon' because of her fringe and slanting eyes. With them were Grandmother's two other bachelor brothers, who had come from town to meet the prince.

In the last carriage, with her son Sina, came my mother's first cousin Hamdiye, who taught at the school on the island. She had been married to my Uncle Cevat, and their son, Sina, was Nejad's age; although he lived with his mother and stepfather, the principal of the local school, Sina spent every day of the summer playing with us at Grandfather's house and, therefore, was very much part of the Büyükada cousins.

When all the children had arrived, Aunt Hakiye, who was unpacking a straw hamper with her teenage son Shakir's help, told Miss Tina to take us swimming before lunch. 'Mother,' Shakir asked wistfully, 'can't I go swimming, too?' 'No,' replied Aunt Hakiye. 'You are not a child. Now stay here and help me.' Aunt Hakiye was always good for a task. As the oldest sister, and the first woman member of the City Council, she demanded attention and service from everyone. We children, therefore, avoided her as much as possible.

Miss Tina and Seher, one of our *beslemes*, led us down the steep, crooked path over the pine roots to the horseshoe cove, where the trees hung over the water like women washing their long hair. Seher, a massive woman, simply stood like an outcrop of rock and let the water cool her tired feet.

As we splashed in the turquoise waters of the little cove, a large yacht drew near, dropped anchor, and lowered its sails. From its deck my cousin Fureya, Aunt Hakiye's lovely daughter, called, and we waved back with cries of welcome. A few minutes later she stepped out of the dinghy on to the rickety wooden pier, looking stunning in a pair of white duck trousers and a cherry-red blazer, her dark hair piled on top of her head like a crown. Behind her came her husband, Kılıç Ali, good-looking except for his huge, protruding belly, which resembled an overblown balloon ready to pop. A deputy in Parliament, he was a close friend of President Atatürk.

Soon it was time for the meal. The children, neatly dressed once more, clustered at one end of a great carpet depicting in stylized form the beauty of a Persian garden, its streams and flowers. Over the soft, radiant colours of the carpet a linen cloth had been spread, and on the cloth was a multitude of dishes – *börek, dolma, köfte* . . .

Hushed for once, we children could think only of food, but the adults, gracefully disposed around the dishes, dipping and reaching and munching, kept up an endless flow of chatter.

They discussed where Nissa and Emir Zeid would live. From his father, Sherif Hussein (later King Hussein of the Hijaz), Emir Zeid had inherited two properties in Istanbul. The first was a handsome *yalı* in Yeniköy, a village on the Bosphorus near town, and the other a ruin on top of a hill further up the Bosphorus near the Black Sea.

When Emir Zeid's great-uncle, the grand sherif of Mecca, had died in 1893, his father Sherif Hussein had expected to be named grand sherif. But to his great disappointment the Ottoman Sultan Abdulhamid had named another member of the family and, regarding Sherif Hussein as a potential troublemaker in Mecca, had ordered him to live in the capital, Istanbul, where he could be watched.

As a sop the sultan had given the sherif a completely furnished *yalı*. Located directly on the Bosphorus, these old wooden *yalıs* were and are still greatly sought after, with lovely big windows to catch the summer breezes off the water and pleasant gardens on the landward side. Spurning the *yalı*, Sherif Hussein, a man of independence and determination, had built the other house far from the sultan and his spies, to his own taste, on a high, windswept hill overlooking the village of Büyükdere (Big River).

The moment the subject of Emir Zeid's homes came up, the Shakirs were anxious to give Mother and the emir unsolicited advice, which they loved to do.

'Of course you will choose the *yalı*. A *yalı* has so much character,' said Ayşe.

'To live on the Bosphorus has always been my dream,' remarked Mizou.

'To give up the *yalı* and live on top of a hill near the Black Sea would be total madness,' exclaimed Suat.

I watched my mother to see how she would react to all this counsel. She simply reached for a crisp *börek* and quietly said, 'We are thinking of the house on top of the hill.' It was the first I had heard of her intention. 'Oh, I hope she doesn't go through with it,' I thought, for I too had already embraced the idea of living in a *yalı*.

Like a flock of birds, the Shakirs swooped down.

'My dear, you can't be serious!'

'But Nissa, it's a total ruin, so remote, so cold in winter, a Wuthering Heights.'

'There are wolves up there.'

'Inaccessible. Think of all the work!'

'And the expense!'

'To fix that old wreck will be a herculean task.'

Raising her arms, Nissa exploded: 'You are all impossible! It has an extraordinary location. Besides, Zeid was born and raised there.'

'Only until I was nine, for we returned to Mecca in 1908 when the Young Turks deposed the sultan.' Then, putting his arm around her, Emir Zeid added gently, 'Nissa, my dear, the Büyükdere property certainly has a spectacular view, but your family is right. You will find it much easier to move into the *yalı*.'

Everyone sighed with relief.

To change the subject, Mother deliberately turned to my cousin Fureya. 'How did your dinner party for Atatürk go last Thursday?'

'Very well. The new cook is excellent, and Atatürk seemed pleased.'

'The cook had nothing to do with it. Fureya is a perfect hostess,' Kılıç said with pride. 'The president enjoyed himself thoroughly.'

'Did he drink a lot of *rakı*?' Suat asked mischievously.

Ignoring Suat's comment, Fureya continued, 'He thanked me profusely, and even complimented me for putting flowers in the bathroom.'

'How refined of him to notice such a detail!' said Ayşe.

'He is a sophisticated man,' Hakiye stated. She, of all the sisters, had known him the longest.

'And *so* charming,' added Nissa. 'What charisma!'

'I often wonder what would have become of this country without Atatürk,' said Emin, scratching his temple with the handle of his cane.

'We would have been finished,' answered Ahmet. 'After the Great

War the Allies would have partitioned the country and doled it out, as the British did the entire Middle East.'

'Uncle Charles says Atatürk has a mother complex and that he saved his country, his motherland, because it meant saving his mother,' Aliye interjected. The other adults all exchanged knowing glances, and Nejad poked me with his elbow. 'Uncle Charles', as Aliye always referred to him, was her lover, Charles Berger, a Hungarian violinist and a disciple of Freud. She had met him ten years before, when he had come to the Büyükada house as Cousin Fureya's violin teacher, and had immediately fallen in love with him. Berger in turn was smitten by the ivory-skinned, golden-haired twenty-one-year-old Aliye. However, as he felt that an artist should not be tied down by marriage, Aliye had to be content to be his mistress. To her mother's and sisters' consternation she embarked on a scandalous love affair, visiting him twice a week at his studio-apartment in Istanbul, heavily disguised in black hat and veil but deceiving no one. By now the family had accepted the situation and talked of Charles Berger freely, often forgetting themselves in front of us children.

'Oh, Aliye! You and your half-baked Freudian theories will drive me insane,' scolded Suat.

'Mother complex,' exclaimed Ahmet. 'What does that mean?'

'You're being ridiculous, Aliye,' remarked Ayşe, coming to her husband's support.

Now they all turned their attention to Aliye, the general irritant, the *enfant terrible* of the family.

'For heaven's sake, Aliye, get that mop of hair off your forehead so we can see your eyes.'

'Yes. Why do you insist on hiding those beautiful eyes?'

'And what about all that paint on your face? You look like an Easter egg,' complained Suat.

Grandmother, who was always the one to smooth the frictions between her expressive and temperamental family, interrupted: 'Now, now, children, please don't pick on your little sister.'

'Oh, I don't mind,' replied Aliye, shrugging. 'I'm used to it. Uncle Charles says as long as I am the youngest, everyone will pick on me.'

'Aliye, I do wish you wouldn't refer to Monsieur Berger in front of the children,' exclaimed Hakiye prudishly, quelling giggles from us with a severe glance.

Ahmet, also annoyed at the references to Aliye's lover, abruptly rose to his feet, pretending that his old wound was bothering him.

'One of your boys got me,' he said jokingly to Zeid, patting his hip where an Arab nationalist had put a bullet in him when Ahmet was acting governor of Baghdad.

'Not a very good shot, I'm glad to say,' Zeid answered with a laugh, and Ahmet launched into the story of how he had forgiven the would-be assassin and even taken him into his service.

'Being governor of Baghdad almost cost me my life twice,' Ahmet said, but before he had a chance to continue, Ayşe interrupted.

'No need to go into that now,' she said, reaching for some grapes and passing them on.

When everyone had finished, the servants cleared away the dishes and the tablecloth, and the people from the nearby kiosk served Turkish coffee on swinging brass trays. So much food, such healthy sea air! It was siesta time. Eyelids drooped. Uncle Emin, leaning his stiff back against a tree trunk, was already asleep. Others sought trees of their own, spread out blankets, propped up pillows, and sank into rest. Soon the glade was covered with slumbering forms.

At tea-time, the kiosk people lighted a samovar and served tea in stubby, tulip-shaped glasses. As a finale, each of us children recited a short poem. I recited 'Titty Mouse and Tatty Mouse', but my seven-year-old cousin, Erdem, stole the show with his rendition of 'The Little Bluebird'. Then Uncle Suat wound up his portable record-player, and he and Mizou gave a spirited rendering of the tango over the stone patio of the kiosk. They were marvellous dancers, slim and graceful. We all clapped like mad.

So the glory of the day waned. The sun was low and red, and as we returned home, clip-clop, clip-clop, over the marble surface of the sea came the many ferries and launches of the evening hour, bearing people from the city back to their summer houses on the island.

2

Büyükada – 1914

For my mother, life at the Büyükada house had not always been a series of sunlit Chekhovian days, as it had been for me. That haven also harboured memories of a momentous tragedy. Whenever Mother spoke of her childhood on the island, her mood invariably became dark and her lively green eyes clouded with grief.

'It was never the same afterward,' she'd say.

I knew the word 'afterward' referred to the killing of her father Shakir Pasha by her older brother Cevat.

As a child, Cevat was doted on by his parents and his Uncle Cevat Pasha, who had no children of his own, and given all the advantages of a good education. Once his primary education was completed, he was sent to Robert College, a boys' preparatory school founded by American missionaries in 1863 in Istanbul, and then on to Oxford University. He had hated the confinement of boarding school and found Oxford no better. Moreover, he detested the cold, wet, grey English weather and was delighted to return, whenever possible, to the sunny blue skies of Büyükada. In a letter to a woman he loved many years later, he wrote:

When I was about seventeen, on my way to Istanbul on holiday from Oxford, leaving the terrible climate of London and Paris behind, I reached Marseilles, where the ship was waiting to take me home. The Mediterranean stretched out before me in all its vastness, glittering in the brilliant sunshine. I leapt aboard in such haste that I left my luggage on the dock. A few days later, near Sicily, the ship sailed into a fleet of fishing smacks at night. Each boat carried a lantern. The stars in the sky and the stars on the sea sparkled at each other, and a fisherman started singing in one of the boats. The icy hell of Oxford was far behind me.

As I riffled through my mother's many journals and diaries and memoirs which she kept all her life, not in any particular order, I found, to my delight, several entries about Cevat's visits:

I was six or seven years old when my brother arrived from Oxford, dashing in his double-breasted Chesterfield coat with its velvet collar and wearing white spats. I cannot say he was handsome. He had the oddest face. The upper part seemed to be crying, while the lower part looked as though it were laughing. It was as if one had cut out the top part of a tragedy mask and had glued it to the bottom of a comedy mask. He spoke in a booming voice in that marvellous Oxford English; each word, crisp and clear, exploded in the air. As my brother carried himself with great authority, he looked much taller than he actually was. I felt like an insignificant midget next to him and needed to show him that I was a person to reckon with, so I said, 'Let's play a game where I can show you that I am stronger than you are.' 'All right,' he said, amused. I rose on tiptoe and with my two fists punched him in the stomach as hard as I could. It hurt him so much that he turned pale, and tears filled his eyes. I was shocked to have hurt him so, but now we were equals, and we became friends.

Back at Oxford for his second year, Cevat fell in with a group of wealthy, upper-class young Englishmen and, enjoying the lifestyle they represented, set out to emulate them, running up huge bills at the tailor and bootmaker. Pleading bad health and high medical bills, he was always asking his father for more money. Shakir Pasha, a hard-working self-made orphan, was incensed by Cevat's playboy behaviour.

When Cevat came home the next summer, Nissa was witness to a very disturbing scene in her father's study. After his retirement from the army, Shakir Pasha spent most of his time locked up in his library writing a four-volume *History of the Ottoman Empire*. As a child, Aunt Aliye remembered peeping through the keyhole and seeing her bearded father bent over a pile of papers, writing by gaslight. 'I loved to put my ear against the keyhole and, in the silence, listen to the scritch-scratch of his pen,' she told me once. On the day Nissa happened to be in the study – how, I don't know, for children were strictly forbidden to enter – Grandfather, seated in a big armchair behind his massive desk covered with bills, was giving Cevat a sharp dressing-down.

'What are all these bills?' Grandfather demanded, banging his fist on the desk. 'Did I send you to Oxford to buy fancy clothes and ride horses? If you do not apply yourself to your studies and cut out these expenses and extravagances, I will take you out of Oxford. You are nothing but a lazy spendthrift.'

Cevat, looking forlorn, stood silently in front of his father's desk. His face turned crimson, and he held his head back, trying to prevent the tears welling in his eyes from rolling down his cheeks. 'My heart went out to him,' writes Mother.

Shakir Pasha had hoped his chastisements would change Cevat's attitude; but they did not. Again in England, Cevat continued his extravagant lifestyle, and finally the irate pasha ordered him to leave Oxford and return home. Instead of complying, Cevat went to Rome and enrolled himself in the Academy of Fine Arts. 'I have found my vocation,' he wrote home enthusiastically. 'Art is my life. For the first time, I am happy.'

His bliss was complete when he fell madly in love with an artist's model, a beautiful Roman girl named Aniesi. As he knew his father would disapprove of his marrying at the age of twenty with no means to support a family, he took photographs of Aniesi to Istanbul while his father was away and begged his mother to plead his cause. During this visit, Nissa remembers sitting on the floor next to Cevat's armchair and watching him sketch.

This event, unimportant as it seemed to be at the time, launched Nissa on her life-long passion for art. When in the mid–1940s she started to exhibit her works, many journalists asked her how she had become interested in painting. She told them her brother Cevat had inspired and encouraged her:

One day when I was eight, I watched him sketch in pen and ink the classic profile of the girl he loved. I was fascinated to see how the thin, delicate, black pen-strokes gradually created a living person on paper. I was mesmerized and driven by a desire to do the same. My brother tore a sheet from his sketchbook and gave it to me. Then, handing me a pencil, he told me to draw anything I wanted. That very day I sketched the entire living room with all its furnishing down to the lamps on the tables and the design of the oriental rug. When I showed my brother the sketch, he was impressed. 'That is very good, Nissa,' he exclaimed. 'I love your bold strokes, and, for your age, you have an uncanny sense of perspective.' Then, patting me on the head, he added, 'You have talent, child. Get a pen and pencil. Keep them with you at all times and sketch anything that catches your fancy. But, above all, keep at it.'

Mother never forgot this advice. From then on she sketched continuously, and a beautiful watercolour portrait she made at the age of fourteen of her grandmother is always exhibited along with her many other paintings.

Just before Shakir Pasha returned home from Ostend, Cevat departed for Rome, leaving his mother the onerous task of obtaining his father's permission to marry Aniesi. Many times Aunt Ayşe overheard her parents fighting into the night, her father's angry voice emanating from their bedroom. 'I felt so sorry for Mother,' she told me. 'Cevat should have been man enough to talk to Father himself instead of letting our poor mother take all that abuse.'

In the end, Shakir Pasha gave in to his wife's entreaties, permission for the marriage was reluctantly granted, and Cevat married Aniesi in Rome. One of the rooms on the top floor of the Büyükada house was refurbished for the newly-weds. Radiant with joy, the prodigal son and his pregnant wife arrived from Italy, and in 1912 their daughter Mutara, Shakir Pasha's second grandchild, was born.

Cevat had brought with him a large crate of nudes that he had painted at the Academy in Rome. Although Grandmother painted landscapes and still-life on silk, which she framed and hung in the house, she was horrified to see paintings of nude females. This was scandalous, particularly in a society where women were still hiding their faces behind veils. Before Grandfather had a chance to glimpse them, she had the nudes banished to the attic. Pretending that they were going to play with many old music-boxes which were stored there, Nissa and Aliye often went up to the attic to observe their brother's portrayals of the female body, while the music-boxes tinkled and twittered.

Refraining from painting more nudes, Cevat turned to a study of miniatures at the Academy of Fine Arts in Istanbul. As his artwork produced no income, Grandfather had to continue to support him and his family. Father and son fought over money matters and what Cevat was going to do and be in life. Shakir Pasha believed that, like all responsible men, his son should find a job, earn an income and take care of his wife and child, but Cevat would have none of it. All he wanted was to be a painter, an artist, and not waste his time with some stupid job. And he certainly did not want to be a soldier like his grandfather, his father and his uncle, brilliant as they may have been. Such statements Shakir Pasha took as an affront, and he bombarded his son with criticism and constant reprimands.

The arguments between father and son were further aggravated by the loss of the Shakir Pasha fortune through a bad investment.

Grandmother's brother, Great-Uncle Mithat, while stationed at the Gendarmerie in Salonika, a rapidly developing commercial and resort city on the Aegean Sea with a large, enterprising Jewish population, had praised the city to his brother-in-law Shakir Pasha and convinced him, in view of its promising future, to invest in a touristic project. As a result, the pasha sold all the income-producing commercial real estate which he had inherited from his childless brother, and with the proceeds started to build a *palazzo*-like luxury hotel on the Salonika corniche. Its main feature was a huge dome above the marble lobby, to accommodate Cevat Pasha's enormous crystal chandelier.

Great-Uncle Mithat's advice to build a hotel in Salonika turned out to be disastrous. The first problem concerned building costs, which so far overran estimates that, to complete payments, Grandmother had to sell a pair of cabochon emerald earrings. Complete disaster came with the outbreak of the first Balkan war in 1912, when Greece, Serbia and Bulgaria attacked the Ottoman Empire in a *blitzkrieg* from three directions. Greece swiftly captured Salonika, ending almost 500 years of Turkish rule, and during the battle a Greek patriot planted a bomb in Grandfather's hotel and blew off its chandeliered dome.

In the wreck of the hotel, Shakir Pasha lost almost all his wealth, and under the severe financial strain the arguments between him and Cevat became more violent. Cevat, who could no longer stand his irate father's tirades, began to fight back, and their quarrels became emotional shouting matches. Grandmother tried to intercede, to no avail. While she watched them rip at each other like two animals, all she could do was bleed inside.

The only good thing which resulted from the Salonika fiasco was that my Aunt Ayşe married Ahmet. A graduate of Staff College and a classmate of Mustafa Kemal, Ahmet was commander of the Salonika Gendarmerie. One day Great-Uncle Mithat, who was something of a show-off, wanting to impress his commanding officer, invited Ahmet to take a stroll with him along the corniche. There he pointed out the partly completed hotel. 'That belongs to my brother-in-law, Shakir Pasha,' said Mithat boastfully. 'I was the one to suggest that he build it.'

'Good for you,' replied Ahmet, and jokingly asked, 'Does the pasha have any marriageable daughters?'

'His oldest daughter is already married to an officer, but his second daughter, Ayşe, who is much more beautiful, with long blonde hair and a yoghurt-like complexion, is not. She is the pasha's favourite daughter, and he calls her "my princess". It will take quite a man for him to give her away!'

Then and there Ahmet decided that one day Ayşe would be his wife.

At the end of the second Balkan war, in 1913, Ahmet was promoted to commandant of the Istanbul Gendarmerie. Remembering Mithat's description of Ayşe, and confident that Shakir Pasha would be impressed by his new position, he asked his cousin to approach the family on his behalf. Receiving encouragement, he then presented himself at the Büyükada house to ask formally for Ayşe's hand in marriage.

During this visit, Ayşe, who was not allowed to see her suitor until the pasha had given his approval, peeked into a room to catch a forbidden glimpse of him, but managed only to see him from the rear, silhouetted against the light through a window. Intimidated by his rigid, erect military bearing, his highly polished boots, and the enormous handlebar moustaches sticking out on either side of her suitor's head, Ayşe later implored her father not to accept. 'I don't want to get married. Please, Father, don't force me,' she begged, tears pouring from her dreamy blue eyes.

But the pasha was adamant. 'My dear daughter, he is a fine, honourable young man with a future and will make you a good husband,' he replied. Then he added more kindly, 'I hear you peeked in and caught only a glimpse of him. But wait until you see him in person. He is very handsome.'

Like all girls at the time, Ayşe had no choice but to marry the man her father had chosen, and she was betrothed to Ahmet, whom she eventually grew to love and respect.

In late May of 1914, Grandfather decided to take Cevat, Suat and Lala to the ancestral farm in Afyon Karahisar for the annual stock-taking and to collect money and provisions for Ayşe's forthcoming marriage. Five years before, Hakiye's wedding to Emin had been put on in grand style, and in spite of being in financial straits Shakir Pasha hoped to give 'his princess' a memorable wedding too. As he wanted to say goodbye to his younger daughters before leaving for the farm, special permission was obtained for Nissa and Aliye to leave the French convent school in town, where they were boarders, and Lala fetched the girls and took them to Büyükada. Many years later, Nissa, recalling that departure, wrote:

We stood in the clearing in front of the house. I remember leaning against one of the large pine trees. My father kissed each one of us goodbye and gave Aliye and me a round tin box of English lemon drops. As I watched him depart through the wisteria-covered red garden gate, followed by my brothers Cevat and Suat and Lala, who was leading our dog, Tom, I felt extremely sad. I don't know why, for this was not the first time my father had left us. Since his retirement from the army, he travelled a great deal. But this time I knew I was seeing him for the last time.

3

The Killing

When I decided to write this book, I wanted to find out how the
family first heard of Shakir Pasha's death. I searched through Mother's
journals to find any mention of the event. In notes she made for a
memoir she never finished, I found a description of that night:

> One June night in 1914, as war clouds were gathering over Europe,
> I was lying in my mother's big brass bed under the mosquito
> netting, listening to my favourite *kalfa* tell me a fairy-tale by
> candlelight.
>
> When my father was away from the house, Aliye and I were
> invited, alternately, as a treat to spend the night with my mother.
> Could anyone be happier than I? The linen sheets under me
> smelled of fresh lavender; the mosquito netting enveloped me like
> a tulle womb; and *kalfa* was an extraordinary story-teller. She knew
> how to modulate her voice and pace a tale . . . When she came
> to the dramatic parts of the story, she'd roll her eyes ominously,
> making them look like half-moons in the night.
>
> Mesmerized by *kalfa*'s honeyed voice that night, I was trans-
> ported into the fairy-tale and imagined myself travelling with the
> banished princess of the story to a magical city where, after a long
> and arduous journey, we had decided to ask for shelter. However,
> before we had time to reach the door, I heard a series of loud
> knocks. 'Who could be rapping?' I thought, still engrossed in the
> fairy-tale. 'We haven't reached the door yet.'
>
> Knock! Knock! Knock! Clear and sharp came the noise. Emerg-
> ing from my reverie, I realized that someone was actually knocking
> on the front door downstairs. *Kalfa* had stopped her story and was
> listening intently. 'Who could be calling at this time of night?' I
> wondered.

Suddenly a gust of wind seemed to sweep through the house. Doors opened and banged shut, and a babble of voices filled the air. A few minutes later the bedroom door was flung open, and into the room ran our governess, Miss Schreiber. 'Come on, Nissa, get up, get up,' she ordered as she pulled me off the bed. 'We have just received word that the pasha is very sick and is on the way home from the farm. The room has to be prepared for his arrival.'

Shakir Pasha never arrived. Instead, early the next morning, his best friend, Sait Pasha, came to the house with a telegram. It announced that Shakir Pasha had been killed at the farm by a bullet fired by his son Cevat.

That fatal morning Nissa saw Grandmother on her knees in the middle of the living room, rocking back and forth, pulling at her hair and crying, 'Allah help me! Allah help me!' and Ayşe ripping Cevat's photographs from their frames. Tearing them to bits, she flung them on the floor and stamped on them as if she were putting the subject to death. Nissa was perplexed and frightened. What was going on? Why this bizarre behaviour? But before she had a chance to find out, Aliye and she were sent to their aunt's home on the mainland until after the funeral. They were told only that their father had had a heart attack at the farm and were not allowed to ask further questions.

When Shakir Pasha's body arrived on the island, after a simple service at the local mosque, he was buried in the hill-top Muslim cemetery which he had had built.

Cevat was tried and convicted of manslaughter and sentenced to fourteen years in prison. At the trial Grandmother pleaded his cause. Testifying as a character witness, she repeated her belief that Cevat could not possibly have intended to kill his father, no matter how much they had quarrelled. She maintained resolutely it must have been an accident. Lala, who was at the farm during the shooting, testified that he had seen nothing for he was fast asleep and was awakened in the middle of the night by gun-shots. In the end the magistrate ruled that it was neither premeditated murder nor an accident, but instead a shooting in the heat of passion after a violent argument.

The affair caused a nationwide scandal, and the whole country speculated as to what really had happened at the farm.

*

Trying to get at the truth behind Cevat's killing of Grandfather is, I find, very much like the Japanese film *Rashomon*, where the viewer listens to witnesses, each believing they are telling the truth, recount different and contradictory versions of the same event. The truth becomes many-faceted, ambiguous, confusing, and, finally, unknown.

Some people thought that Shakir was having an affair with his son's young wife and that brooding jealousy drove Cevat to murder. In the film about Cevat, *Blue Exile*, released in 1994 and proposed by the Turkish government for the Academy Awards, this is the theory put forward by the screenplay. I do not agree with it.

Other people said that Cevat had embezzled money from Grandfather's account and that he was so petrified of his father's wrath on discovering the theft that he killed him.

A few whispered that it was cold-blooded murder.

Many said it was an accident.

Most thought it was an impulsive act spurred by sudden, uncontrollable rage.

Cevat insisted it was self-defence.

Sina, his son, believes it was an act of defiance.

Uncle Suat was the only member of the family present at the farm on the night of the shooting. His grim version of the tale, whispered to me in bits and pieces over the years, was that Cevat drugged them all, Suat, Lala, and even the dog, Tom, killed Grandfather while the household slept, and in the morning tried to make it look like a political assassination or the act of a burglar. Whenever I gently broached this version of the story to the family, I was bombarded with instant uproar and protestation.

'How could Suat say a thing like that?'

'Obviously when he saw his father covered with blood, he went out of his mind and imagined the whole wild tale.'

'Poor Suat! He was so shaken up by his father's death that he was always fainting and throwing wild fits of incoherent babbling afterward.'

I never heard Cevat's version from his own lips. However, he carried on a voluminous correspondence with Azra Erhat, an essayist and authority on classical mythology. Their exchange began on the subject of Homer and gradually became more personal.

In 1957, in a letter to Erhat that refers to the shooting, Cevat wrote:

I have many things to tell you, all at the tip of my tongue. I don't want to be unfair to myself or to justify myself unduly. But what is the truth as it appears to me?

I was rebellious over many matters. It was as if they held an iron bar in front of me, and bent it in two. 'We're strong,' they said. I couldn't stand it any more. 'I'm strong, too,' I said, and took the bar and bent it back again.

The choice between roads to salvation or perdition is not always one's own. That fatal night, my father and I quarrelled over many complicated subjects. As my father was always afraid of assassination, he kept many guns on the farm. At the peak of our quarrel, I could see that he was about to reach for a gun. I seized one myself and shot without aiming. So there were two shots, his and mine, one after the other, but almost simultaneous. He was the one to die, and I was destroyed by more than death. I felt terrible pain. I lost my belief in myself. From that moment on, I felt I was a lie. Even now when people praise me, I am angry.

When this was published in a collection of Cevat's letters to Azra Erhat, my aunts and uncles were up in arms. 'Our father would never have pointed a gun at his son,' they insisted. 'That is not the way it happened.' And once more they started to recount their own versions.

I have never been able to extract my mother's view of the killing, because for seventy years she has pretended to know nothing and has refused to discuss the matter. In the late summer of 1983, when I was collecting material for this book, Mother and I spent two weeks at the Royal Orologio Hotel in Abano Terme, Italy, where we were taking mud treatments. Interviewing her in the garden one afternoon, I got up my courage and asked her, 'When did you find out that Uncle Cevat killed my grandfather?'

She looked me straight in the eye and said, 'I know of no such thing.'

'Oh, come on, Mother,' I said, 'everyone knows the story; he went to jail for it. He even admitted it in letters and interviews that have been published.'

She did not budge.

'*We* knew when we were children,' I added, trying to push her into admission.

'What did you know?' she asked, perturbed.

'One summer I was having a tea party for my dolls under the magnolia tree in the Büyükada garden when Cousin Nermidil ran over. "Guess what!" she said. "Uncle Cevat killed Grandfather." She then hopped on her red tricycle and pedalled toward the pond with the golden fish.'

'Children playing games! I know of no such thing,' Mother repeated.

'You choose not to know,' I insisted.

'Perhaps I do not *want* to know,' she said, and turned her head away with finality. Out of respect for her pain, I did not press her further.

I think Uncle Cevat must have felt that, for his own survival, he had to destroy his father. Shakir Pasha had become the barrier that prevented him from living his life as he chose; so in a moment of blind fury he lost all control and smashed it. There is evidence to this effect in a letter that Cevat wrote: 'In jail I used to dream of my childhood. When I woke up, I was glad to be awake even though I was in prison. That is, I was glad to be saved from him.'

What really happened at the farm on that fatal night, no one shall ever know.

4

War Years – 1914–18

The killing of my grandfather heralded years of chaos for our family and for Turkey. The family was inconsolable in its grief and horror at the unthinkable event, mortified at the scandal. Shortly after, war broke out. Ahmet, my Aunt Ayşe's betrothed, knew that Turkey could not remain neutral indefinitely and that he would soon be called to active duty. He urged that he and Ayşe be married immediately, and refused Ayşe's offer to release him of his commitment because of the disgrace surrounding the family. 'We are betrothed. You will be my wife, and I shall be faithful to you until the end of my life,' he declared gallantly.

Relieved and pleased that her future son-in-law was a man of character, Grandmother immediately had the local Greek dressmaker sew a simple white dress for Ayşe to wear at the small family gathering, where the *imam* from the next-door mosque would perform the religious ceremony. On the wedding day, however, in spite of her mother's entreaties, a sobbing and crying Ayşe refused to wear the new dress and insisted on being married in the black one she had worn since her father's death only a few weeks earlier.

'It was awful,' Mother told me, shuddering, 'just awful! In the midst of the cries emanating from Ayşe's room I heard shrieks coming from the garden and ran to see what had happened. Suat had fainted. He was lying in a flower-bed, all white like a marble statue which had toppled over, surrounded by servants who were trying to revive him. After Father died, Suat had a tendency to have convulsions and faint like that.' Then she added philosophically, 'Two sisters, one year apart in age, are married in the same house. One has a fairy-tale wedding – trees all over the garden lit with Japanese lanterns, a hundred guests seated at one table along the oleander path, the orchestra playing in the grotto, and the bride being showered with gold coins – and my poor sister Ayşe has a wedding like a García Lorca tragedy. That's life for you!'

That autumn Nissa and Aliye were sent back to the convent school. Away from her grieving family, Nissa found peace of mind, and the kindness of the nuns helped her during the difficult days after her father's death. She loved watching the nuns file through the courtyard on their way to Mass, and their absolute silence and reverence filled her with a sense of deep religious mystery. However, her haven came to an abrupt end when Turkey entered the war on 5 November 1914, and the authorities, now at war with France, caught up with the harmless French nuns. One day in early December the Reverend Mother entered the classroom and said, 'Children, Notre Dame de Sion is closing, for we are at war. I want you to collect your things and go home.'

The closing of the French convent was only one small consequence of war, but for Nissa it seemed of overwhelming importance. Even after seventy years, her account, in French and devoid of commas or even full stops, gallops across the huge pages of her journal in a series of scratches and blots!

I ran up to the music room to get my violin and met Aliye and the others at the front door. Our Lala was waiting for us with our bulldog, Tom. With Tom carrying our schoolbags in his huge jaws, we set off. I cried as I left, for I loved the convent. I looked up through my tears at the lighted windows of the houses we passed in the street and wondered if the people inside had heard of the terrible tragedy. How could those gentle nuns overnight become our enemies? It was incomprehensible to me. That was the first time I realized the absurdity of war.

After the closing of the convent, Grandmother's chief concern was the resumption of her daughters' French education, so necessary for young ladies of social standing at the time. She enrolled Nissa and Aliye in the Pension Braggiotti, a very expensive school run by a local Levantine lady. At the same time, Suat was attending the Galatasaray Lycée, a boys' school founded in 1868 for the Ottoman élite. With three children in private schools and the astronomical rise in living costs due to war-time shortages, Grandmother found herself short of funds. She had no income but her late husband's pension and rent from the few floors unoccupied by her family in the Shakir

Pasha apartment house in town. Letting all her staff go, except of course for the two *beslemes*, who were family, she saved coal by shutting off rooms in the apartment and having the household double up.

That winter all the men of the family were called to active duty. Emin was posted to the Russian front where, early in 1915, the Tsar's troops invaded the eastern provinces of the Ottoman Empire. Great-Uncle Nedim, Grandmother's youngest brother, was sent to Gallipoli where England and France launched a massive military and naval attack, and Ahmet was appointed acting governor of Baghdad, the headquarters of the Thirteenth Army, where a British invasion from the Persian Gulf was imminent.

With her husband dead, her eldest son in prison, and her sons-in-law gone to war, Grandmother had to contend by herself with her two eldest daughters. Neither Hakiye nor Ayşe could conceal the wrath they felt toward their brother Cevat. 'How can my mother be so solicitous of Cevat?' 'How can she forgive him for the heinous crime he committed?' 'Why does she go to visit him in jail at every occasion?' were questions they discussed often. They frequently confronted their mother on this subject, and after one especially violent argument Grandmother ordered both Hakiye and Ayşe out of her house and would not speak to them for weeks. So as not to lose her mind, poor Grandmother joined a *tekke* where she found solace in prayer and in helping the sick and destitute.

Speaking of the war years, Aunt Aliye, who was no more than a child then, has told me how poor they were and how she hated to wear patched clothes and old shoes to school. 'The city was so dark,' she'd say, shivering, 'and I was always cold because there was never enough coal.'

Mother, on the other hand, did not complain. She enjoyed studying under Madame Braggiotti and, as she did not want to ask Grandmother for money, she made hand-painted postcards and sold them at the local shop in exchange for paints, brushes and notebooks.

Of all the sisters, Aunt Ayşe had the most to report. Whenever we talked of World War I, she'd say in a tone of infinite sadness, 'My dear child, if only you knew how much I suffered! After my father's tragic death, the pain I felt was so sharp it numbed me. Even my fingers were frozen, and I could not play the piano for a long period. Without time even to mourn him, that dreadful war descended upon us, and the next thing I knew your Uncle Ahmet was shot in Baghdad by an Arab nationalist, and as if that were not enough, he was court-martialled for disobeying the war minister's orders and almost executed.'

In 1915 the British, anxious to secure the oil resources of Mosul in northern Iraq, had advanced north from the Persian Gulf toward Baghdad. Enver Pasha, the Ottoman minister of war, had ordered Ahmet to defend the city on the far side of the Tigris River. Ahmet assessed the situation: the British had a superior army and more and heavier ammunition and guns than he had; his army had been decimated by a recent epidemic of cholera; he was being asked to defend an area which was totally exposed. Knowing that his troops would be far better able to resist attack behind the river, Ahmet, acting on his own initiative, pulled them back, thus saving them from total destruction. Enver Pasha, who had locked horns twice before with the independent and dogged Ahmet, took this opportunity to court-martial him for disobeying orders. The prosecutor demanded the death penalty, and Ahmet was convicted. Just before he was to stand before the firing squad, however, the War Department received a telegram from the German Allies, signed by the head of the joint German-Turkish command, General von Hindenburg, praising the clever defender of Baghdad and recommending that he be rewarded for his initiative and valour. Over Enver's objections, Ahmet was released and shortly after named acting governor of Syria.

When we talked of those years, Aunt Ayşe would recount the horrors she had experienced during her travels by coach, accompanied by Lala, through war-torn Anatolia to join Uncle Ahmet. On one trip she had seen a column of Armenians being relocated from their homes in eastern Turkey to Syria, and in Sivas, an important province in central Anatolia, she had witnessed a famine in which 30,000 Turks had died from starvation, their bodies bloated from eating grass, scattered over the countryside.

Aunt Hakiye, the stoic of the family, never talked much of the war. While Uncle Emin was away at the front she worked diligently as a volunteer nurse in an army hospital and concentrated on her little daughter Fureya, whom she adored.

After the bloody Gallipoli campaign, which lasted a full year, the Turks, under the command of Mustafa Kemal, defeated the Allied forces and compelled them to withdraw. Gallipoli resulted in the temporary eclipse of its main British protagonist, Winston Churchill, and the political triumph of its not-yet-famous Turkish commander, later known as Atatürk. The success at Gallipoli had relieved pressure on Turkey in the West; in the East the Russian Revolution of 1917 resulted in the withdrawal of enemy forces there. However, without any respite, Turkey had to defend a third front in the south against the Arabs.

The Ottoman Empire was like a salad made up of *millets* – separate, self-governing ethnic groups retaining their own languages, religions and cultures. The Arab *millet* (what is now Syria, Lebanon, Israel, the Occupied Territories, Jordan, Iraq and the countries of the Arabian peninsula) was at the time of the Great War, because of its size and population, the most important. Most Arabs were Sunni Muslims like the Turks and regarded the sultan not only as the head of state but also as the caliph, their spiritual leader. In spite of the bond of Islam, however, Arab nationalism had been slowly fermenting for the past half-century, and Great Britain, determined to drive the Turks out of the Arab lands and searching for a way to take advantage of this Arab nationalist movement, turned to Emir Zeid's father, Sherif Hussein.

Following the deposal of Sultan Abdulhamid by the Young Turks in 1908, Sherif Hussein had returned to Mecca after an absence of sixteen years, and at the age of fifty-six was named emir of Mecca. Gradually becoming disappointed at the Young Turks' policy of 'Turkey for the Turks', called Pan-Turkism, and convinced that they intended to reduce the influence of the non-Turkish minorities, especially the Arabs, he began to favour the idea of Arab nationalism. Shortly before World War I, he sent his son Abdullah to visit Lord Kitchener, the British agent in Cairo, to tell him confidentially that, in the event of war against the Ottomans, the Hashemites would support Britain. This was music to Kitchener's ears. Later, in a series of letters to Sherif Hussein, Britain offered military support to him and his four sons, Ali, Faisal, Abdullah and Zeid, if they would lead a revolt of the Arab tribes against the Ottomans and promised, after victory, all Arab lands to Hussein and his descendants.

In 1916 Sherif Hussein proclaimed the Arab Revolt and declared the independence of the Hijaz from the Ottoman Empire. T. E. Lawrence, 'Lawrence of Arabia', was assigned to assist and advise Sherif Hussein and his sons. In the first phase of the Revolt, Emir Faisal and Colonel Lawrence, at the head of an Arab army raised from the tribes by the Hashemites and supplied by Britain with guns and ammunition, captured Aqaba, an important Turkish port on the

Red Sea, now in Jordan. This opened the second and most effective phase of the Revolt – their drive toward Damascus, the capital of Syria. Following the railway line, they pushed north into Jordan, where Emir Zeid was the first person to enter Amman, and onwards toward Damascus. During this period, a British force under the command of General Allenby was slowly occupying Palestine and Lebanon. On 1 October 1918, Faisal and Lawrence, accompanied by Emir Zeid, entered Damascus to great jubilation.

Two days later, General Allenby arrived in Damascus with news which stunned the Arabs. Behind their back, the British and French had signed the Sykes-Picot Treaty of 1916, by which France was to rule Syria and Lebanon while Great Britain was to have a League of Nations mandate over Palestine, Jordan and Iraq. Moreover, the Balfour Declaration had virtually promised Palestine to the Zionists. As these events completely contradicted the promises made by Great Britain to Sherif Hussein, he and all the Arabs felt betrayed by their friends and allies.

The Turks, on the other hand, regarded the 'betrayal' of Sherif Hussein by the British as his come-uppance for having attacked the motherland when it was weakest. For the Arabs to break away, as Greece and the Balkan countries had already done, meant the complete dismemberment of the empire, and the Turks regarded Sherif Hussein as the culprit who had helped bring this about. Even Mother, when she wanted to hit Emir Zeid below the belt, screamed, 'This is your punishment for blowing up a train full of wounded Turkish soldiers, your own mother's people!' Emir Zeid's mother, Sherif Hussein's third wife, was the grand-daughter of the illustrious Ottoman grand vizier Reşid Pasha, who in 1839 had promulgated the earliest constitutional document in any Islamic country, to be followed by the *Tanzimat*.

Emir Zeid rarely talked of his role in the war. He was by nature a very modest man. Moreover, we were Turks. It would have been inconsiderate of him to brag about his victories over our people. However, when any of us complained about any minor hardships he would say, 'You don't know what suffering is! Did you ever have to drink camel piss in the desert because you were so thirsty your tongue stuck to your palate?'

By the end of 1918, the 500-year-old Ottoman Empire had shrunk to little more than the Anatolian peninsula and Rumelia, a tiny foothold in Europe. Istanbul, once the capital of conquerors, was itself conquered and occupied by the British, French and Italians.

During the early days of the Occupation, Uncle Emin, who had been promoted to commandant of the Bosphorus, in charge of all shipping in and out of Istanbul, used his position, in spite of the watchful eyes of the British, to smuggle guns to Anatolia, where a war of independence was fomenting. The French had established a regular boat service between Istanbul and the Black Sea port of Samsun in Anatolia which facilitated the smuggling operation.

One winter afternoon in 1919, as the ferries were not running to Büyükada, a common occurrence due to the coal shortage, Nissa, then a young girl of eighteen, decided to spend the night at her sister Hakiye's apartment in the Shakir Pasha building in town, as she had done on many other such occasions. When she rang the bell, Hakiye at once opened the door a crack and signalled her to be quiet.

'Don't go into the living room,' she whispered, mysteriously. 'Emin has important visitors. We'll sit in my room until the gentlemen leave.'

When Hakiye told Nissa that one of the guests was Mustafa Kemal, the Gallipoli hero, Nissa could not resist peeking through the keyhole of the living-room door. He was sitting erect on an overstuffed, dark red velvet armchair with a high back which framed his handsome head. His golden hair was neatly combed to the side, and his big, piercing, steel-blue eyes shot from under his thick, wing-like eyebrows. He was wearing a simple, well-cut grey suit, and his elegantly crossed legs revealed trousers pressed to a knife-edge and highly polished shoes. Nissa was impressed by the good looks and elegant posture of this hero and hoped that one day she'd meet him.

The other guest was Seyfeddin Bey, Aunt Mizou's father, who had been the Ottoman consul-general in Marseilles and who had a French wife. The third man was a French boat captain whom Seyfeddin Bey had brought to meet Mustafa Kemal, and who was being bribed to smuggle guns to Samsun.

In May 1919 King Constantine of Greece, protected by British and American warships, landed an army at Izmir, Turkey's second largest city located on the Aegean Sea. Dreaming of reconquering Constantinople, the city named after the first Constantine, he became the first Christian king since the Crusades to set foot on Anatolian soil. In Istanbul, in the big square in front of the Blue Mosque, a large meeting took place to protest the dismemberment of Turkey, and Halide Edip, a renowned writer and a friend of the Bloomsbury Group, with her head uncovered, urged the people to fight against the Greeks. It was the first time a Muslim woman had appeared in public without the *çarşaf*. The response of the citizens to Halide Edip was instantaneous and wholehearted. Four days after the Greek landing, on 19 May, now celebrated as a national holiday in Turkey, Mustafa Kemal landed at Samsun and, through sheer force of personality, rallied the whole nation behind him to launch the 'War of Independence'.

When Uncle Emin discovered that the British had become suspicious of his arms shipments, he, like many other Ottoman officers, deserted the sultan's army and fled to Anatolia to join Mustafa Kemal and fight in his Army of Independence. Ahmet was not so lucky. In May the British arrested him with a group of prominent Turks – a former grand vizier, the speaker of Parliament, the chief of the General Staff, several ministers, professors and writers (about 115 in total). Charged with various crimes, they were sent into exile on Malta, where they were held for three years. None was ever tried or convicted.

In 1920 the Allies dismissed the Ottoman Parliament and ministries and took control of all departments of government and municipal administration. With the sultan reduced to a powerless figurehead, a puppet, the Turks experienced the heavy hand of their conquerors.

5

Enter Izzet–Melih

Somehow in this chaos Nissa found herself. Once she completed the necessary courses for the *brevet superior*, she entered a painting school for women which had been established during the reign of Sultan Reşad (1909–18). Although conditions in the city were dismal, and the daily journey from Büyükada to town by ferry in the winter took from two to five hours, after which she had to climb a long, steep hill to the academy, Nissa began an ecstatic year.

She loved standing at her easel all day, till long after the others had gone home and the white-bearded old porter had begun pushing his broom around her feet. Then she'd roll up her drawings and run down the hill, her head bursting, her lungs filling again with fresh air after the stifling atmosphere of the classrooms, and jump on the ferry for home. During the peaceful sea voyage her headache would vanish and she would be able to climb up from the dock in the best of spirits.

Nissa was a beautiful young woman of eighteen by now. Although she was of medium height, she looked tall, for she carried her head high and moved with great assurance. Her classic face was framed by wavy chestnut hair and illuminated by big green eyes, fringed with thick, black lashes. A wide smile revealed perfect white teeth which gleamed like shiny, shelled, fresh almonds.

Like all Muslim women of her age and older, she had to wear the *çarşaf* but, headstrong and independent as ever, she soon dispensed with the veil portion by tossing it back over her head. However, dealing with the issue of marriage was not so easy. The way marriages were arranged appalled her. For centuries women spies or *voyeuses* had made it their business to spot likely brides and report their names and addresses to go-betweens, who in turn would match the girls with unmarried sons of appropriate families.

44

In this way Nissa was 'noticed'. While she commuted to the academy, she was spotted by two *voyeuses*, who had the audacity to follow her to her house to discover who she was. That done, they reported her to a couple who were looking for an appropriate bride for their son. Satisfied with Nissa's credentials, the couple then asked a close friend of Grandmother's whom they happened to know slightly to act as go-between. Shortly after, the friend went to the Büyükada house and reported to Grandmother that a good family was interested in Nissa as a bride for their son, an engineer who had just completed his university training in Germany. She added, 'He is tall and handsome as Apollo,' to prove which she presented a photograph, 'and the family promises the bride a fully furnished house.'

When, later, Grandmother told Nissa about the visit, Nissa acquiesced, for she was fond of the go-between and did not want to disappoint her. Presently the prospective groom and his family arrived for tea. As good-looking as reported, the young man interested Nissa until she showed him some of her latest art-school work, including sketches of the Discus Thrower and other nudes which she had tacked on to the walls of her room. Her suitor blushed to the roots of his hair and was struck dumb with embarrassment. Nissa told Grandmother after they left, 'How naive he is! How bourgeois! If I am to marry, I want a real man, not a shy boy, a man who can appreciate art, who has culture and intellect.'

'Suit yourself, my dear child,' Grandmother said, shrugging her shoulders, for she had absolutely no intention of imposing husbands on Nissa and Aliye, as had been done to her and her elder daughters. Besides, she knew that Nissa and Aliye, although totally different in temperament, were both strong-willed and would do exactly as they pleased, regardless. 'So why not let them pick their own husbands?' Grandmother thought. 'Anyhow, times have changed.'

As if a genie had heard Nissa, a few days after the engineer's visit she was told by Seyfeddin Bey that Izzet-Melih, the young, dynamic president of the Imperial Ottoman Tobacco Monopoly, a writer of considerable achievement who spoke and wrote French like a Frenchman, intended to call on the family to meet her.

Nissa was thrilled at the thought of his coming to call, for she had read Izzet's books and remembered seeing him years before as he drove by her nuns' school in an elegant landau, his *fez* rakishly tipped to the side, wrapped in a fur-lined coat. As his landau had passed Notre Dame de Sion, the sight of the uniformed young girls tittering at its gate had pleased him, and he had smiled at them as he twisted the tip of his handlebar moustache.

My father, Izzet-Melih, was born in 1887 in Jerusalem, a *sanjak* of the empire, where his father Esad Bey was *defterdar*. Prior to being posted to Jerusalem, Esad Bey had served in the mid–1880s as *defterdar* in Crete. There he had married the daughter of a wealthy landowner, Uzun Melek Bey. The latter owned three villages in the Khaniá section of the island and was the exclusive distributor for the entire Mediterranean of Yemen coffee, considered the best in the world. Mother has reluctantly admitted that my father's Cretan ancestors were superior to hers – simple islanders.

Father's paternal ancestors had come from Konya, the capital of the Seljuk Turks and also the home of the renowned mystic Sufi poet, Mevlana, and the seat of the Whirling Dervishes.

After attending primary school in Jerusalem, Izzet was sent to the Galatasaray Lycée in Istanbul, and, after graduation, to study law in Paris, where he developed a life-long love for all things French, especially its literature and its actresses. In the old empire there were plenty of opportunities for educated, enterprising young men, and when Izzet returned from Paris he started working for the Régie Ottomane, a French-owned tobacco company whose patrician Jewish president, Mr Weil, became his mentor and role model.

As a young bachelor Izzet lived virtuously in a three-storey wooden house in Şişli, a fashionable residential section of the city, with his widowed mother and aunt and an unmarried sister, working diligently at the tobacco company and helping to support them, since the old ladies had only their deceased husbands' pensions.

Opposite Izzet's house, a young woman named Seniye lived with her prominent and much older husband and their two little daughters. From her window across the street, Seniye watched Izzet's comings and goings and set her cap at him. Without any compunction, she sent her maid to deliver to him a hand-written message to meet her at the glove counter of the Bon Marché, a shop on the main street in Pera. Izzet was somewhat startled by her forwardness; however, intrigued, for he had heard of her beauty, he showed up at the Bon Marché on the appointed day and hour. There she was, standing at the glove counter with her two little girls. As he approached, she lifted her veil, and Izzet was overcome, dazzled by this red-headed, translucent-skinned enchantress. After a few more rendezvous and a great deal of scheming, Seniye abandoned husband and children and married Izzet. In 1912 they had a daughter they named Remide.

Going up the executive ladder in leaps and bounds, assisted by Mr Weil and the seductive and ambitious Seniye, Izzet became president of the Tobacco Company at the age of thirty. He showered Seniye with gifts and jewels and loved her with a passion he never felt for another woman. Father had a theory that in certain cases the skin of a man and the skin of a woman worked together so remarkably that there would be a kind of electrical discharge, and passion would be generated. 'C'est une question de peau,' he told me in his old age. Certainly, the skins of Izzet and Seniye flourished magnificently.

After the war Seniye and Izzet, Remide and the English governess travelled to Europe. At the Hotel Danieli in Venice, Seniye came down with the Spanish flu and was treated by a handsome Italian doctor. She fell madly in love with him and embarked on a passionate love affair. I suppose their skins sizzled, for Seniye lost all reason. Izzet, devastated, decided that the best thing would be for them to return home immediately, but Seniye refused to go. Remide, then aged eight, who was in her mother's bedroom at the Danieli at the time, told me many years later that Father, tears pouring down his cheeks, had implored her mother, Seniye, not to leave him. He had pointed out the mistake she was making by staying behind for a married man with two little children, a Catholic to boot, who would never marry her. He had warned her she would repent her move bitterly, but Seniye, ablaze with passion, had adamantly refused to listen to reason or common sense. The last time I saw my half-sister Remide, in Ankara, where she lived and worked at the French Embassy, she said bitterly, leaning on her cane, 'The only thing my mother cared about was sex. She thought nothing of abandoning me for a good lay. Animals are more responsible toward their cubs.'

Unable to sway Seniye, Izzet returned to Istanbul with little Remide and her governess, feeling rejected and utterly miserable. Ready to forgive her and take her back, he hoped and waited six months for Seniye's return; when she did not come, he divorced her, broken-hearted.

Madame Seyfeddin Bey, Aunt Mizou's French mother, had met Izzet-Melih, the dapper francophile, at the Alliance Française in Istanbul and liked him instantly. How could this handsome, sophisticated young man look so sad? When she found out that the wife he loved had deserted him, she decided to 'help out' and told him of Nissa. 'I know a beautiful, well-educated young girl of good family who is of marriageable age,' she said. 'Seyfeddin Bey was a close friend of her father, Shakir Pasha, and knows the family well. If you are interested, he would be glad to act as go-between.'

Izzet-Melih was interested. Yes, the best way for him to forget would be to get involved with another woman – the hair of the dog that bit him. He asked Seyfeddin Bey to contact the family on his behalf.

When Izzet-Melih presented himself at the Büyükada house, he was received by Grandmother and her four daughters in the formal lower living room, full of Cevat Pasha's stiff, mother-of-pearl inlaid furniture from Damascus. This gloomy room with its heavy, bottle-green velvet draperies, fringed with hundreds of pompoms, had a special redeeming feature. Its entire far wall had been made into a grotto, with half-moon-shaped shelves filled with moss and earth from which grew geraniums and ferns. Water constantly trickled down its rough terracotta surface like a mini waterfall. To the left of the grotto wall was the piano and to the right a comfortable seating arrangement for those who wanted to listen to it. To enable his daughters to read their music easily, Shakir Pasha had installed a skylight in that area. The many house plants in blue and white Chinese pots thrived with the light from above and gave that end of the room a greenhouse effect.

As a child I used to think, 'This living room represents the two sides of life, the dark and the bad, and the light and the good.' When my dolls misbehaved, I sent them for punishment to the dark side, and when they were good girls, they could sit on the bright side.

On the day my parents met, Suat had gone to meet Izzet at the ferry landing. When they entered the living room, where Grandmother and her daughters were waiting, Izzet gallantly kissed all the ladies' hands, including Aliye's, who was only seventeen at the time. A typical Turkish gentleman would have kissed only Grandmother's, the older lady's, out of respect, but Izzet, the product of French education, automatically kissed them all. Grandmother led him to an armchair near the piano and one of the *beslemes* served everyone Turkish coffee in tiny Meissen cups. While Nissa sat opposite Izzet sipping her coffee, he examined her closely and was most impressed by her extraordinary beauty. Many years later, telling me of their first meeting, Father said, 'One would expect anyone who has such perfect classic features to be remote and cold like a marble statue. Yet your mother had such a vivacious personality! That reinforced her beauty and made it come alive. Her charm could skin a peach.'

My mother, on the other hand, told me how delighted she had been with Father's good looks, impeccably tailored clothes, sophisticated manner and conversation. 'He was the perfect boulevardier,' she said, 'and when I showed him my sketches, he complimented me. "You should visit the museums in Europe," your father said, and I knew he meant, "When we are married, I will see to it that you do." '

After Ayşe had regaled the group with one of her favourite Chopin mazurkas and Hakiye, not to be outshone, had played Mozart's Turkish March with great *éclat*, the family moved to the upstairs living room. There, taking Izzet by the arm, Nissa showed him her mother's landscapes painted on silk, her brother Cevat's miniatures, and the watercolour of her grandmother that she herself had made at the age of fourteen. The samovar was lit, and the tea table, which had been set with Grandmother's best linen and the Rosenthal china that came out only for special visitors, was covered with finger sandwiches, salted and sweet wafers and a large chocolate cake. Grandmother poured the tea. Nissa cut the cake while Aliye, being the youngest, passed the tea. When she offered Izzet his cup, he looked up to thank her and was moved by her haunting, innocent, lavender eyes set in her pale face. As he reached to take the cup, their hands touched and Izzet felt an immediate electric charge. He had an overwhelming urge to take this young nymph, this mermaid with her long, flowing, golden hair, into his arms and protect her, for she seemed as vulnerable as a little bird lost on a stormy night. As Nissa approached, cake plate in hand, Aliye glided aside and, like an eclipse, Nissa's classic face replaced Aliye's. 'Thank you,' Izzet said, accepting his cake, and, seeing Nissa's face at such close range, he thought to himself, 'How lovely she is! I cannot wait for her to be my wife and to kiss those perfectly shaped lips. What I felt for the little one a moment ago was nothing but a momentary impulse.' Bothered by these conflicting emotions, Izzet rose from his chair and walked over to talk with the two elder sisters.

When he enquired politely about their husbands, Hakiye told him that Emin was in Anatolia fighting with Mustafa Kemal. Like all Turkish intellectuals, Izzet was a fervent admirer of Kemal, not only as a great soldier but also as a man who appreciated literature. Izzet had sent the hero all his books, with passionate, flowery dedications, and he too hoped to join him soon. Ayşe told him that her husband, Ahmet, had been exiled to Malta, where he was interned with many of Izzet's friends, writers and journalists. Apolitical though he was, Izzet launched into a bitter criticism of the British occupiers who, like most colonizers, treated the Turkish people as their inferiors. The conversation then shifted to lighter subjects, and Suat entertained the group with his witty stories.

The visit over, Izzet left much impressed by this warm, sophisticated, music- and art-loving family, which reminded him of characters in the Chekhov plays he had read. During the ferry ride back to the city that evening, while reviewing the events of the afternoon, Izzet briefly recalled the strong attraction he had felt for Aliye but immediately pushed it out of his mind.

My parents' wedding was celebrated in Izzet's town house, where the religious ceremony also took place, performed by a kadı. It was a quiet affair, attended only by members of both families and close friends. Once again Grandmother strained her resources in order to give Nissa a suitable trousseau of linens and china and silver, which she supplemented with unusual pieces of furniture from the Büyükada house, including one of the six screens the Japanese emperor had sent Cevat Pasha, a couple of gilt, throne-like armchairs and a tall blue and white Ming vase, which Izzet was to use as a stand for his many canes.

After the wedding Nissa joined Izzet's household, which consisted of his widowed mother and aunt, his eight-year-old daughter Remide, her English governess and a staff of servants. The ghost of his first wife Seniye lingered everywhere.

6

The Early Twenties

Nissa soon discovered that the members of her new household were not very friendly. Her crotchety, demanding mother-in-law ridiculed her because she was young and simple. Izzet's first wife Seniye had known all the ploys of sex appeal and beguiled men and women as a matter of course. While Seniye had worn elaborate, *décolleté* gowns around the house, Nissa, only nineteen and pregnant with her first child, wore simple, dark, high-necked dresses. The old lady, who missed Seniye's colourful persona, would mockingly exclaim to her sister, 'Well, well! Look at our new bride. What a plain Jane she is!' and the two widows, always in black, would cackle like two crows.

Izzet's daughter, Remide, rejected by her own mother, continually showed her resentment at Nissa's intrusion into her life. Once, in a fit of pique, she threw Nissa's pink diamond ring down the lavatory; the plumber had to be summoned to retrieve it. 'This is *my* mother's house,' she kept saying on every occasion, '*my* mother's, not yours!' Even the governess turned out to be a disappointment, a timid, ignorant Englishwoman whom Remide ordered about.

Worst of all, Izzet was caught up in the frenetic social whirl of the occupied capital. The worse conditions became for the common people, the faster and more frivolous became the social scene. To the British, French and Italian officers and their families present at the soirées and balls had been added a new, exotic element – *émigrés* from the Russian Revolution. From all the Russian Black Sea ports shiploads of White Russian men and women and children and whole regiments of soldiers arrived. Many of the women had been members of the old nobility, and though some were penniless and reduced to working as governesses or servants, others had brought their jewels or had transferred their fortunes before the collapse and were able to join Istanbul society. The beauty and refinement of the Russian women dazzled the Turks, including Izzet, who regularly left his pregnant wife alone at home and went out on the town.

One night, Nissa got out of bed and sat in the cold on the steps outside the house and waited. In the early morning she caught Izzet as he crept in from an assignation. Shocked to see her sitting in the street, Izzet tried to explain his late arrival. 'An old Galatasaray schoolmate is getting married and his close friends threw a party for him at the Chat Noir. You know what a bachelor party is; it lasted for ever!' She wanted very much to believe him, but she knew he was fibbing. Later she saw his handkerchief was stained with lipstick marks, but she did not confront him. Instead, that morning, after he had left for his office, she packed a bag and moved to her mother's home. She intended to get a divorce rather than put up with his philandering and lies.

Although Grandmother and her sisters sympathized with her at first, after a few days they began gently to bring up questions of her expected child, forgiveness and wifely duty.

'These things happen,' Grandmother advised Nissa. 'Remember what I had to put up with? Your father's Belgian mistress in Ostend whom he visited every year? You even brought me a letter he had written her, which he had given you to post, for you thought it was wrong. Still, I looked the other way for the sake of my marriage, the family, my children. That is the wise thing to do. If every woman whose husband is unfaithful got a divorce, there would be few marriages left in the world.'

Understanding the wisdom of her mother's advice, two weeks later Nissa reluctantly returned to Izzet, who had called every day, bouquet in hand, asking for forgiveness, and tried to ignore his indiscretions. In store for her lay many more serious infidelities with which, however, she learned to live.

The most disgraceful affair she had to endure occurred barely a year after her marriage, towards the end of her pregnancy. One afternoon at a tea dance in a friend's home, Nissa felt nauseous and, abruptly leaving the dance floor, ran upstairs to the ladies' room. As she opened the door of a sitting room leading to it, she glimpsed two figures close together, silhouetted against the rays of the dying sun. The moment the couple heard the door open, they sprang apart, and Nissa was flabbergasted to see it was Izzet and Aliye.

'What are you doing up here?' she demanded, nonplussed. 'What the hell is going on?'

Aliye, ruffled, tried to make light of the situation. 'Nissa, my dearest, it's nothing. It really is nothing, believe me. I happened to come up to go to the ladies' room and found Izzet here looking at the books. As a joke he tried to kiss me. You know Izzet will flirt with anyone and everyone. It doesn't mean a thing. Believe me, there's nothing to worry about. Please, please, don't be upset.'

Izzet calmly corroborated Aliye's remarks. 'She is right,' he added. 'It doesn't mean a thing. We were just playing around.'

Embarrassed for them, Nissa let the matter drop, but she seethed inside. How could Izzet pursue her sister? Weren't there enough other women? But, worse, how could Aliye, the baby sister whom she worshipped, the closest person to her in the world, act so treacherously? The pain she felt was excruciating.

Nissa and Aliye had been inseparable since childhood, bound by a deep-seated attachment, almost a passion. One day the two sisters could fight like wildcats, saying hurtful things, making cruel accusations, throwing objects and pulling hair, and the next behave as if nothing had happened, solicitous of each other's feelings.

No two sisters were ever more unalike in looks and character. Despite their identical upbringing – they shared the same room and governess, went to the same schools, had the same Qur'an and piano teachers – they experienced life totally differently. Nissa was the strong-willed sister who always knew her own mind and took by storm what she wanted when she wanted it. She charged through life like a fearless tigress. Aliye, on the other hand, worked out an opposite style early on, partly as a defence against Nissa: she made herself a master of indecision and helplessness. I have seen her stand in her room in hat and coat for an hour, irresolute over whether to go out or not. How to explain her power? It was the power of a very small, helpless bird. 'Help me,' she would say, looking around forlornly, with those big innocent eyes. 'I don't know what to do. Help me! I cannot do it. I do not know how.' In that way she got everyone to assist and protect her.

As a child Aliye behaved in such a fey way that one day Grandfather decided to take her to a doctor. Off they went, terrified little Aliye alone with the bearded old pasha whom she scarcely ever addressed. At the doctor's, she was left in the examination room and told to undress. But nannies and maids and elder sisters had always undone those remote buttons and ribbons and laces; now she stood rigid, waiting for help. She could not even undress herself. The doctor and the patriarch conferred: if not imbecility, certainly close to it, they decided. To her infinite relief, Aliye was taken home. Her father expected nothing more of her, and the family regarded her as a simpleton. 'Poor little Aliye,' they'd say, 'Alyosha, Alyosha,' and forgave her all her indiscretions. Actually Aunt Aliye was a highly intelligent woman, adept at manipulating people. In life, like Nissa, but in a very different guise, she did as she wished, when she wished it, regardless of consequences.

For years I felt I could not confront my mother about this painful affair. It was only during one of our last conversations that I got her to admit how much it had hurt her.

'I had just given birth to Faruk, a year after my marriage. Your father came to the hospital with Aliye to see me after the baby was born. Of course, he was overjoyed to have a son, and Aliye hugged the baby with such love! The three of us shared the joy of my first-born. But when your father and Aliye left the hospital room together, I knew they were going somewhere . . . Suat had already told me about their affair. Suddenly I burst into tears. The young nurse attending me could not understand what had happened. Here I was in the best private room, surrounded by bouquets of flowers, having just given birth to a lovely, eight-pound, healthy baby boy, and having just received a visit from my handsome, loving husband and sister – crying my heart out!

'How could she have known that the pain I was feeling was so acute that I wished I had died in childbirth?'

No one's chaos can be permanent, and the Aliye 'escapade' ended with the intervention of Grandmother, the older aunts and Suat, and the appearance of Charles Berger on the scene as Fureya's violin teacher. Nissa healed emotionally and found solace in her new baby and a new home without her in-laws. Izzet had found her a splendid apartment in Şişli, named Sebuhyan after its Armenian owner, with parquet and marble floors, central heating (new in those days) and a lift like a bird-cage. There, in a spacious room which she converted into a studio, Nissa set up her easel and painted as often as she could between all her social and family obligations. A self-portrait she made during that period, with bobbed hair, white face and dark, cherry-red mouth, was displayed for years on many different walls of our homes, and, like several of her paintings, eventually disappeared, resurfacing later at auctions in Istanbul, London and Paris.

Just about that time, Cevat was released from jail. His health had deteriorated, and he was coughing up blood. Once he had tried to commit suicide. 'Let me die,' he wrote to Grandmother, 'or get me out of here.' In spite of her strenuous efforts to obtain a pardon for Cevat, Grandmother had been unable to accomplish anything. However, when a general amnesty was declared in 1921, he was released after serving only seven of the fourteen years to which he had been sentenced.

Nissa, who loved Cevat and was grateful to him for having started her on painting as a child, first saw him after his release from prison dressed in a black cloak and a wide-brimmed hat, 'so romantic', sitting in the porter's lodge at the Shakir Pasha apartment. He had come to see his mother and was waiting to be told whether it was 'convenient' for him to go upstairs. Nissa felt it was so humiliating for him to sit like a servant in the porter's lodge, waiting for clearance, that she went in, threw her arms around him and told him that she loved him.

After his release, like his mother, Cevat joined a *tekke* and worked among the poor. Then, moving to Üsküdar on the Asiatic shore of the city, he lived with Grandmother's oldest brother, Vecihi, a veteran who had been blinded in the 1911 defence of Tripoli. Cevat married the old soldier's daughter, Hamdiye, his first cousin, and had a son, Sina, by her. While he worked as a journalist, he also translated English books and plays into Turkish. Shaw's *Man and Superman* was his favourite; he quoted from it constantly. He also drew political cartoons, produced the first colour magazine covers in Turkey, and in his spare time painted miniatures.

That summer another prisoner returned home, Ayşe's husband Ahmet. After being detained for three years in Malta, with no charges brought against them, Ahmet and fifteen other prisoners escaped in a small motorboat carrying a load of pigs to Italy. The fee charged by the boat owner – 2500 lira – had been raised in Istanbul by the prisoners' relatives, toward which Ayşe had contributed a piece of her jewellery. As the prisoners had expected, the Maltese authorities did not search the boat because they thought that no Turks would ever ride with a load of pigs, which Muslims, like Jews, consider unclean.

Having reached Italy safely, Ahmet made his way to Munich,

where Ayşe joined him. Returning later to Turkey in a Lloyd Tristino steamer, before entering the Istanbul harbour, he disguised himself as an Italian waiter to avoid capture a second time by the British, who still occupied the city. He then sailed on to Samsun.

And from far-away San Francisco there arrived on the Orient Express an unexpected addition to the Shakir family – a tall, glamorous American beauty, Syida Spreckels. Named for her Egyptian grandmother, Syida was the ex-wife of the California sugar heir Jack Spreckels. She had met Suat at the bar in the Excelsior Hotel in Rome. He had swept her off her feet, and they had had a whirlwind romance in the Eternal City. After returning to the United States, she then left country, home and husband, and, taking her only child, six-year-old Geraldine, followed Suat to Istanbul.

'We were having dinner at the Sebuhyan apartment when the doorbell rang,' my mother recalls. 'The maid came to tell us that a tall foreign lady and a child were at the door, asking for Suat Bey. "I told the lady that Suat Bey did not live here, but she did not understand. She kept repeating, 'Suat Bey, Suat Bey.' "

'Intrigued, I went to the door to see who this person was. An elegant woman in a cloche hat and chinchilla-trimmed coat, holding the hand of a dishevelled blonde child, stood in the hall in front of a mound of luggage. It looked as if they had come to stay! When the lady saw me, a puzzled expression crossed her face. "Is Suat Bey here?" she asked in a small voice. She probably thought I was Suat's wife and that he had not told her he was married. With Muslim men, one never knew.

'To put her at ease I immediately said, "My brother Suat isn't here at the moment, but please do come in. We'll telephone him, and he should be right over." Relieved, she flashed a luminous smile, revealing a splendid set of teeth. "What a gorgeous creature!" I thought to myself. "Suat certainly knows how to pick women."

'As she stepped into our vestibule, Izzet arrived, curious to know what was happening. "This is my husband," I said, introducing them. Izzet, after looking her over with approval, gallantly kissed her hand. "*Madame*," he said, "it's a pleasure. Let me take your coat." I then took the child, who looked so tired and had smudges on her face, to my room, where I bathed her and put her to sleep in my bed. As I was doing that, I heard Suat's voice: "Syida, my darling, what a marvellous thing to do. What a wonderful surprise!" '

Although Uncle Suat lived with Grandmother and Aunt Aliye in the Shakir Pasha apartment, he had given Syida my parents' home as his address. He must have sensed that Syida might follow him to Istanbul and wanted to make sure she had a good first impression. He did not want her to be confronted by the antiquated Shakir Pasha apartment, his stocky, old-fashioned mother who did not speak English, and his slightly fey and frowzy sister. He needn't have bothered. Syida was so madly in love with Suat that she would not have cared if he had been a *fakir* who lived in a tent with a couple of goats.

Shortly after her arrival, Suat and she were married in a civil ceremony, after which they moved in with Grandmother and Aunt Aliye. In the summers, like all the Shakirs, they came to the Büyükada house. Everyone loved and appreciated Syida for being so good-natured and flexible, and for fitting in with such ease and élan. The family always held her up as a role model.

When I was an overgrown teenager, Mother would say, 'Syida was as tall as you, Shirinaki, yet she was so graceful. She knew how to handle her height. You should have seen how elegantly she crossed her long legs. Now pull in those long legs of yours and try to sit like her. Don't walk into a room as if you are marching. Glide in. Syida floated into a room like a chiffon scarf held up by a breeze. You should have seen Syida and Suat dancing the Charleston at the Yacht Club. Everyone stopped and watched. They were divine.'

Around this time, a new crisis erupted in Nissa's life. One day on her way back from the Istanbul Academy of Fine Arts, which now accepted women, a zealous artist friend told her that Izzet's first wife Seniye had returned from Italy and that he had set her up in an apartment and visited her there. After being rejected by her Italian lover, Seniye had returned to Istanbul and thrown herself at Izzet's feet, crying and begging forgiveness, telling him that her passion for the doctor had been folly and that she loved only Izzet. Once more he had fallen under the spell of her skin.

This time Nissa issued an ultimatum: Izzet either had to end his relationship with Seniye or she, Nissa, would take her son and leave. Izzet chose the first alternative, and for a time things calmed down.

These were days full of national celebrations, and my parents were caught up in them. After three years of continuous warfare against the invading Greeks, the Turkish armies finally gained the upper hand, defeated the Greeks and chased them out of Izmir into the Aegean Sea whence they had come.

Uncle Emin, having entered Izmir as chief of staff of Fahrettin Pasha's army, was promoted to general and made commandant of the city. Twenty-eight-year-old Hakiye joined him there with her daughter Fureya and her little son Shakir. They lived in a lovely house in the Karşıyaka section of Izmir, which had survived the great fire that had erupted after the recapture of the city. Izmir was a highly civilized port city on the Aegean Sea, where many sophisticated, educated Turkish, Levantine, Greek, Armenian and Jewish families had cohabited harmoniously for centuries. Engaged in shipping and the export of tobacco, its residents had connections all over the world. Hakiye felt very much at home among people who were as worldly as any she had known in Istanbul.

One of the first ladies she befriended was Latife Hanım, a twenty-three-year-old, highly educated daughter of a prominent, wealthy local businessman, who was soon to become Mustafa Kemal's wife.

On 20 September 1922 Mustafa Kemal, now called the Gazi (the Conqueror), entered Izmir in an open car decorated with red and white carnations, to a frenzied welcome, and went directly to army headquarters, which was a beehive of activity, its staff officers trying to deal with a thousand problems that required immediate attention. The devastated country had to be administered, and a million important decisions made.

In the midst of all this turmoil, Latife Hanım, wearing a purple silk *çarşaf*, but without veil, made her way through the throngs in the streets, past the guards, orderlies and aides-de-camp, into the Gazi's office. He was taken aback by the forwardness of this young woman, who looked him straight in the eye and announced that she was the daughter of Uşakizade Muammer Bey. This was a lady of evident breeding, no woman of the streets, not one of the flirtatious young girls who threw seductive glances from behind their veils. He asked her to sit down.

She spoke candidly: 'My parents are spending the summer in Biarritz, and we have a large, comfortable house in Göztepe, one of Izmir's suburbs. You and your staff would be much more comfortable there, away from the noise, confusion and uproar of the city. As you know, the fighting here has not yet completely subsided, and there are still smouldering fires everywhere.

'I will personally see to it that you are well taken care of.' Then she added passionately, 'When I heard that our troops were nearing Izmir, I left my law studies in Paris and came home as fast as I could, because I wanted to witness your victory in person. Look,' she said, opening a locket around her neck, 'I keep your picture with me all the time.'

Kemal was thoroughly intrigued by this self-assured, poised and sophisticated young woman, and accepted her offer. The White Palace, as her home was called, was a fairly large structure on a hill overlooking the bay of Izmir and the sea beyond. Surrounded by vineyards and lovely gardens, it suited the Gazi well. His personal comforts were looked after, the food was good, and Latife ran a splendid household with a well-trained staff. She not only took care of his personal needs and his health; she also became his secretary. Every morning, after having read the local and foreign newspapers, she personally carried breakfast to the Gazi, and, as he ate, she gave him a summary of the news. 'My newspaper,' he called her. With her fluency of both English and French, she translated his diplomatic correspondence. His mind was stimulated by her insight, intelligent comments, observations and brilliant arguments.

Latife stimulated Kemal not only intellectually but also physically. A masculine mind in a feminine body was a combination he had not encountered in many Turkish women. His passion was ignited; he desired her and made advances. Although she was madly in love with him, she refused to become his mistress: she would be his wife or nothing. Since he wanted her, he agreed to marry her.

Hakiye and Emin, now called Emin Pasha, were among the very small inner circle of friends invited to Kemal and Latife's wedding, held at the White Palace in the early afternoon of 29 January 1923. A *kadı* married them in a quiet ceremony attended only by her family and a few very close friends and aides. Latife wore a simple dress with a veil to cover her hair and white gloves, and held a single long-stemmed rose. She was not a beautiful bride; in fact, she was short and stocky, but she had big, intelligent eyes and a formidable intellect. Personality, more than looks, were her great asset. The Gazi married her because he admired her as the symbol of the modern Turkish woman. She would be a role model for the new nation. After the marriage ceremony the governor of Izmir shook Latife's hand vigorously and in a voice full of emotion said, 'You have conquered the Conqueror of Izmir.'

The first time the newly-weds went out, they called on Aunt

Hakiye and Emin Pasha. Although it was tea-time, Hakiye offered them champagne, which she had kept on ice for the occasion. When the people in the neighbourhood saw all the guards and cars in front of the commandant's house, they realized that the Gazi was inside and gathered below the balcony. 'Long live our Gazi!' they shouted. 'Long live Mustafa Kemal Pasha!' The Gazi walked to the window and raised his champagne glass in a toast to the crowd.

'Kemal,' Latife shouted in a scolding tone from across the room, 'don't show yourself to the people with glass in hand.'

Aunt Hakiye was shocked. 'You cannot tell a man like Mustafa Kemal how to behave,' she told me. 'Besides, Latife should have called him "my pasha" in front of other people, as tradition requires, and not used his first name. Then and there I knew the marriage couldn't last.'

She was right. The marriage lasted only another two and a half years. The Gazi never remarried.

With victory over the Greeks won, in the late summer of 1922 Refet Pasha, one of Mustafa Kemal's great generals and minister of war, to the frenzied cheers of thousands packed in the streets and hanging from the roofs, had entered Istanbul at the head of an army and ended four years of occupation. The *mehmetciks* were elated at their reception, and as they marched through the city, led by Refet Pasha on a horse, they beamed like a cast of actors receiving a standing ovation. Nissa was beside herself with joy and wanted to hug each and every one of them. After such a long period of degradation under the heels of the Allies, national pride and honour were finally restored.

In an audience with Sultan Mehmet VI, Refet Pasha advised the ineffectual monarch to dissolve his government, as Turkey could not continue to have two governments – the National Government established by Mustafa Kemal in Ankara and the sultan's in Istanbul. Intimidated by the stupendous reception Refet had received, and fearing for his life, the sultan approached the British. On 17 November 1922 he was slipped out of the city on one of their battleships and sailed into oblivion, to San Remo, Italy. Thus ended, most undramatically, a dynasty which had ruled for over six centuries, paving the way for the birth of a new nation.

In July 1923 Nissa gave birth to her second son, Nejad, and four months later, on 29 October 1923, Turkey was declared a republic and Mustafa Kemal elected its first president.

7

Sadness and Trouble

Although my parents' marriage was far from perfect, Nissa and Izzet shared a tragedy that temporarily brought them closer together. A little more than three years after their marriage, Remide, a difficult twelve-year-old, contracted scarlet fever. Nissa felt duty-bound, especially because Remide was a maladjusted stepchild, to nurse her personally at home instead of sending her to an isolation hospital. The result of her kindness was that Faruk, her first-born, caught the highly contagious disease and died, aged two and a half. He was adorable, judging by his photographs, with big, luminous, hazel-coloured eyes and golden-brown hair.

I have in my possession a book of my father's short stories, the pages brown with age, the hard binding covered with *petit-point*, work of the loving hand of his third wife. The story, called 'The Greatest Agony', brings out graphically what he felt when he took Nissa away after little Faruk's tragic and sudden death. They caught the *SS Leopolis* for France, and as the ship prepared to clear the harbour they looked up from the deck to the hillside where Faruk lay buried, under the inscribed verses of a famous poet friend, Abdulhak Hamit, in the old graveyard of Eyüb overlooking the Golden Horn. Later, on the boat, Father wrote:

How did your mother and I not die in that house of mourning? Why didn't we go mad when we saw your little body, white and rigid as marble, the sweetest smile set fast on your little face? We lived a night as long as centuries next to the room in which you lay dead. And we even slept! We were choking with agony and yet we slept . . .

We are escaping, Faruk, we are going to far other seas, far other lands, far other skies. We are leaving your little body, light as a

61

bird's, lying on a hillside in Eyüb, and we think of when we were last on these waters, steaming towards Şişli and the house filled with your laughter. Now we are on the Sea of Marmara. Our ship's prow parts the bright blue water. Behind us lies the unforgettable spectacle of my beloved Istanbul. Faruk's poor mother rests her head on my shoulder and looks up at my face. Her eyes are full of tears.

I feel a warmth in my wounded heart. The thick layer of ice around my great pain melts a little. In the endless emptiness of catastrophe I am not alone. Like two friends, we will remember and weep together.

Over sixty years later, speaking of her pain, Mother told me, 'I felt I was a tree whose branches were being hacked off with a big axe. The agony was like nothing I have suffered before or since. I was immunized for life.'

Father has recounted how, in their room at Claridge's in Paris, my mother screamed on several occasions, 'I am burning, Izzet. I am afire,' then ripped her clothes and fell to the floor, and how he then held her in his arms, wiped away the flood of tears and tried to calm her down as best he could. 'Your poor mother suffered a great deal. The loss of a child is something one never gets over.'

In Paris, Izzet tried to divert Nissa by taking her to the theatre, to elegant restaurants and to visit his literary friends – all to no avail. They soon returned home, where Nissa concentrated on painting all day, for that was her therapy. When she painted, she immersed herself totally in her work. Some life force seemed to penetrate her and, as if her body were a conduit, release itself in colours on the canvas. At tea-time the Shakirs and friends would call to keep her company, to cry with her if necessary or laugh with her as need demanded. If she was satisfied with her current painting, she would show it to them for their comments.

Just about this time, another event, her brother Cevat's arrest and exile, upset Nissa profoundly. Cevat's 'Kafkaesque' arrest was ironically a result of the Kurdish Revolt in 1925. The Kurds, who lived in the eastern part of Turkey and Syria as well as in northern Iraq and Iran, distinct in both race and language from ethnic Turks, Arabs and Iranians, revolted against the recently founded republic. Fanatically religious Sunni Muslims, the Kurds claimed to be fighting a religious war against the 'Infidel Republic of Ankara', but their real aim was to carve out from Turkey's eastern provinces an independent Kurdestan. Within two months they wiped out the Turkish garrisons of two provinces. Once again rallying his new nation solidly behind him, Mustafa Kemal took personal command and put down the rebellion. Unfortunately, the constitution had to be suspended, and the president was given dictatorial powers by Parliament. He set up a special court called the Tribunal of Independence and in the year that followed tried many of his political enemies. Uncle Kılıç Ali was one of the judges and unwittingly played a role in shaping Uncle Cevat's destiny.

Uncle Cevat, who had been released from jail four years before, was living in Üsküdar with his cousin-wife and his two-year-old son Sina and working for a newspaper called *Tan*, whose owner, a prominent journalist, was regarded as a leftist. About the time of the Kurdish Revolt, Cevat published an article based on a story he had heard in prison. It was about conscripts during the war who deserted from troop trains when they passed near their villages and, when caught, were hanged or shot out of hand, without trials. Far from being a political indictment, Cevat meant the article to be a paean to the longings of young men so homesick that they risked death for desertion in order to see their loved ones once again.

In view of the Kurdish Revolt, however, the general paranoia which gripped the country at that time, and the leftist newspaper in which it was published, the government considered Cevat's article insulting to the military and 'subversive' and arrested him. The circumstances of the arrest were bizarre.

'It was the eve of Şeker Bayram, and I'd bought some boxes of sweets for the household, which I had stuffed into my pockets . . . I was returning from a long, hard day's work at the newspaper . . . and looked forward to relaxing at home while painting my miniatures after dinner.

'The corner room of the house in Üsküdar overlooked on one side the sea, the Leander Tower and the Topkapı Palace, and on the other side the street. As I was about to take off my coat, I was informed that the police were at the door asking to see me. I was surprised. Through the front window I saw two plain-clothes men near the tree where I used to take my son Sina to enjoy the fresh air. Then through the side window I saw two other plain-clothes men. It was like a nightmare. What grave crime had I committed to warrant the appearance of four policemen? With my coat still on, I opened the door.

' "You must come with us to the police station," said one of the men.

' "Why?"

' "They'll tell you why at the police station."

' "But is it something serious? I want to know."

' "We don't know. The police chief will tell you."

'At the police station, when I asked the chief why I had been arrested, he said, "You'll find out in due course," and abruptly dismissed me. I spent the night on a bench in the police station, and at dawn a huge man appeared and shouted, "Come along. We're taking you to the Haydarpaşa Station to catch the Ankara train." They were taking me to the capital to face the consequences of my crime. But what *was* my crime? What *had* I done?'

The grim comedy continued until Cevat found himself facing the dreaded Tribunal of Independence, where he was finally told what his crime was. When they sentenced him to imprisonment for sedition, his distraught mother dispatched her younger brother Nedim to Ankara to plead with Judge Kılıç Ali, who had been a comrade of his in the Tripoli war. The latter, who did not yet know the Shakir family (but who later married my cousin Fureya), interceded as a favour to Nedim and was able to have the sentence reduced to three years internal exile in Bodrum. Then a tiny, sleepy fishermen's village in the southern Aegean, Bodrum, in ancient times, had been called Halicarnassus, the great capital of Mausolus.

In his book *Blue Exile* Cevat describes his arrival and first night in Bodrum:

I immediately rented a small peasant house, a one-room, white-washed stone structure, where I was allowed to live as long as I stayed within the village limits and reported daily to the *gendarme*, who represented the only state authority there. That first evening I spent in Bodrum I was alone for the first time in weeks without the guards who had escorted me on the endless, tedious journey from Ankara. When I opened my door, I saw the sunset over the sea and the scarlet rays of the dying sun falling on the shores and the islands. Against the sky stood the old Crusader fortress in the bay, black and sharply silhouetted. The whitewashed houses on the shore had turned pink and the sea a dark violet. I could hear the rustling of the vine leaves and the murmur of the sea. The seaweed strewn on the shore was like silver filigree. I went out on the little beach in front of the house and plunged my hands into the sand and the sea, letting first one and then the other stream through my fingers. As if in a religious ecstasy, I fell on my knees and felt my spirit rising out of my inanimate body like a million twittering birds. As in a flash of lightning I saw the sea for what it was – the same sea that, in my early childhood, I had seen at Phalernon near Athens when my father had been ambassador to Greece. I had come home to the sea.

I rushed into the village and bought a bucket and a rope and began hauling water out of the well in the little courtyard. I splashed water everywhere over the cobbles of the courtyard, and when I had done this several times I returned to the beach and hauled out buckets full of sea water, which I then threw about in the same manner on the sand and then up further and further on the shore, until I was totally exhausted.

Long after the three years of internal exile were over, Cevat continued to live in Bodrum. Deserting his cousin-wife, he married a local girl, a Cretan like his mother, whose family had been relocated from the island in the population exchange of 1912. They had three children. Writings flowed from his pen about the adventures of the fishermen, the tragic lives and deaths of the sponge divers who, to eke out their living, dived fathoms under the sea without oxygen, all for the price of a sponge worth perhaps one hot meal. Many, as a result, got the bends, and some died. Under his pseudonym 'The Fisherman of Halicarnassus', Cevat wrote fifteen books of fiction, essays, short stories and other pieces, and numerous articles on many different subjects. He became widely known and loved in Turkey for pointing out the homely joys and sorrows, the struggles and successes of the little people of Turkey, and for being a champion of Anatolian civilizations.

Cevat's most cherished intellectual passion concerned Homer. The point he stressed about him was that, as Homer was born in Anatolia, an Ionian, he represented Anatolian heroism. The Trojans, he said, were as much the heroes of the *Iliad* as the Achaians, the mainland Greeks. These theories he worked out in the minute detail and obsessive style of a fundamentally isolated man who built up his knowledge piece by piece away from the marketplace of scholarship.

Another of Cevat's many interests concerned the greening of Bodrum. When he first arrived there, the village was bare of trees. Though he had few means, he denied himself necessities to buy books on horticulture, which he read until they fell apart. When he was permitted to leave Bodrum, he visited Istanbul to obtain seedlings and seeds. Within an hour of his arrival back in Bodrum, he would go about the village on his mission of bringing green to the peninsula, planting and watering and tending. He carried fertilizer from the neighbouring islands down to a *kayık* and transported it to Bodrum and his beloved plants; if the weather was bad, he would load donkey baskets with good earth in the hills and bring it down to the trees. He became a teacher of gardening. His 300-page notebook went from village to village and hand to hand so that other villages would become like the Bodrum he was realizing out of his dream – a white town shaded by tall trees, with bougainvillaea on the walls and oleanders near the water. When he eventually left it, the peninsula was a heaven of citrus, especially grapefruit, and there were tall palms and eucalyptus giving shade. The beautiful groves one can now see in the village were his work too. A combination of Ernest Hemingway, Mark Twain and Thoreau, he was a philosopher, a poet, a sage, a naturalist, and a highly vocal champion of the dignity of the individual.

8

Nissa, Star of Istanbul

After about a year and a half of mourning for Faruk, in a complete reversal, Nissa gave up painting temporarily and plunged into the very active Istanbul social scene, so different in atmosphere from Occupation days. While the Turks were celebrating the republic, the foreign ambassadors, who were soon to move to Ankara, the new capital, at that time a primitive country town, were giving farewell parties in their beautiful old residences, which they hated to leave.

At this time Nissa discovered she was expecting me, but that did not keep her from going out till the very last days of her pregnancy.

'So much champagne was drunk in your honour, so many toasts!' "To the baby!" "*Pour le bébé!*" "May its *kismet* be good!" No child has been more toasted. No wonder you turned out bubbly like champagne!' she told me.

I was born on 3 March 1926, between two acts during the opening night of *La Parisienne* by Henri Becq, performed by a French theatre company led by two popular stars of the day, René Alexandre and Gabrielle Robin. For the gala opening my father had taken a box. Before the show my parents dined with Aunt Hakiye and Uncle Emin. During the dessert Mother felt she was going to burst. The buttons down the front of her satin evening gown started popping in all directions.

'"Aïee, I think the child is descending,' she cried. Then, turning to my father, she added, 'You had better go to the theatre alone.' He left without any qualms. Soon after, Mother, like a demented circus horse, starting running around the dinner table, screaming, 'Give me a pair of scissors. Scissors! Scissors!' When Aunt Hakiye handed her a pair, she cut her dress all the way down the front. Uncle Emin turned beet-red. Aunt Hakiye threw Mother's chinchilla cape over her and rushed her to the Manara Clinic. Like all Istanbul society,

Dr Manara was also at the theatre. When word reached him, he and my father hurried to the clinic, the doctor slipped a white smock over his tuxedo, and I, who was in a great hurry to make my entrance into this world, was born. Dr Manara then duly returned to the theatre in time for the second act interval. The news that Madame Izzet-Melih had just given birth to a baby girl spread around the lobby. Count Bonarelli, the cultural attaché of the Italian Embassy went from box to box announcing my birth and, like a soothsayer in a fairy-tale, predicted, 'Baby Shirin is going to be a great tragedienne called *La Chirina*.'

A charming prediction, but, for the time and place, ridiculous. The first Turkish Muslim actress, Afife, had appeared on stage two years before only to have the police raid the theatre. The poor woman had had to escape the scandalized public and the ensuing riot through the back door. At the time of my birth it was unheard of for a Muslim girl to become an actress, for acting involved a public display of one's person exactly as is forbidden in the Qur'an. But times have changed, and, yes, I did become an actress – not a great one, perhaps, but enough to fulfil Count Bonarelli's prophecy.

Although my birth brought a temporary happiness, the basis of my parents' marriage stayed the same. Izzet continued to do as he chose, and Nissa put up with it and lived her own full life. By the time I was born, she had become a totally different woman from the naive schoolgirl Izzet had married. The numerous European trips they had taken had enriched her and given her *savoir faire* and self-confidence. Many times she has told me that these trips were the redeeming feature of her marriage.

'Seeing and learning were my elixir,' she said. 'Your father and I got on much better away from home. We went everywhere. "Where do you want to go?" he would ask me, and we'd go to Madrid to see the Prado, to Florence where I nearly lost my mind when I first saw the Fra Angelico frescoes, to Holland where we visited many museums and where I discovered my favourite painter, Bruegel.'

In Paris, because of Izzet's reputation as a writer, they were included in the literary salons. Nissa bought clothes from the Paris couturiers. Everywhere they went they stayed in the best hotels, the great palazzos. On the Riviera they partied with maharajahs, princesses, British lords and ladies, and American millionaires.

In Istanbul they were much sought after, especially by the diplomats who, whenever a visiting dignitary came, invited them as representatives of the modern Turkish couple. Thus my parents met and got to know many prominent Europeans in politics, journalism, and particularly the arts.

Considered by then the most beautiful woman of Turkey (old ladies still tell me they remember her doing the Charleston at a ball, lovely in a fringed, bugle-beaded Chanel dress), Mother was admired and courted by many, including her hero, Mustafa Kemal.

One summer day my parents went to a big luncheon the French ambassador, the Comte de Chambrun, was giving in honour of a group of French journalists who were touring Turkey. At the time everybody was writing articles about '*la nouvelle Turquie*' and its charismatic leader, Mustafa Kemal, who had converted the old, sprawling Ottoman Empire into a dynamic, compact, Western-oriented republic. When they returned to Büyükada in the late afternoon, they saw the president's yacht, *Ertuğrul*, anchored in front of the Yacht Club, where they were staying that summer. Almost as soon as they reached their room, the renowned writer Hamdullah Suphi, Izzet's Galatasaray classmate and his best friend, knocked on their door.

'I am with the president's party,' he announced. 'He saw you enter the club and asked me to invite you to his table.'

My parents were thrilled; at last they were going to meet the great man. So much had happened in the eight years since Nissa had seen him through the keyhole at her sister Hakiye's home and Izzet had sent him his autographed books!

In the large salon the president was seated in the middle of a long table surrounded by ministers, deputies, aides and, as always, journalists and writers. Obviously they had been drinking *rakı*, for the table was covered with a multitude of *mezes*.

The *rakı* table is a special Turkish way of socializing and has its own definite protocol. People sit around a table for an extended period of time, talking and sipping *rakı* with or without water and picking at a variety of cold *mezes* – *feta* cheese, dried mackerel, mussel and eggplant salads and *dolmas*, to name but a few – laid in front of them in little dishes. Later, during the course of the evening, one by one, is served an array of hot *mezes*, such as small *böreks*, little *şiş kebabs, köftes*, fried liver cubes and oysters. There is no dessert as such at a *meze* table, for there are no courses. Fruit in season is on the table throughout the meal and is picked at like the rest. Many *rakı* aficionados accompany their first sip with *feta* cheese and a cube of melon.

When Nissa approached the table, everyone got up. Some changed places to allow her to sit next to the president. She immediately felt the animal magnetism he emanated which people now call charisma, and when, with his piercing, steel-blue eyes, he looked at her, she felt a chill run down her spine. 'He was by far the most fascinating man I ever met,' she has often told me.

As soon as Nissa sat down, Mustafa Kemal complimented her on her deep tan and asked her what she would like to drink. When without hesitation she replied, 'Whatever you are drinking,' she sensed a feeling of relief among those at the table. Later Hamdullah Suphi told her that, just before she had arrived, the president had asked the same question of the mayor's wife. Before she had had a chance to answer, the mayor had interjected in a righteous tone, 'My wife does not drink, sir.' The president had taken this as an affront, and in front of everybody, had given the mayor a tongue-lashing: 'Is your wife mute that you have to answer for her? Has she no right to express herself?' On and on he had gone. Therefore the group was relieved that Nissa had given the proper answer.

The *rakı* table was the president's favourite social activity. During these sessions, some of which had lasted until the early hours of the morning, he held forth at length on all subjects and asked his guests leading questions to generate stimulating conversation. With the mayor subdued and Nissa seated next to him, the president, again in good humour, threw out several subjects for debate, and a lively discussion ensued, in which everyone expressed their opinion in an effort to outshine the others.

During this period, when the president was in residence at Dolmabahçe Palace in Istanbul, the rococo, wedding-cake-like edifice on the Bosphorus, my parents became part of his social circle, and Nissa was greatly flattered by the attention he showed her. He even included her in his poker games. Convivial by nature, he loved human company. He was also a womanizer, but Nissa, unlike other women who threw themselves at his feet, steadfastly resisted his advances and won his respect. 'If you want it to be platonic,' he had said, 'so be it!'

The most important evening my parents spent with Mustafa Kemal was an August night in 1928 when they were invited to a conference at the Dolmabahçe Palace. The purpose of the meeting, which included men of letters, scholars, journalists and deputies, was to reform the alphabet. The Turkish language for hundreds of years had been written in Arabic script because the Qur'an had been written in Arabic, although that language, in fact, was not well suited to the sounds of Turkish. While there had been a few earlier attempts to change to the Western, Latin alphabet, all had been bitterly opposed by the Islamic authorities. Only Mustafa Kemal had the will and popularity to push through such a sweeping reform.

The conference was held in the palace ballroom. Nissa was seated on the president's right, at a long banquet table set beneath the mammoth chandelier. Opposite them stood a series of blackboards with the new Latin letters written on them. There was much discussion as to which letters should be assigned to the various sounds of the Turkish language. The French cedilla (,) was suggested for the consonants 'c' and 's', and after a good deal of talk it was incorporated. Next, a symbol for the Turkish sound 'u', as in the French 'tu', had to be found. It was almost dawn and everyone was exhausted. 'We have no choice,' said the president. 'We have to take the German umlaut,' and everyone agreed. He then scribbled something on a card. The minister of the interior, Şükrü Kaya, picked it up, read it, and handed it to Nissa. 'The president has written your name for the first time in the new Turkish alphabet,' he said. It was her name in the new Latin characters and with the new umlaut – Fahrünnisa.

That was the first use of the umlaut in new Turkish. Mother put the card in her purse and later lost it or gave it away, as she did everything else. Later she 'arabicized' her name to Fahrelnissa, which does not require the umlaut.

The task completed, the members of that amazing conference looked out and were surprised to see the sun rising over the waters of the Bosphorus. Kemal turned to Nebile, one of his adopted daughters, and asked her to chant a hymn. In the hush of dawn, her nightingale voice filled the ballroom. It was a moment of ecstasy, and according to Nissa, 'Tears poured out of the president's beautiful steel-blue eyes.'

A private launch carried my parents and their friends back to Büyükada. When they reached the island, they were still so exhilarated after that extraordinary night that they could not go to bed. Instead, they hired three carriages and made a tour of the island, as the whole Turkish nation woke up to a new era.

9

A Paris Interlude

Mustafa Kemal embarked on a long series of drastic reforms, more far-reaching than any society has undertaken in history. He abolished the Caliphate, the institution by which the sultans had claimed leadership of the world's Muslims, and secularized Turkey. To take the place of the *Sharia*, the religious Muslim law, the National Assembly adopted a new civil code modelled on the Swiss code. A law was passed requiring all men to wear hats; the wearing of the traditional Turkish *fez* became a criminal offence. Although in 1925 he publicly ridiculed the veil and, by the example of the women around him (Latife had ridden open-faced on a horse next to his car), encouraged women to do away with it, Mustafa Kemal never legislated against the veil, for he was clever enough to realize that was an extremely sensitive subject in a country which had held to Muslim traditions for centuries.

Among his reforms he also set out to nationalize foreign-owned companies. One of the first, in 1925, was the Ottoman Tobacco Company, and Father lost his job. He was still a wealthy man, however, for he received a large bonus from the French owners for his twenty years of service; he had invested well in the New York stock market; and he still served on the boards of several foreign banks and corporations which were not nationalized until years later.

Many of Father's close friends, writers like Yakup Kadri and Hamdullah Suphi, had been appointed ambassadors, and now that the president had befriended him he too was hoping to be offered a good position with the new administration. Especially encouraging was an invitation from the minister of the interior, Şükrü Kaya, to discuss 'the possibilities'. After tea they went on a boat ride up the Bosphorus. As their private launch passed the Dolmabahçe Palace, the minister pointed at Mustafa Kemal standing on its balcony and said, 'Look! The president is waving at you,' and they waved back. Obviously the president knew the purpose of the boat ride. However, no offer was forthcoming.

Mustafa Kemal appreciated Izzet as he did all men of letters and culture. 'I have read with great interest and pleasure your books,' he wrote on a marvellous photograph he gave Izzet of himself in uniform wearing the black astrakhan *kalpak*, which Father kept in a silver frame on his desk all his life. I think, however, that although my father, for an extended period of time, had smuggled aircraft engines to Anatolia from Germany to assist the War of Independence, Atatürk never forgave him for not having put his total trust in his victory by leaving everything behind and joining him in Ankara in the early days, as had many others. Great men demand total loyalty, and to those who give go the rewards.

When I asked Mother why my father had not been patriotic enough to leave everything behind and join the War of Independence, she replied, choosing her words with care, for she wanted to be absolutely accurate, 'He thought about it seriously and decided to go. He even wrote Atatürk a letter in that regard, but then when the Greeks captured Eskişehir and things looked hopeless, he lost heart. We had a lovely home; he had an excellent position and a good salary. It was a good life in Istanbul. Leaving it all behind and going to Ankara, with no guarantee of the future, seemed like madness at the time. He asked me what he should do, and I am ashamed to say I did not encourage him.'

I was amazed that Mother had given such advice, for I would have thought the opposite of her. She was a bold woman who made fearless decisions and plunged into situations regardless of consequences. Therefore I can only assume that she herself did not want to leave the sophisticated life of Istanbul and live in a small Anatolian town such as Ankara then was.

When he received no offer from the new government, Izzet decided to go to Paris for an extended stay. Leaving me, aged two, and my five-year-old brother Nejad behind with our nanny, the maid, the cook and Aunt Aliye to oversee us all, my parents set sail for France. Izzet had two objectives – to look for business opportunities and to work at the Académie Française on his doctoral thesis on the French writer Henri Bataille. For this work he was awarded, in 1938, an honorary doctorate from the Académie; for his literary work he was given Les Palmes Académiques.

73

If Nissa's passion was painting, Izzet's was writing, which he had been doing since childhood. When he was twelve he published verses and started a children's newspaper, and at fifteen he published a magazine and was invited to become the youngest member of a literary circle, Fecri Ati, in Istanbul. His first and most popular novel, *Tezad* (*Contrast*), published when he was twenty-two, became an instant success and went to four printings. When his second novel, *Sermed*, which he also wrote in French, was published in Paris, the famous French writer Pierre Loti wrote the foreword. Like Loti and many French writers of the time, Izzet's prose style was exotic, ornate, mysterious, amorous and suggestive, rather than explicit. Izzet wrote essays, short stories and articles on every subject but politics, which he intensely disliked, and even a one-act play called *Leyla* (*The Disenchanted* in its English translation), which was produced in several languages. In it Izzet contrasted the psychological make-up of two women – a Muslim and a Christian – who loved the same man. The play was first performed as a curtain-raiser by the Blanche Toutain Company at the Variété Theatre in Istanbul. That same year, the renowned artistic director of L'Oeuvre Theatre in Paris, Lugne Poe, came to Istanbul, met Izzet, and decided to produce *Leyla* at the Sarah Bernhardt Theatre in Paris. Suzanne Despres, one of the many actresses whose photographs adorned Izzet's study, played the lead. When the play was published in French in 1912, it included a long treatise on the Turkish theatre by Izzet.

How my father found the time to write so prolifically between his job, his travels, his family, his social life and his womanizing is beyond me. I have retained the image of him as an elegant man, always impeccably turned out, either reading in his big wing chair or writing at his desk in his book-filled study, surrounded by photographs of prominent people which had been dedicated to him. He was extremely proud to have been made, in 1957, a permanent member of the prestigious Société des Gens de Lettres. Toward the end of his life, when his mind was failing him, it was heart-breaking to watch him at his desk trying to write; all that came out were illegible doodles and scribbles.

During his early student days in Paris, Izzet had attended plays and had numerous liaisons with well-known actresses, one being the diva Mme Lampé; another, Marie Bell, burst into peals of laughter when she saw Izzet in long-johns and bought him his first pair of boxer shorts from Sulka.

The true extent of Father's conquests of French ladies came to me when I was an apprentice in 1948 in a summer stock theatre in Maine. The French mother of the producer had come to visit her son. When she heard I was Turkish, she told me how she had gone to Istanbul in the early 1900s with her famous actress-mother Réjanne, who was to perform there, and how she had had the most exotic romance with a dashing Turk. Of course, it turned out to be Father, who, considering Mother Réjanne much too old, had courted her daughter.

In Paris, while Izzet was researching his thesis, Nissa enrolled at the Académie Ronson to study art with the well-known painter Roger Bissière, who immediately recognized her extraordinary talent. Late one afternoon at the atelier after the students had finished painting nudes from the model, Bissière went around to comment on their work. When he complimented two Japanese students whose easels were next to Nissa's, she was surprised, for she thought their nudes uninspired, flat and dull. Later she asked the master why he had liked those paintings so much, and he replied, 'That is the very best those two students can do. So of course I shall compliment them.'

When Bissière came to Nissa's easel, he took a long look at the nude she had painted, then picked up her canvas and smashed it on the floor. Nissa was horrified. How could he do such a thing? Had he gone mad?

'You can do much better than that,' he said. 'I know you can. This is just a copy! Don't you know that you should never copy nature?'

'Then why do we have a model if I am not to copy her?' Nissa asked brazenly.

'The model is simply a means. If, and I mean *if*, you have a story to tell, *if* you have a melody within you, it is through her that you will express it.'

When a painter friend later asked Bissière why he had treated Nissa so harshly, he gave this explanation: 'I had to shake her up for her own good, so she could find her truth. She is a woman of society. I do not want her merely to dabble with art as a hobby. She is a real painter, with great talent, and she should make it her profession.'

As soon as my parents had left for Paris, Aunt Aliye had moved in with her bits and pieces to play mother to Nejad and me. The only unmarried sister, living with Grandmother and with no funds of her own, she depended for clothing on hand-me-downs from her sisters. Aliye continued to visit Charles Berger twice a week, and my pious and puritanical grandmother had no choice but to put up with her daughter's indiscretion. What was she to do? Throw her out? Berger had totally captured Aliye's soul, and her passion for him had become her vocation. For him she gave up many prominent and wealthy suitors. Her love for Berger became a legend, and, although the affair was regarded as scandalous, it tickled everyone's romantic instincts.

Four years into the affair, when she was twenty-five, during my parents' absence in Paris, she became aware of a rival – Berger's piano accompanist. Tortured with jealousy, unable to eat or sleep, Aunt Aliye finally decided to take matters in hand. She found a pistol belonging to my father and went to the rival's house in Üsküdar on the Asian shore. She hid behind a tree and waited. The house was perfectly quiet. No one seemed to be there. All at once, through a window, she saw Berger and the woman entering the living room. Berger sat in an armchair while the woman knelt and put on his socks and shoes. Convinced they had just made love, Aliye went mad. She ran to the front door and rang the bell. When her rival answered the door, Aliye fired the pistol at her. The bullet went through the woman's thigh, and she survived.

Another terrible scandal to rock the Shakirs! 'ALIYE SHOOTS MARIE!' screamed the headline in enormous black letters, and once again the family was disgraced. To everyone's relief, Marie, who was married and a mother, did not press charges and no legal action was brought. The whole affair was treated as an 'unfortunate accident'.

Berger stood by Aliye, for he knew that if he abandoned her now she would go to pieces, possibly even lose her mind. Perhaps he was moved to discover the depths of her passion for him and the extent to which she was willing to go. For whatever reason, their affair continued as before.

The moment my parents heard the shocking news they rushed back from Paris to assist Aliye and take over our care. The Shakirs too rallied around Aliye. They did not condone her conduct, but they understood it. Of all the family, the most sympathetic was Suat. 'Passion,' he once told me, 'is like a terrible disease. When it possesses you, you are at its command, and it can make you do frightful things.' At the time of Aliye's scandal, Suat had just returned alone from his second trip to the United States, having lost Syida for good. During their seven-year marriage, Syida had put up with a lot – living with in-laws in old-fashioned houses, a chronic shortage of funds and, worst of all, Suat's infidelities. On this trip, when Suat indulged in a highly publicized affair with Syida's best friend, the famous Hollywood actress Bebe Daniels, Syida decided she could stand no more and sent Suat packing back to Istanbul. According to her daughter Geraldine, however, she never stopped loving him.

Once Aliye's scandal had subsided and my parents had settled back into their routine Istanbul life, they suffered another major setback. In the fall of 1929 the New York stock market collapsed, and overnight stocks lost 25–30 per cent of their value. Izzet, who had invested all his money, buying on margin, lost his fortune. One of his neighbours, Mr Süleymanovitch, committed suicide, like many others, by jumping out of a window. All of Istanbul held its breath. How was Izzet-Melih going to react to the financial misfortune? Might he be the next to jump? Nissa remembers how moved she was when he put his head in her lap and cried like a child. To cheer him up, and to spike all the prophets of doom, she suggested they dress up to the hilt and drive around the city in their Alfa-Romeo town car, the Italian chauffeur Manuel at the wheel, and personally deliver invitations to a tea dance she hurriedly organized.

Nissa's bold front, however, did not deter harsh reality. One of my first recollections as a child is of two burly men hauling away our player-piano, which Manuel used to pretend to play to entertain Nejad and me. Soon after, the Alfa-Romeo, Manuel, and our fabulous Bolu cook departed like the piano. (All good Turkish cooks are male and come from the town of Bolu. They never give away their recipes but pass them on from father to son.)

Within six years Izzet had lost his son, his job and his fortune. They say troubles came in threes, but for him there was to be a fourth . . . this time of his own making.

10

Enter Emir Zeid

Father was now desperate to find a job. Mr Weil, the French chairman of the board of the Ottoman Tobacco Company, who had many contacts in the European business world, came to his rescue and helped him find a new position as director of the Electric Tunnel and Street Car Company of Istanbul, a subsidiary of Sofina, a Belgian holding company. Relieved, and wanting to leave behind their bad memories and start afresh in a new home, my parents moved to the Hayırlı (Lucky) apartment block opposite the art deco Park Hotel in the Ayaz Paşa section of town.

It was a large apartment with a balcony facing the street in front and a glassed-in porch at the back, overlooking a graveyard which, like many at the time, was being excavated for new building sites. There, as far away from the hubbub of the household as possible, Nissa set up her easel, for she intended to spend long hours painting.

Shortly before my parents moved, King Faisal I of Iraq – as a special gesture of Atatürk – had appointed his younger brother, Emir Zeid, as the first minister from the new kingdom of Iraq to the republic of Turkey. Emir Zeid's two younger sisters, also by Sherif Hussein's Turkish wife, had accompanied him from Iraq, but instead of living with him at the Iraqi legation in Ankara they chose to live in Istanbul, and rented a flat in Ayaz Paşa.

In the early 1930s Ankara was a city filled with blocks of Bauhaus-inspired cement buildings and populated by bureaucrats and diplomats, with few cultural amenities. The Turkish poet Yahya Kemal said, 'The only good thing about Ankara is that you can always go to Istanbul.' Emir Zeid agreed with the poet and went to Istanbul as often as he could to visit his sisters, whose flat in the Park apartment was immediately adjacent to my parents' new home and on the same floor. The adjoining balconies almost touched. It was there that Emir

Zeid first laid eyes on Nissa, and when Madame Polychroniadis, the Greek minister's wife, gave a luncheon in his honour, he met her.

'My friend Militzia insisted I come to the luncheon,' Mother told me. 'She said a colleague of theirs, the new Iraqi minister, a bachelor and a Hashemite prince, had just arrived from Ankara, and they were giving a luncheon for him. "Nissa, you and Izzet Bey must come; you always enliven a party." '

'I really did not feel like going to the luncheon. It was a busy week and I was in the middle of a new painting. Moreover, what did I care about meeting some Arab prince? I had met plenty of princes in my time. But so as not to disappoint Militzia, who was one of my best friends, your father and I attended the luncheon. I wore a robin's-egg-blue silk crêpe dress with a short white vest and a white turban. My shoes matched my dress.'

Mother always remembered in great detail what she wore and how she looked. The image she portrayed was of paramount importance to her, and once she created it it was permanently etched in her mind's eye. She always tried to look her best. Her bed table was cluttered with boxes of powder and rouge, eyebrow pencils, tubes of mascara and eye-shadow. The moment she awoke, she reached for her silver hand mirror and started to 'prepare' herself by combing her hair and putting on her face for the arrival of the person bringing her breakfast tray, whoever it might be.

Even on her death bed, when she was expecting a visit from the Turkish ambassador she insisted that I pencil in her eyebrows and put rouge on her cheeks. When, because she was too ill, the nurse and I could not put on her the silk lavender bed jacket she wanted to wear, for she felt the colour became her, she grew very agitated. Only when we finally pinned it on her nightgown with safety-pins did she quieten down and breathe normally.

Mother was conscious not only of her looks but also of everyone else's around her. 'That colour becomes you,' she'd say the moment you walked into her room, or, 'That skirt makes you dumpy', or 'I like the way you've draped that scarf.' 'Your hair should be shorter', 'Your eyebrows need plucking', 'Put the rouge below your cheek-bones' – she would advise anyone and everyone. To please her, we all tried to look our best and wear clothes we knew she would like. My sister-in-law Majda has complained that she and her children could not drop in on Mother 'unprepared'. I think Mother's obsession with colours, clothes and appearance had to do with her strong aesthetic sense and her trained artist's eye, for vain she was not.

At the luncheon in honour of Emir Zeid given by the Greek minister and his wife, the conversation at the table was, as it always is on such occasions, very lively; but the emir barely spoke. He just stared across the table at Nissa with his big, black eyes. Being used to sophisticated, cosmopolitan men like my father and his friends, who dressed impeccably, were great conversationalists, made witty remarks and automatically courted the ladies, Nissa was not in the least impressed by this quiet, dark man in his simple, loosely cut, grey suit and black tie. (After his mother's death, Emir Zeid wore only black ties.) Yet, as she kept running into him at the many social functions, he began to intrigue her. 'He was so different from everyone I had known. He looked at me in a way no man ever had before. This mysterious, dark, quiet prince began to haunt me.'

At a party the Italian ambassador gave for the officers of some visiting naval ships in the gardens of the former Italian Embassy in Istanbul, Nissa noticed Emir Zeid standing under a pine tree, observing her. Touched by something in his demeanour, she felt the urge to go over to him.

'Your Highness,' she said, 'would you like to play tennis with me and my friends?'

'I would,' he said, then added, 'I would very much like to,' and smiled. It was the first time she had seen him smile.

'Pick me up tomorrow around ten, and we'll drive to Tarabya to the Sümer Palas courts.'

That was the opening Emir Zeid needed. From then on he deliberately set out to court Nissa until he made her fall in love with him.

That summer an Austrian diplomat rented several *takas* (the ubiquitous little one-cylinder wooden motorboats painted in bright colours like slices of watermelon, lemon and lime, throbbing *taka, taka, taka*) to take his guests across the Bosphorus for a picnic. My parents and Emir Zeid were, as usual, among the guests.

'I was in love with Zeid by then,' Mother told me. 'How did I know I was in love? Because I dreamt about him several times. I dreamt we were Siamese twins and we were stuck together and he kept me warm. The day of the picnic I sat next to him in the *taka*. I was wearing a halter-neck dress, and when Zeid slipped his arm under my jacket and wrapped it around my bare back, I felt the same warmth I had felt in my dream.'

In Göksü, a little village on the Asiatic side which has a sweet-water stream flowing down the hills into the Bosphorus, they lunched on spitted lamb and an array of other foods, and drank wine. After desserts and coffee, Emir Zeid suggested to Nissa they go on a boat ride up the creek. He borrowed a little rowing boat tied at a small pier some way off from the picnic grounds and rowed with such vigour that they flew across the water. (Zeid had been a member of the Balliol College crew at Oxford.) When they arrived at a deserted spot, Zeid beached the boat, and they strolled along the beautiful shore where the reflection of the weeping willows lay on the water. 'Kiss me,' Nissa suddenly said. Zeid kissed her with such vigour that her head spun.

Now that both Zeid and Nissa were in love, nothing could deter them from embarking on a clandestine romance, which turned into a full-fledged affair. All their friends aided and abetted, for they knew that Izzet had often been unfaithful to Nissa and that, for once, it was her turn.

In the spring of 1933 Mother had arranged for Nejad and me to go to Grandmother's on Büyükada, as usual, while she and Father were to visit Bucharest at the invitation of Hamdullah Suphi, then the Turkish ambassador to Romania, who had written to them, 'I can't wait to show off our Turkish queen Nissa in Bucharest.'

My parents were also going to oversee the publication in Romanian of Father's popular novel *Sermed*, for which Mother had designed an exotic poster. Nissa was eagerly looking forward to the trip and had had several dresses made especially for the occasion. According to her, as preparations were underway, Father made up a tale as to why he had to go to Bucharest alone. He told her that Sofina, the owners of the Street Car Company, had asked him to go to Brussels to discuss important plans for the company and that he would be able to spend only a few days in Bucharest. As the ambassador's estranged wife would not be there, it would be inappropriate for Nissa to stay in the Turkish Embassy alone with him. And off Izzet had gone to Romania.

By leaving her behind, Izzet gave Nissa the justification for her next move. She immediately found a tenant for our apartment in town, leased a house in Yeniköy, and then informed Nejad and me that she had a delightful surprise for us – a summer on the Bosphorus. To us, the 'delightful surprise' was a blow; we would greatly have preferred to go to Büyükada.

Nissa had a definite reason to spend the summer in Yeniköy: it was just the right place for her to be with Emir Zeid. All their friends in the diplomatic corps who had come from hot Ankara were spending the summer in the *yalıs* and handsome mansions nearby, surrounded by the lovely parks and gardens which had been built or purchased in the mid-nineteenth century by foreign governments as summer residences for their ambassadors. Emir Zeid and Nissa played tennis at the Sümer Palas in Tarabya, a turn-of-the-century hotel surrounded by masses of hydrangeas in glorious Monet blues, mauves and pinks. Often they sailed on those brisk, masculine Bosphorus waters, so different from the balmy, feminine Marmara Sea around Büyükada, and went to parties up and down the Bosphorus at their friends' homes.

While Mother was enjoying her romance with Zeid, who was totally devoted to her, Miss Tina took Nejad and me swimming to an old white clapboard bath house on the waterfront in Tarabya, the village above Yeniköy, which at the time still had two sections, one for women and one for men. We watched the big ships coming up the Bosphorus until, at the last moment, they swerved north on the next leg of the journey to the Black Sea. The water traffic was fascinating – tankers, ferries, tramp steamers, yachts, *kayıks*, schooners and *takas* transporting their cargoes. Nejad and I enjoyed the Bosphorus life and did not miss Büyükada as much as we had feared.

Only my father, newly back from Brussels to find his town apartment rented out for the season, and forced to go to work from Yeniköy by ferry, grumbled at the arrangement. But Mother was not in the least put out by his complaints. For once she had got the better of him.

It was nice to see her so happy and active that summer. Every day she went swimming and lay in the sun for hours. Once she fell asleep and was seriously sunburned. To ease the sting that night, she covered her face completely with yoghurt, leaving only holes for eyes, nose and mouth.

'Mother,' I exclaimed, giggling, 'you look like a clown.'

She advanced in her wet, white mask and slapped me hard on the cheek. 'How dare you make fun of your mother!' she said. I began to sob.

'She's only a child,' cried Father, embracing me. 'She did not mean to insult you.'

From then on I learned to watch my words with Mother and began to discover that she could not tolerate criticism.

All throughout their married life my parents had fought constantly, and their quarrels had a hard edge lacking in those marital rows that compose themselves eventually as a nice, rough feature in the total landscape of a good marriage. For the most part these quarrels concerned Father's infidelities and money matters. Mother was a terrible spendthrift; in all ways she was extravagant. For her, money was good for only one thing, to spend fast and completely, never thinking where the next sum would come from. Father, on the other hand, was frugal. He budgeted his expenses carefully, and saved and invested his money. Every night, in his beautiful handwriting, he entered his daily expenses to the last penny in leather-bound note-books. These notebooks read like diaries, for, by the various entries – Sulka bill, train tickets, toys for children, restaurants – one could tell the story of his life.

That autumn, back in the Hayırlı apartment, my parents' arguments increased in intensity. Once I heard their raised voices, followed by a terrible crash. Racing into the living room, I saw my mother, white-faced, unconscious, lying on the floor with her arms flung over the edge of the carpet, surrounded by red roses and broken chunks of crystal from the vase she had brought down with her in her fall. Mother had a tendency to pass out when things got out of control. Perhaps it was her way of avoiding painful situations, or an outward manifestation of her tormented psyche. Whatever the reason, when I saw her unconscious, lying among broken glass, I screamed in utter terror. My father stared at me blank-faced, and then he started to comfort me. All the while Mother did not stir, and, as I was still screaming, Miss Tina and the Greek maid Theodosia arrived. At this point Mother's eyes opened. She looked around blankly and asked what in the world was happening, as if she remembered nothing. Relieved, I calmed down.

A few days after that incident, when Nejad and I returned from the park, we were surprised to find Mother seated in street clothes on the sofa in the drawing room, looking as lovely as ever. Tears dripped steadily on to a big sketch pad on her lap and splotched the swirls of red with which she was filling the page, and for a moment I thought she was crying blood. Then I saw the bottles of India ink and the pens and the tumbler of blood-red water, and, as I came stealthily nearer, I saw that she had sketched a mass of flames with nasty little devils among them. It looked like a scene from Dante's *Inferno*. In the background she had printed in large red letters, 'Never Ever Lie'. When she saw how puzzled I was, she patted my cheek and said, 'This is to hang in your room, to remember never to lie. I might not be here to remind you. This will.'

I found the sketch a frightening and perplexing piece of work. Why should I lie? I was a child, and she treated me as a child, scolding and then instantly forgiving my faults. And what did she mean by 'I might not be here'? It was the first indication to me that something was wrong; confirmation was not long in coming.

One day after dinner, shortly after the 'hell sketch' incident, my father sat me on his lap and said, 'Shirin, I am going to Europe on a long trip. While I'm gone, your mother is going to move you all to a beautiful new apartment opposite the park where you play every day. Before I return in November, your mother will leave. She and I are separating; these things happen in life.'

'How can Father be so calm?' I thought to myself. There was something very incongruous about the whole scene. Here we were in his comfortable study, the strains of a Viennese waltz coming from our radio, Mother seated in a wing chair, perfectly calm, sipping her camomile tea, and Father was telling me casually that their marriage was over! If, after one of their violent fights, he had told me they were separating, it would have made more sense.

I was scared. What about us? What was to become of us? Father had said nothing about plans for the children. Where were we to live?

Jumping off his lap, I went over to Mother and stood in front of her. My voice quivering, I said, barely audibly, 'Mother, are you going to go away and leave us behind?' A pained expression crossed her face. She took a deep breath and with genuine feeling said, 'I am not leaving you. How could I possibly do that? Don't worry, Shirinaki, your father and I will do everything in our power to see to it that you and Nejad are never denied a parent. You will have two homes instead of one. You'll be constantly visiting one of us, and you know that visitors are special people and that they get special treatment.' She then embraced me, holding me tight to her bosom as if she wanted to transmit to me all the warmth and love within her. Then she kissed me on both cheeks. She smelled so good, as always, of Guerlain's Mitsouko. 'Trust me. All will be well, Shirinaki,' she added tenderly. 'Now run along. It's way past your bedtime.'

Despite being forbidden, for Nejad had the mumps, I slipped into his room and sat on his bed. 'Did they tell you?' I asked him. 'Did Father tell you they are separating?'

'Divorcing is the word,' said Nejad importantly. 'Of course they told me, but I don't believe they will. Look at them. They are living together as if nothing has happened. People who are getting a divorce are usually furious at each other,' Nejad added as if he were an expert in such matters.

That night I went to bed not really believing the separation would actually take place. 'They'll make up as usual,' I thought to myself; 'they always do.' Hadn't Mother walked out on Father and gone to Grandmother's several times and always returned? After fights, hadn't they stopped talking for days on end and then made up as if nothing had happened?

However, as planned, Father left for Europe. Mother once reluctantly described her final hours with him. 'Imagine,' she said, shaking her head in disbelief, 'that night before he left for Europe, he wanted to make love to me. "As a farewell," he said, "for the last time."' She let him do it, for she wanted to prove to herself that he had no hold over her.

The next morning she saw him off. When his ship to Marseilles started to pull away from the dock, Izzet raised his Homburg with one hand and waved goodbye with the other. Hit suddenly by an excruciating pain, Nissa started to sob and choke, and when Izzet's figure gradually receded in the distance, and the man with whom she had spent thirteen years of her life – good or bad – became a mere speck, she nearly fainted. Angry with herself for being so distraught, she went on a wild shopping spree.

Soon after his departure, the household, consisting of Mother, Nejad, myself, Miss Tina, Theodosia and our Armenian cook Paulina, moved to the new apartment. Mother prepared it to the last detail for Father's return, arranging his books, lining his dresser drawers, and neatly laying out his shirts.

That October, in honour of the tenth anniversary of the Turkish republic, Mustafa Kemal suggested that Istanbul citizens entertain their countrymen from the provinces. Mother, to distract Nejad and me – and probably herself – during this difficult transition period, invited a peasant family to stay with us and enjoy the festivities. The visitors, never having seen electricity, constantly switched the lights on and off, and kept going in to the kitchen to admire our Frigidaire. They marvelled at the radio. They could not get used to the idea that people wore shoes indoors, because in village houses shoes are left at the door to preserve the cleanliness of floors, on which people sit, eat and pray. Suddenly and silently they would arrive beside us in their stocking feet.

On 29 October 1933, the whole nation celebrated. Overlooking the parade route we had a large wrought-iron balcony which we festooned with flags and a string of red and white electric lights. When the parade came near, we all crowded on to the balcony, sang partriotic songs and waved to the soldiers with their flags and their bands. Afterwards we sat down to a sumptuous four-course luncheon prepared by Paulina. My cousins Nermidil and Erdem had come over to watch the parade with us, and they, the two peasant children, and Nejad and I then played hide-and-seek and took turns bicycling up and down the long corridor.

Life at the Cumhuriyet apartment was so pleasant in every way that I was more than ever convinced that the threatened separation would not take place. Father would return from Europe as he always did, and we would live happily ever after. But sure enough, before his return, Mother moved two blocks away to the Shakir Pasha apartment to stay with my Aunt Ayşe and Uncle Ahmet until the divorce came through.

She sent most of her personal possessions into storage, taking only her paints and clothes with her, but she did not remove from the hall the tall Ming vase where Father kept his canes. 'I couldn't do it,' she told me. 'I couldn't remove his canes.'

Nejad and I settled into a routine of spending the day at Aunt Ayşe's with Mother and our cousins Nermidil and Erdem and returning to Father's for the evening meal and the night. We seemed to have the best of two worlds. However, after the divorce, which was a brief affair handled by one lawyer, when Mother, accompanied by Grandmother, left for Athens to join Emir Zeid, we finally realized that our family was permanently broken up. To live without a mother felt like living without a limb.

When King Faisal I of Iraq, before he died in September of 1933, had heard about his younger brother's liaison with a married woman with two children, he had been angry and had tried to break up the affair by asking Zeid to leave Turkey and go to Egypt as minister plenipotentiary. Emir Zeid, however, had refused, resigned as minister to Turkey and sailed to Greece, ostensibly to look after some lands he had inherited from his Turkish maternal ancestor, the great Reşid Pasha.

In Athens, Mother and her prince were married; and in July of 1934 Mother brought her new husband to Büyükada to meet her family. With Emir Zeid, who gave her the freedom to do as she pleased, Nissa entered a new phase in her life.

11

Villa of the Sherifs – 1934

In spite of all the Shakirs' objections Mother had decided to live, instead of in the *yalı*, in the villa on the hill overlooking the Bosphorus which Sherif Hussein had built. One summer morning shortly after Grandmother's picnic for Emir Zeid, she said, 'Come, Shirinaki, let's go to town. Then we'll drive to Büyükdere, for I want to show you the fabulous site of our new home.' There had been so much talk about this property that the thought of seeing it thrilled me.

At the ferry landing Mother and I jumped into Emir Zeid's Studebaker, and off we went. There were few cars in Istanbul then, and the present corniche had not yet been built, so we zoomed along the hills lining the European bank of the Bosphorus until we arrived at the village of Büyükdere (Big River) which overlooks a wide bay. In the village itself are the summer embassies of Russia and Spain and summer homes of prosperous Turks. Mother pointed up to a thickly wooded property on the very top of a hill with a massive stone wall circling it like a coronet. 'The villa's up there,' she said. It looked remote and unattainable. 'How are we ever going to live up there?' I wondered. 'How will anyone ever come to visit us? They don't have cars like us.'

We drove as far as we could up the winding road that Sherif Hussein had dynamited through rock forty years ago and then trudged up a steep path to a landing in front of a wrought-iron gate, where we stopped to catch our breath. I was mesmerized by the heart-stopping, panoramic view of the Bosphorus and its surroundings. Below us was Büyükdere Bay with water traffic manoeuvring around the curve, the hills on the Asian shore seeming to come forward to the ones on this side to form a lake out of the strait. Grazing on the slope just below were flocks of sheep. The wind howled, a thousand birds sang, and the trees crowded up and rattled the window glass of the dilapidated old house. Mother was right. This was an extraordinary site.

As we entered the musty interior of what had been the *selamlık*, the men's quarters, where Sherif Hussein had received his guests, we looked in dismay at its peeling walls, battered tile roof and ruined floors.

Behind the *selamlık*, hidden from view by trees, was a solid iron door in the middle of a stone wall that ran the width of the property. When Mother pushed open the heavy gate, I saw an overgrown alley lined with mulberry trees leading to the top of the hill, where the property ended. On both sides among the spruces, chestnuts and oaks lay the burned-out ruins of the two large buildings which had once made up the *harem*, the women's quarters.

After having seen the condition the property was in, I wondered how Mother could ever make it habitable, but as usual she rose to the challenge. As her contractor she hired Grandmother's brother, Uncle Mithat, and gave him a millon instructions. A sober, efficient ex-soldier, he went nearly out of his mind, for Mother wanted everything 'quick, quick, quick'. First Uncle Mithat hired gangs of labourers to hack out the old road. The moment access was established, plumbers and masons went to work. Electricians had to bring wiring all the way up the hill to provide electricity for the first time. Carpenters repaired walls and floors and installed new windows and doors, and painters swarmed all over the house. Great big wood-burning tile stoves for heating the rooms and cast-iron cooking stoves arrived by boat and were hauled up the hill, along with sinks and bath-tubs.

That autumn, during the remodelling of the Büyükdere property, which proceeded with lightning speed due to Uncle Mithat's efforts, Emir Zeid and Mother stayed with Aunt Hakiye at the Shakir Pasha apartment. I moved back to Father's, only two blocks away, and Nejad entered boarding school. So in the large Cumhuriyet Apartment there were only four of us – Father, myself, my governess and Theodosia, who now served as both cook and maid. My half-sister Remide was long gone. Already divorced from her first husband, with whom she had eloped after running away from the nuns' school, she was now living in sin with a consumptive young man of good family. Since she had disgraced Father's name, he refused to speak with her, and we were not allowed to see her either.

My governess, Miss Tina, continued to tutor me in English,

history, geography and arithmetic. I desperately wanted to go to school like Nejad and my cousins, Erdem and Nermidil. When would they ever send me? My only compensation was that I accompanied Mother on many forays into the Grand Bazaar where she purchased quantities of furnishings for the new house.

At that time in the Bazaar there was a plethora of exceptional objects available, attributed to three causes – the Russian Revolution, the collapse of the Ottoman Empire, and the Westernization of Turkey. The Russian émigrés disposed of their jewels and objets d'art through merchants in the Bazaar, and so did the descendants of the Ottoman imperial family. When Atatürk turned West, the upper-class Turks modernized their homes, selling precious items associated with the old mode of life and replacing them with the simplest forms of 1930s furniture, art-deco objects, and Gallé lamps.

Taking the opposite approach, as could be expected of Mother, she went on an orgy of collecting antiques – old pistols and Qur'ans, brocades, miniatures of sultans in ivory frames, old scissors, antique watches, elaborately carved and gilded turban stands. When she was exhausted from shopping, we would lunch near the university under what must be the biggest elm tree in the world. Birds hopped around our feet and fluttered up and down from the branches of the tree. Then Mother would get out her sketchbook and black china-ink bottle and pen and would begin to sketch. I did not know how life could be happier.

In late November, to everyone's surprise and Uncle Mithat's infinite relief, the army of workmen in Büyükdere dispersed, and the Studebaker glided up to a neat entrance with polished marble steps. Beyond stood a warm, tight house ready for occupation. Slowly, with all the possessions Mother had acquired in the Bazaar, the house came alive and glowed with colour.

In the winter, as wolves came down the Bulgarian shore from the forests of the Ukraine to prey on the flocks of sheep pastured along the European side of the Bosphorus, two gigantic wolfhounds were purchased and, with their spiked collars, were let loose at night to prowl the hill-tops and keep the wolves at bay. How snug it was sitting in the villa around big warm stoves and listening to the roaring of the wind and the howling of the wolves! How happy we were at last!

So the winter passed, and the trees budded and flowered, and one morning in late May Mother announced that she was pregnant. The idea of having a little brother or sister thrilled me. Emir Zeid was excited at the prospect of being a father and, like all Middle Eastern men, hoped for a son to carry on his name.

On the night of the July full moon Mother and Emir Zeid gave their first party in the new house. Mother hung little Japanese lanterns, like the ones she remembered from Hakiye's wedding in the Büyükada garden, in the trees and bushes, and set little wrought-iron tables and chairs on the terrace and along the slopes overlooking the Bosphorus. There were marvellous things to eat and drink and lovely plates to eat off and fine Baccarat glasses to drink from. Guests wandered around, the women in bright summer prints and the men in white linen suits, drinking in the spectacular views. The party was the talk of the town.

The summer progressed happily for all of us. Nejad and I gathered mulberries in the woods, walked down the hill to swim at the bath house and played with a swarm of friends, but when Miss Tina emigrated to France, things changed for me. Mother immediately hired an athletic young White Russian as my next governess. At first Miss Tatiana was helpful. She encouraged me to climb trees, something Miss Tina never let me do; I owe to her my acquaintance with Büyükdere's finest trees and marvellous vistas. Later, however, when she discovered I was a constant bed-wetter, she decided to discipline me by having me write out 200 times for each flood, 'I will not make pee-pee in my bed again.'

Confined to the villa while doing my penance for bed-wetting, I became finely attuned to what was going on there – actually not much. From my window every day I saw Emir Zeid in khaki shorts, pruning trees. Besides that, he spent his time puffing on his pipe, reading newspapers and drinking *raki* in the evenings. He was a loner. I noticed that he and Mother rarely conversed and that he always slipped away from a crowded room. He came alive only in the company of other men, for he liked to trade jokes and talk politics with them.

As for Mother, instead of being relaxed after having fixed up the villa and given her first grand soirée, with plenty of leisure time to paint and to enjoy the delights of Büyükdere, she seemed restless. Since her marriage to Zeid, they had been constantly surrounded by people, and Nissa had kept busy planning and doing. When they were finally left to their own resources, with nothing particular to do or to look forward to, she felt at a loss and, according to a diary entry, was tormented by the realization that her marriage was not what she had hoped it would be and was searching for a solution. 'Zeid spends his days pruning trees, and I paint. We are living on a faraway hill like old retired people; yet we are still in our mid-thirties. This is not the sort of life we should be leading. Zeid should get back in harness. He must return to work and take part in the world again in places where important decisions are made.'

As always, Nissa found a way out. She persuaded Emir Zeid to ask his nephew King Ghazi to give him a diplomatic post, and the king named him as the first Iraqi minister to Germany.

They closed the villa, on which they had spent so much energy and money and where they had lived barely a year, and, taking only Mother's favourite 'collections', left for Berlin.

To abandon the villa was one thing. To be abandoned oneself was quite another. I don't remember Mother's departure for Berlin, nor the closing of the villa. I only remember being delivered to Father's and standing in the entrance hall, feeling terribly alone. Now all I had to look forward to was some vague promise that one day Mother would return and take me to Berlin.

12

Berlin – 1935–8

Berlin in the mid-1930s was a plum post for any diplomat. Germany was emerging once more as a major power, and many people all over the world were mesmerized by Adolf Hitler and his Nazi cohorts, their parades and marches, their pageants, swastikas and banners, their 'Sieg Heils' and black-uniformed stormtroopers. At the time, very few suspected that the toy-like German soldiers would turn into a killing machine and that the war Hitler started would result in the death of 50 million people.

When in autumn 1935 Nissa arrived in Berlin, she immediately realized that this was an arena of major players, and decided to become one. As Iraq was a small country which had gained its independence from the British Mandate only three years earlier, its representative would normally receive little attention. This presented her with a difficult challenge. When the wife of Mussolini's ambassador, Madame Attolico, snubbed Nissa by not returning her call – a breach of protocol – Nissa vowed she would make the lady ask to be invited to the Royal Iraqi Legation.

As Nissa was pregnant with Raad, she had to wait at least six months to launch her campaign. Meanwhile she concentrated on setting up a new legation and hiring a staff. She visited museums and art galleries in Berlin, as well as in Nuremberg and Munich, and steeped herself in German culture and literature. She became a devotee of Rilke and was enthralled with Nietzsche's *Thus spoke Zarathustra*, which she kept by her bedside and constantly quoted. Wanting to continue painting, she enrolled in art classes and set up an easel in one corner of her bedroom. A portrait she painted during this period, of a young woman, still hangs in Fureya's home. It is so classical that no one can believe it is her work.

Nissa had always loved opera more than concert music. The heroic and the grandiose appealed to her, for at heart she was a romantic. In Wagner's operas she found all the fire and fury and emotional stimulation she loved. On the record-player in her bedroom she constantly played arias from *Tristan und Isolde*, and every time she listened to the *Liebestod* she wept.

Once Raad was born, in February 1936, and after a slimming cure at the sanatorium in Dresden and a trip to Paris to purchase the latest fashions, she was ready to make her début in Berlin society. The perfect occasion arose – a formal dinner Hitler was giving for the diplomatic corps at the Reichskanzlei. When Nissa and Emir Zeid, in white tie, sash and numerous decorations, entered the Reichskanzlei they were overwhelmed by the profusion of flowers. Hundreds of azaleas were massed together to form a carpet in the great entrance hall, and bouquets of yellow roses everywhere perfumed the air. They joined the slow-moving reception line. When Nissa found herself facing Hitler, he recognized her as the woman with the perfect profile he had noticed in the diplomatic box at a recent performance of *Die Walküre*. Moved by Nissa's beauty at close range, he held her gaze with his hypnotic eyes, which he made lustrous with drops of belladonna, for what seemed to her an eternity; then, saying, 'Welcome to Berlin, your Highness,' he bent stiffly and kissed her hand. Nissa was flattered by this attention, for he had not so honoured any of the ladies ahead of her. His normal greeting was a handshake and a perfunctory nod. Everyone wondered who was this shimmering beauty in her silver-lamé Chanel gown and diamond tiara, who had held the Führer's attention for so long.

The reception was followed by a sumptuous dinner at a big, horseshoe-shaped table. After the meal the ladies retired to the drawing room and Nissa found herself sitting next to Emmy Göring who, soon after, invited her to tea. Nissa had made her mark!

At Emmy Göring's tea party at Carinhall, Göring's elaborate estate named after his first wife, a Swede, were several wives of leading Nazi ministers. Nissa was the only foreigner present, which seemed odd to her. When tea was over Marshal Göring joined them, dressed in a burgundy velvet smoking jacket with quilted satin lapels and silk sash. Everyone in the room, both visitors and servants – the latter were dressed in green and gold livery, looking like footmen in a Lehár operetta – seemed to stiffen at his presence. Nissa wondered why they were intimidated by him. To her, the pudgy Göring looked like a tenor in an opera.

After he had exchanged the usual pleasantries, Göring looked around with obvious pride and asked Nissa, 'What do you think of my house?' Not impressed by this extraordinary baroque palace with its naked display of endless, eclectic possessions and priceless artefacts, she swallowed and politely replied, 'It is quite fantastic' – but then could not refrain from pointing at a landscape painting over the door and adding, 'But I certainly don't like that painting.' She had thought it hideous the moment she had entered the room, and when it came to art, she could not be diplomatic.

There was a stunned silence. Then the wives of the Nazi ministers started to protest that Nissa was wrong, that the picture was beautiful and well-placed over the door. Göring, however, didn't seem offended, and perhaps even appreciated her frankness. 'Come, I want to show you the rest of my paintings. I have quite a collection,' he said, taking Nissa's arm and, followed by all the ladies, he proceeded to escort her on a tour of the house. Nissa was much impressed by the quality and quantity of the art works. 'How can Göring have acquired such a fabulous collection in so little time?' she thought. 'Wherever did he get the money?' She did not know that most of the art was stolen or 'bought' under duress from the wealthy Jewish families who were already fleeing Germany.

The walls of one room of Carinhall were covered with magnificent Persian tapestries, and another was lined with different maps of the world. In still another, five or six half-grown lion cubs were playing. Göring let them jump all over him, caressing them and fondling them, while the women watched goggle-eyed.

They then climbed a narrow winding staircase and arrived in a large room on the top floor which contained an amazingly intricate model-railway network. Stepping up to a platform, on which was a console, Göring pushed button after button; trains started running about the tracks, and bridges opened and closed. There were even model planes on wires that dropped bombs on the trains. Then Göring beckoned Nissa to join him. Standing on the platform next to him, she pressed several buttons at once with both hands as if she were playing a chord on a piano. Immediately, chaos ensued. Trains were derailed and toppled over. Rails broke loose and houses were overturned. The ladies uttered shrieks, but Göring simply laughed, pleased that Nissa was enjoying herself.

When Mother told me of her visit to Carinhall many years later, we both shook our heads in disbelief. 'Who would have thought that that buffoon, with his chubby beringed fingers, playing with his lion cubs and his trains, would turn out to be one of the main architects of Hitler's evil Reich?'

During the Berlin Olympics of 1936 the city bustled with celebrities, enthusiastic fans, and revellers from all over the world. Caught up in the excitement and gaiety, Nissa felt privileged to be living in Berlin. The hard-to-get tickets were readily available to the diplomatic corps, and she made a point of attending as many events as possible. As much as she enjoyed the games themselves, she relished even more the chance to be seen.

At the end of the Olympics, the American ambassador gave a huge reception in honour of the American athletes, and Nissa was horrified to hear that none of the black athletes had been invited – not even Jesse Owens, the American track star who had won more gold medals than anyone else. She considered it the most shocking incident she experienced in Berlin. What if she had been there during *Kristallnacht*, which occurred only six months after she left Berlin?

When the games were over and the city was slowly subsiding to its normal pace, Nissa decided it was time to bring Nejad and me to Berlin. As always with Mother, action followed immediately on thought, and she wrote to my father that same day. Her letter reached him at a crucial time in his life. Uncertain of his own immediate future – for the Electric and Tram Company, of which he was director, was about to be nationalized – and knowing that his children would have greater opportunities living with their mother and Emir Zeid in a city like Berlin, he consented.

At the end of that summer when Nejad and I returned to Father's apartment from Büyükada, Father did not break the news to us immediately. First he took us to a photographer, where we had little individual pictures taken (for our passports, we realized later). The next day Aunt Aliye arrived with a dressmaker, who measured me for a winter outfit. At the same time, my father took Nejad to the tailor and arranged to have a tweed suit made for him. We were puzzled by all this attention until that afternoon, when Father seated us on the formal sofa in the living room and, while the maid served us tea and cakes, told us that Mother was coming to take us back with her to Berlin.

'This will be an enriching experience for both of you, your first contact with a foreign land and culture,' he told us. 'Don't be critical because things are different and unfamiliar to you. Keep an open mind, learn and benefit from all you see.' Suddenly his voice broke, and his face wrinkled from the effort not to cry. 'But you won't forget your father,' he said. Then, after a long, awkward pause, he added tenderly, 'I shall miss you children. I shall miss you a lot.'

Overcome by the momentous news and by Father's rare show of emotion, I began to cry. Then Nejad broke into a sob, and Father let his own tears overflow; a few trembled at the tips of his long eyelashes. Pulling the pristine white linen handkerchief from his breast pocket, I wiped first his eyes, then mine, and passed the handkerchief to Nejad who blew his nose loudly.

Soon Mother arrived in Istanbul in high spirits. A week of farewell parties with Grandmother and my aunts and uncles added to the excitement and heightened our anticipation. On the day of departure, the entire Shakir clan came to the railroad station to see us off. The Orient Express waited by its platform, its monstrous black locomotive enveloped in clouds of steam and smoke, its elegant coaches with their beautiful interiors of polished wood and brass, immaculate upholstery and plush carpeting waiting to receive us. Our compartments were crammed with flowers, baskets of fruit, boxes of chocolates, books and magazines the Shakirs had brought.

For two nights and three days the train sped north-west through spectacular scenery, across parts of Greece, Bulgaria, Yugoslavia, Austria and Czechoslovakia, and then north into Germany. For hours Nejad and I watched the mountains change into plains, the rivers to lakes and back again, while Mother read, sketched and wrote in her diary. On the evening of the third day the train pulled into the huge iron and glass sleeve of the main station in Berlin. On the platform stood Emir Zeid wearing a grey striped suit and homburg, looking ambassadorial, with a chauffeur beside him fitted out in a dark uniform with brass buttons and a cap featuring the Hashemite crown. Alongside were a couple of burly porters for the luggage.

To two children from Istanbul (Nejad was then thirteen, I ten), the first and most amazing impression of Berlin at night was the colour and glow of the sky, illumination such as we had never imagined, towering buildings blazing with electric light, wide avenues full of speeding traffic. Istanbul, apart from one or two main streets, was at that time still very dim and quiet after nightfall; dark lanes surfaced in cobblestones burrowed between its little old houses. Yes, there were several apartment buildings like the one Father lived in, but they were not characteristic.

When we arrived at the Iraqi legation, a pleasant four-storey town house set back behind a low iron fence on the Fasanenstrasse in Charlottenburg, we were shown to our rooms on the top floor. Emir Zeid had provided books, toys and sweets. Blue pyjamas for Nejad and a pink nightdress for me lay on our beds. Emir Zeid's thoughtfulness and warm welcome filled us with gratitude.

The morning after our arrival, we were blissfully asleep under our eiderdowns when our door flew open. The intruder announced herself as Fräulein Gerlach; then this battle-axe of a governess ordered me out of bed and into the bathroom, where she vigorously scrubbed me with a stiff brush and cold water. Nejad was next. This was our introduction to what became a daily regimen. 'Battle-axe' wore grey suits and a grey bun and sensible black button shoes, and had a black habit of shouting, 'Nein!'

We asked to see our new baby brother. 'Nein!' We wanted to burst into Mother's room. 'Nein!' We asked for cheese for breakfast. 'Nein!'

After our breakfast, served by the butler in the dining room, Fräulein Gerlach disappeared briefly. Unable to contain my curiosity, I ran upstairs to the second floor and opened the door opposite Mother's room. Sitting on a potty on top of a changing table was my new brother, Raad, a jolly little Buddha, a delicious sausage at eight months old. Curly-haired and black-eyed, he was the very image of Emir Zeid. His *Schwester*, in an immaculately starched white uniform, stood at attention beside the table waiting for the princeling to perform. When all was done and finished, and his little red buttocks had been oiled and powdered, the nurse allowed me to hold Raad in my arms and feel how warm and solid he was. He examined me fearlessly, holding on to one of my curls. Just then Fräulein Gerlach, towing Nejad by one hand, marched in with a series of 'Nein's. She quickly hustled me out of the room.

Fortunately, Mother could not tolerate Fräulein's 'Nein's any more than we could and three months later she fired her. Her successor, a timid, pale Dane, spent hours watering the plants on the verandah next to Emir Zeid's office on the ground floor, and Mother, convinced that she was in love with Emir Zeid, soon let her go also. Then came an agreeable Spanish woman who was more of a companion and chaperone. We liked her, for she did whatever we wanted.

Eager for her children to have beautiful clothes, Mother took Nejad and me to the KaDeWe on the Kurfürstendamm. This, like the Wertheim, was an immense department store, a palace of consumer goods. In one afternoon I was outfitted with many *dirndl* dresses, skirts and pullovers for school and a velvet party dress or two. Nejad acquired *lederhosen*, a camel-hair coat and a dark blue party suit. For the first time, we both had extensive wardrobes.

From the start, I loved everything about school, to which I had been looking forward for half of my young life. The French Lycée (Französische Gymnasium) in Berlin was a big, four-storey, red-brick building on the River Spree, around the corner from the Reichstag, near the Unter den Linden and the Brandenburger Tor. It had been founded in 1685 by French Huguenots who had fled France after Louis XIV revoked the Edict of Nantes, which had briefly granted non-Catholics religious freedom. The gymnasium was a boys' school, and only girls of Huguenot descent and from the diplomatic community were allowed to attend. In my class there were thirty-three boys and only three girls.

Soon I discovered that I was a hit with the boys. Every morning when I entered the classroom, I saw chalked on the blackboard a heart pierced with an arrow, drops of blood dripping down, inscribed: *Friedrich liebt Shirin*, or *Otto liebt Shirin*. It was calf-love, of course, but at eleven it seemed deep and important, and it stirred my romantic longings. I soon picked an older boyfried, Joachim Cyliax, a classmate of Nejad's. He was a Bavarian, with chestnut-coloured hair and eyes, and always dressed in *lederhosen*. Every day I found in my desk a love-letter, unbelievably romantic for a boy of thirteen, with a box of delicious chocolates from one of his father's chain of sweet shops. At last, in return, I wrote *Ich liebe dich auch* ('I love you too') on my most flattering photo, put it in a red wooden heart-shaped frame with a little door that clicked open, and gave it to him. Although the exchange of gifts and letters seemed very grown-up, the only thing we managed to do when we saw each other was to blush. Tongue-tied, we never actually exchanged a word. At last, at one of my parties, during a game of 'spin the bottle', Joachim kissed me on the cheek, and I felt as if a burning cinder had touched it.

By 1936, the third year of the Hitler era and the year I entered school, the approved greeting was the Nazi salute – 'Heil Hitler', with right arm raised. Foreign students were not required to say 'Heil

Hitler', but if we ran into a teacher in the corridor we had to stop and raise our right arms in the Nazi salute.

By the way a teacher saluted, one could tell how he felt about Hitler and the Nazis. When the elderly history teacher entered the classroom, he would say very deliberately, '*Guten morgen, kinder,*' and then, as if chasing a fly, mumble, '*Heil* Hitler' before he sat down. On the other hand, the young French teacher, dressed in a brown shirt with a Swastika on his arm, would click the heels of his spotless black boots, stick out a rigid arm and bellow, '*Heil* Hitler!' This military demeanour seemed out of place in a classroom full of children; yet my classmates, some of whom had started to wear the Hitler *Jugend* uniform with daggers stuck in the belts of their black corduroy shorts, would reply, '*Heil*, Hitler!' in loud, enthusiastic voices, their right arms stiffly raised.

We found Berlin a revelation and a delight, a place where children could have lives of their own. Not only was there children's theatre, where plays were lavishly produced and beautifully acted by professional actors, but also elaborate parties especially for children.

Our first Christmas, Madame Poncet, wife of the popular French ambassador, gave a big children's costume party, to which she invited the children of the diplomatic corps and of the high German officials. Anxious for us to stand out, Mother ordered custom-made white and pink satin outfits, white wigs and red leather-heeled shoes, which Nejad and I wore to the party as Louis XVI and Marie-Antoinette. When in the costume competition we won first prize, she was overjoyed.

For Mother, a party was an artistic creation. She decided to give a children's costume party which would top the one at the French Embassy. For it she hired the best puppet show in Berlin and, as if those in Germany were not good enough, ordered from London, crackers, favours, toys and prizes for every child, and prepared an elaborate table covered with a multitude of cakes and pastries. The living and dining rooms were decorated festively with multi-coloured streamers and heaps of colourful packages.

Nissa's most talked-about party, however, was the white-tie dinner for twenty-four she gave in honour of Baron von Neurath, the foreign minister. When I returned from school that afternoon, I was told by our butler that Mother wanted me to go to the dining room and watch the preparations for the party. This was her method of teaching me 'how things are done'.

The long dining-room table was covered with a hand-made lace cloth which had been dipped in weak tea to obtain the proper shade of ecru. The silver was vermeil, the china Meissen, with an antique Meissen bowl from the Büyükada house filled with lavender orchids as the centrepiece. Garlands of matching baby orchids trailed from the bowl to each of the six branches of the two silver candelabra that stood on either side of the bowl, holding tall lavender candles. By each place setting was a delicate bundle of finger-sized rolls, held together with a slip of mauve satin ribbon, as well as a hand-written menu engraved with the gold Hashemite crown. There was turtle soup, *foie gras* (from the Périgord region of France), lobster (flown in from Amsterdam), pheasant (prepared by the famous German restaurateur Horcher), French cheeses, *bombe glacé* and *petit-fours*. The latter were displayed on the sideboard in little baskets made of orchid-coloured sugar. The dinner was to end with fruit from Cape Town, South Africa. 'Oh, how good the peaches smelled in the middle of winter in this country where fruit is so scarce!' Mother wrote in her diary. 'And those beautiful big black grapes! I was worried they wouldn't keep in their crate until the party, so I had them hung on string in the cool basement, and every day I visited them to see how they were coming along.'

For the party, Nissa wore an orchid-coloured chiffon evening gown, and thus the symphony of lavenders and mauves was completed. When the butler announced dinner and the dining-room doors were rolled back revealing the splendid table, the French ambassador, M. François Poncet, exclaimed, 'This is magnificent, too beautiful a sight not to applaud,' and he clapped enthusiastically, followed by all the other guests. Before the dessert Emir Zeid raised his champagne glass and welcomed his guests with a gracious toast. Then Baron von Neurath thanked Emir Zeid for his hospitality and, turning to Nissa, said, 'Our gratitude to our lovely hostess, the Princess of *The Thousand and One Nights*.' Later, as the guests were departing, the Austrian ambassador, Mr Tauschnitz, whispered in Nissa's ear, 'My dear Princess, you have outdone us all.'

Nissa had achieved what she had set out to do. In less than two years, she had impressed Berlin society with her charm, wit and elegance. She was known as the exotic 'Princess from the East', an artist, a woman of great personality, a lavish hostess. Everyone wanted to be invited to the Iraqi legation, including Madame Attolico.

Nissa's parties, outfits and extravagant gestures became legendary.

She sent Hitler, for his birthday, a gift out of an Arabian fairy-tale: an antique curved dagger with a heavily encrusted silver handle and scabbard, presented on a purple velvet pillow with long silk tassels dangling from its four corners. On another occasion, Frau Bülow Schwante, the wife of a foreign service officer, received a bouquet of pink roses tied together with a pink satin ribbon fastened by an old Turkish ruby-and-pearl-encrusted pin. To people she particularly liked, Nissa framed and sent sketches and drawings she had made.

Emir Zeid, in contrast, won over his colleagues with his easy-going ways and his quiet charm. The Arab diplomats in particular looked up to him and consulted him on political matters. The Germans, who loved titles, were impressed by the fact that he was a '*Königliche Hoheit*' and the paternal uncle of the king of Iraq. Of course, they were aware of Iraq's oil riches which the British had monopolized.

Money gushed from Emir Zeid's bank account like oil from a geyser as Nissa had more delicacies flown in and ordered more designer clothes from the Paris couturiers. One evening, on her way to a big reception again at the Reichskanzlei, she swept into our room in an extraordinary shocking-pink costume, Schiaparelli's latest, topped by a voluminous burgundy-coloured velvet cape. With long bird-of-paradise feathers on her head, she looked like some fantastic character in an exotic ballet, the *Firebird*, perhaps.

In spite of her active social life, Mother did not neglect us. We took trips, as we never had in Turkey. We toured Potsdam, Cologne, the Black Forest, visited the museums, where she explained at length the different techniques of painting, and on Sundays had tea at the leading hotels while listening to string quartets. In the summer, with our governess, we went swimming at Warnemünde, and one winter Mother took us skiing at Garmisch Partenkirchen. However, after three days of bliss on the slopes, she decided that the hotel was wrong and the company not up to scratch, and dragged us away – children's opinions to the contrary definitely not welcome. And one night, at the theatre, when we were watching a bedroom farce Mother considered vulgar, she insisted on leaving in the middle of the first act. As Nejad and I were enthralled with the proceedings, she literally had to drag us away. We were never consulted as to how we felt or what we wanted.

*

One day in late 1937 our geography teacher made an announcement in class. 'We are having a school picnic next Wednesday. Bring your rucksacks along, for we shall be hiking.' Then, after clearing his throat, he added, 'Some of you are not welcome.'

Of course, I assumed that those with poor grades were being left behind, but when I saw my friend Grünfeld, who was at the top of the class, turn red, his hair and freckles and face all one colour, I realized that I was wrong. When I looked around the room, I saw that all the Jewish boys were hanging their heads. Weinstein, who sat next to me, had tears in his eyes.

After school that afternoon, I went straight to my mother's room. She was in bed sketching a cathedral she had recently visited and listening to music. I gave her a peck on the cheek and told her what had happened in school.

'Why does this upset you so much?' asked Mother. 'Obviously the children with bad grades are being left behind. That's how the school is punishing them for being lazy.'

'No, no!' I said. 'That's not the reason. They are simply being left behind because they are Jewish.'

'That's utter nonsense.'

'No, it's not nonsense. When the teacher made that announcement today, all the Jewish boys hung their heads in embarrassment.'

'You are jumping to conclusions. How do you know they are Jewish?' asked Mother.

'I know because, like Nejad and me, they are excused from religion class. Mother, why can't they go on the picnic because they are Jewish? We Muslims are going. It isn't fair.'

'I really don't know,' Mother replied. 'If you feel it is wrong, don't go to the picnic. Now, run along and have your tea.'

Most of my classmates were going to the picnic, including Joachim; the lure was too great. In the end, I went also and put thoughts of Grünfeld and Weinstein and my other Jewish friends out of my mind. Since then, however, whenever the Holocaust has been mentioned, I have wondered what became of those boys.

Some time after the picnic I came down with scarlet fever and, in accordance with German law, was put in the special quarantine wing of the children's hospital. The rooms of that wing had glass walls, and I could see all the children around me. We showed our toys to one another, and at night we signalled in Morse code with flashlights. My room was the attraction of the wing because it was always full of flowers and toys and baskets of fruit. Mother couldn't do enough to cheer me up. Every day she and Emir Zeid, Nejad and our chauffeur Franz came to visit. Forbidden to enter the room, they made faces and signalled through the glass. Along with cards from my classmates, Joachim sent me love-letters and boxes of chocolates, which I gave away to the nurses. I loved the hospital and all the attention I was getting. About three weeks after I entered the hospital, however, complications set in. My throat became swollen, and my fever rose alarmingly. They carried me on a stretcher to treat the swollen glands in my throat with X-rays, but my condition did not improve, my temperature did not fall, and I became gravely ill. As the crisis deepened, Aunt Ayşe arrived from Istanbul to stand by her sister.

'If anything happens to Shirin, I will kill myself. I cannot endure the loss of another child,' Mother told her, tormented by fear and memories of her first child, who had died of the same disease. 'Poor Shirinaki is burning up! They just cannot lower her temperature.'

'Fahrünnisa, my dear, calm down,' replied Aunt Ayşe soothingly. 'We are in Germany, which has great doctors. Faruk was at home, attended by a local doctor. The situation here is totally different. She will recover, you will see. Just have faith. I will pray for her.'

'Nevertheless,' Mother said with finality, 'if she dies, I will kill myself.' And to be prepared for the worst, she began to carry a dagger with her wherever she went.

One morning as I opened my feverish eyes, I thought I was hallucinating when I saw Father looking at me through the glass, smiling and making faces. I was too weak to respond. As soon as he had been alerted to my critical state, he had boarded the Orient Express and come to Berlin. During the three-day journey, he was tortured by the fear of arriving too late.

The X-ray treatment having failed to improve my condition, the doctors next tried hot-potato purée compresses on my neck. The purée, reheated and reused many times, gave off a sour, nauseating stench. Although I begged the nurses to remove the foul-smelling compresses, they said, '*Nein*. This will do the trick.' They were right. About two months after I had fallen ill, my throat at last returned to normal and the fever broke. When Mother arrived that day, she was overjoyed to find me sitting up in bed, pale and thin, but able to respond. In her elation at my recovery, she went out and bought gifts for all the doctors and nurses.

All this while, Father stayed in Berlin, visiting me every day. Though still in the process of looking for a new position, for his company had been nationalized, he was relatively free and able to spend as much time as necessary in Berlin. He had moved to a smaller apartment in Istanbul, and with no family to support he was living fairly comfortably.

Some time after I left the hospital, when I was strong enough, Father, to celebrate my recovery, took Nejad and me to dinner at a fashionable restaurant called the Weisse Traube, which had hanging at its entrance a lamp in the shape of a cluster of grapes. The Herr Ober seated us at a good corner table and took our order. The restaurant, jammed with people, rang with the din of conversation and the rattle of plates and glasses, and waiters scurried around attending to the customers' needs. After three months in the hospital, it was wonderful to be in the bustle of a nice restaurant.

Suddenly, while we were starting on our main course, the loud-speaker crackled, and a stentorian voice announced, '*Meine Damen und Herren, der Führer.*' Immediately Hitler's voice boomed out and, as if God had spoken, everything in the room stopped. The waiters backed up to the walls and stood to attention. Putting down their knives and forks, the diners stopped chewing and listened.

Father gazed about him in amazement. He could not believe that a restaurant would stop serving and force its customers to listen to a speech, even if it were Hitler's. Unable to contain his irritation, he exclaimed, 'This is ridiculous. We came here to eat, not to listen to speeches.' The people at the next table loudly shushed him.

He looked around the room, expecting to see people preparing to leave, irritated and annoyed like himself. No one budged; no one protested; no one looked annoyed. On the contrary, everyone was listening, mesmerized; obviously the Führer's power lay in his phenomenal oratory.

Father rose, threw his napkin and some marks on the table, and tersely said, 'Come on, children, let's get out of here.' We finished our dinner at a little pavement restaurant, where we ate frankfurters, potato salad and black bread. Not Father's style at all.

The speech that had so annoyed him was Hitler's announcement that on 11 March 1938, Austria had become a province of the German Reich. The *Anschluss* had been one of Hitler's ambitions, predicted in the first paragraph of his book *Mein Kampf*. His threat to invade Austria had forced the Austrian chancellor, Kurt von

Schuschnigg, to resign, and three days later Hitler rode in triumph through the streets of Vienna to the cheers of most of the populace. The world saw only the cheering crowds and was spared the brutality inflicted on those who were against this move.

Mother was grateful to Aunt Ayşe for having left her own family and rushed to her side, and took her sister shopping, sightseeing and to concerts. One afternoon when the sisters returned to the legation, Nissa stopped at Emir Zeid's office. He was standing at his desk holding a telegram. 'We have been recalled,' he announced flatly.

'What do you mean, recalled?' she asked, uncomprehending. 'By whom?'

'By the minister of foreign affairs, Mr El-Swaidi.'

'That is ridiculous. How can *he* recall *you*? Why? Ask him why!'

'I wouldn't stoop to such a question.'

'They should be grateful to us for all we've done for Iraq. Instead they recall us! That's justice for you. Ah!' she continued. 'When Mr El-Swaidi came to Berlin, I was ill and did not give a dinner for him. He probably was furious at what he considered a snub, and intrigued against us in Baghdad.'

'I don't think that can be the reason,' Emir Zeid said quietly. 'But whatever the reason, we are leaving.'

'Very well, then,' Nissa said resolutely. 'We will go to Baghdad. We'll go and confront them all!'

None of us ever found out why Emir Zeid was recalled. It was rumoured that the reason was Mother's extravagant spending of government money, but the real reason, I think, was that the British, who were still pulling the strings in Iraq, did not approve of Nissa's friendship with the Nazi leaders. In Iraq, pro-German sentiment was gaining momentum, and the British were nervous at having Emir Zeid, so prominent a member of the Iraqi royal family, in Berlin at this critical time.

When I heard we were leaving Berlin, I was heartbroken, for I had been looking forward to returning to school, to Joachim, to my ballet lessons and to all that Berlin had to offer.

As soon as our departure was announced, a necessary round of official calls and farewell parties followed. One morning in mid-April, Nissa received a telephone call from Hitler's aide, von Kivitz. 'Your Royal Highness, the Führer would like to see you,' he said in his excellent French.

'Oh,' said Nissa, giving herself a moment to think. 'Alone? Or with my husband?'

There was a pause. She decided that von Kivitz's hesitation meant that the Führer wanted to see her alone. 'I accept with pleasure,' she said promptly. (I now think she jumped to conclusions. The idea of having a *tête-à-tête* with Hitler intrigued her. What was the man really like? She wanted to know.)

'April the twentieth at five, five-fifteen, or five-thirty – which time would you prefer, Your Highness?' asked von Kivitz.

Opting for the middle road, she answered, 'Five-fifteen.'

'I should like to remind Your Highness that April the twentieth is the Führer's birthday and all the streets around the Reichskanzlei will be blocked off to traffic. Your car, with licence CD82, will be the only one allowed through.'

'Thank you,' said Nissa, and the conversation ended.

When she told Emir Zeid about this invitation at lunch that day, he was surprised. For a head of state to receive a departing diplomat and his wife was an act of courtesy, but to ask to see the wife alone was unheard of. However, she had already accepted the invitation, and to make her back out would be undiplomatic and rude, so he concealed his misgivings. With his usual equanimity, he raised no objections. Besides, he always let Nissa do whatever she wanted. It was easier that way.

As the day approached, she prepared for her visit with Hitler, planning her conversation and her outfit. She decided to wear a long-skirted black velvet suit, her latest Parisian hat, and throw over her shoulders her silver-fox jacket. 'All in black, that will be dramatic,' she thought. 'What am I going to talk to him about? What am I going to say to Mr Hitler? Oh! I will talk about art. He fancies himself a painter. That's it. I will tell him about the museums I visited in Germany and the art I saw. That will interest him.'

On the appointed day, Nissa was a little nervous. To fortify herself, before leaving the legation, she drank a glass of cognac. Franz, who for some time had been affecting a Hitleresque moustache and hair-style, stood proudly next to the gleaming blue Buick as Nissa climbed in.

The streets were empty of traffic. A few blocks from the Reichs-kanzlei, the police waved them through a checkpoint. As they approached the Reichskanzlei, thousands of people, gathered behind barricades, peered curiously into the car. Who was this woman? Why was she coming alone to the Reichskanzlei on such a day?

The moment the car stopped at the door, officers in highly polished boots clicked their heels and saluted, and von Kivitz escorted Nissa to a huge reception room, at the far end of which she saw Hitler. He was standing on the balcony acknowledging the frenzied *Sieg Heil*'s of the crowd below. Von Kivitz hurried to tell him of Nissa's arrival. Meanwhile Nissa wondered what to do. Should she wait for him or should she walk toward him? Noticing an immense chandelier in the middle of the room, she decided to walk slowly so they would meet halfway. Hitler turned and walked toward her. 'How taut he is!' Nissa thought. 'There is nothing easy or natural about this man.' Just as she'd planned, Hitler met her beneath the chandelier. Bowing stiffly, he kissed her hand and led her to a seating arrangement in front of the fireplace, where an array of cakes and finger sandwiches had been tastefully spread on a small table.

Faced with a two-seater sofa and an armchair, Nissa chose the latter. 'If I sit on the sofa,' she thought, 'he might consider it an invitation for him to sit next to me. What would I do if he tried to hold my hand or make advances?'

Von Kivitz asked Nissa if she cared to have an interpreter. She hesitated for a moment. Although her German was very poor, the idea of talking through someone else bothered her.

'No,' she said bravely. 'Thank you. I can manage without one.' Like all Mediterraneans, she had the knack of making herself understood with the help of eyes and hands.

An officer reached for her fox jacket. 'Would you care to remove your cape, Your Highness?' he asked.

'They want to remove my cape in case I have a concealed weapon,' Nissa thought suspiciously, holding on to it. 'No, thank you,' she answered. 'I prefer to keep it.'

When everyone except the butler had left the room, she removed her cape in a dramatic gesture and flung it on to the polished parquet floor. Like an animal with a million invisible legs, it slid all the way across the room as Hitler and she watched its journey. The butler picked it up and placed in on a chair; he then served her tea. From a different silver pot he poured Hitler some hot chocolate.

To start the conversation, Nissa jokingly said, 'Führer, you are having hot chocolate like a little boy.' He wasn't amused and looked at her sternly. Then, after taking a sip of his hot chocolate, he said, 'I hear you are a painter. So am I.'

Nissa was delighted that he had broached the subject for which she had prepared. She sat back and told him all about the museums she had visited and the art she had seen in Germany. When she said she had particularly enjoyed the Pinakotek Museum in Munich, Hitler made a wry face. 'But it is cold there in the winter,' he said.

She felt she had touched on a subject that displeased him, but she couldn't understand why, since she knew Munich was where he'd risen to power, his operational base in the beginning.

'I do not like much of the art in the German museums,' Hitler continued. 'It is decadent. I plan to build a museum in Nüremberg, and I am encouraging a new movement of nationalistic art. Do you plan to continue to paint?'

'Of course,' she replied. 'Now I still have family obligations, but eventually I shall give myself totally to art.' Then, looking around the large room she added, 'All this gold trim is very Byzantine. It reminds me of St Sophia in Istanbul. I compliment you on the decoration.'

As architecture was one of his passions, Hitler was pleased. He had spent months with the architect Speer on the decoration of the Reichskanzlei. As a youth, he had been greatly affected by the baroque architecture of Vienna, and had painted pictures of many beautiful buildings. He had even had postcards made of them, which he'd sold.

Abruptly, Hitler asked, 'What do you think of the *Anschluss*?'

Nissa had heard that Hitler had cried with joy the day Austria became a province of the German Reich; she had not yet heard of the arrest of Chancellor Schuschnigg and thousands of Jews by the Gestapo. 'It was like a miracle,' she said. 'Not a shot fired – *keine Toten, kein Blut.*'

Hitler smiled for the first time that afternoon; then a shadow crossed his face. He looked down at his black shoes and remarked, 'It's too bad about Chancellor Schuschnigg.'

Nissa did not understand what he meant. There was a long, awkward pause, and she decided it was time for her to leave. A diplomatic call usually lasted fifteen minutes, and she had already overstayed that time. But before leaving, she decided to ask him one leading question.

'Führer,' she said, 'Ambassador Poncet is running around Berlin like Cassandra, lamenting, "There is going to be a war. I can feel it in my bones. War is going to break out." Is it true? Is there going to be a war?'

Hitler did not flinch. 'Monsieur Poncet is the most intelligent and witty ambassador France has ever sent to Germany,' he replied, avoiding her question.

As she rose, von Kivitz appeared out of nowhere and helped her with her cape.

Hitler pointed at a small table by the armchair. 'Where are the yellow roses?' he asked von Kivitz. 'You were going to have a vase of yellow roses put there. You forgot.' And he patted the man affectionately on the shoulder. Von Kivitz blushed and made an apology.

They both walked Nissa to the door. Hitler kissed her hand twice and said, 'Thank you, Your Highness. Thank you for coming.'

'That was my tea party with Hitler,' Mother concluded when she had described to all of us every detail of her visit with the Führer. Then, 'I don't understand why he reacted that way when I mentioned Munich,' she commented.

Emir Zeid explained that after the famous 'Beerhall putsch' in Munich in 1923, Hitler and his henchmen had been jailed briefly by the Weimar republic. 'Obviously, Munich is not one of his favourite places,' he said. 'Yet that's where he wrote *Mein Kampf*.'

'What was he referring to when he talked about Schuschnigg?' Mother asked.

'There are rumours,' Emir Zeid said, 'that Schuschnigg has been arrested and imprisoned by the Gestapo.'

'How can that be?' she exclaimed. 'Everything I have read has said that the Austrians welcomed the Germans.'

'That's what they want you to think,' replied Emir Zeid. 'Don't believe everything they say. Their propaganda machine is very powerful! Did you enjoy your tea party after all?'

'Not particularly,' Mother replied, 'when I think how exhilarating it is to be with Atatürk. Now, *he* has charisma. Hitler has none, for me, at least. There is something cold about the man. His eyes are bottomless, like long, grey tunnels. However, I admire him for what he has done for the German people. Remember when we first came to Berlin, there were still soup kitchens in the streets? But by the time the Olympics took place, only a year later, it was like a new nation.'

'All that is true,' answered Emir Zeid, 'But he will undo everything if he leads them to war. The *Anschluss* was just the beginning, and it looks to me as if Czechoslovakia is going to be the next victim.' Then he added, puffing at his pipe, 'I don't trust Mr Hitler and this whole Nazi scene.'

By the end of the month it was time for us to depart, and the family left Berlin in shifts. Nejad and Aunt Ayşe were the first to set out for Istanbul. Mother, exhausted from all the emotional upsets of the past two months, her health again disintegrating, needed to go away to gather her strength, and left for Prague to visit her old friends, the Kadris. Yakup Kadri, then Turkish ambassador to Czechoslovakia, was a renowned writer whom she had known from her days with Father, and his wife was a close friend. She and the Kadris planned to go on to Karlsbad for the water cure.

As I had been too weak to travel earlier, Emir Zeid and I were the last to leave Berlin. After the three-day train trip, he left me in Istanbul and went on to Baghdad, while I returned once again for the summer to the house on the island.

13

Cevat Comes Home

On Büyükada, I was pleased to find everything as I had left it. Late every afternoon, Grandmother, her daily chores completed, sheer white cotton scarf on her head, sat in her pristine room, which would be ablaze with the rays of the dying sun, and read the Qur'an. And shortly before the evening meal, the same old man selling yoghurt hawked his wares through the village: 'Yoooo yooooghurt!' Day after day and evening after evening, at tea in the house around the samovar or in the garden under the arbour, the aunts and uncles carried on their endless conversations, which usually came to rest on the question of whether Turkey would become involved if the European nations, then drifting toward war, actually started fighting.

In late July Mother returned from Karlsbad in high spirits, bringing lovely gifts for everyone. I have always found her resilience admirable. Happy to be back in the Büyükada house, she spent the days sketching in the pine groves and taking some of the thirty dips in the sea that were recommended to ward off winter ills.

One sweltering August afternoon, all the Shakirs except Grandmother were gathered as usual for tea in the upstairs living room. This would be an ice-cream day, they decided, and dispatched the gardener to summon the vendor, who was found strolling through the streets, carrying two buckets of hand-churned ice-cream suspended from a yoke across his shoulders and chanting, *Donduuuuurma!*

When the vendor arrived in the garden, he lowered his buckets to the ground, sat on a bench, and ladled out, slowly and carefully, *kaymak* and fruit sherbets into the little glass cups the maid had lined up on a large silver tray.

'Make sure everyone in the household gets some. Don't forget the gardener,' Emin told the maid as he accepted his cup.

Aliye, who was extremely close to her mother, with whom she

still lived all the year round, licked the sour-cherry sherbet off her spoon and murmured, 'I wonder why Mother isn't back.'

'Perhaps she missed the three-thirty ferry,' Nissa suggested, putting aside her ice-cream dish and picking up a pen to continue the china-ink drawing on her lap.

'Why did she have to go to town anyway, on such a hot day?' Aliye wanted to know.

'She had a doctor's appointment,' confided Mizou.

'A doctor's appointment!' cried Hakiye, surprised. 'She didn't tell me anything was wrong.'

'Nor me,' added Ayşe. 'How do you know she went to the doctor?'

'I found out by accident,' Mizou answered. 'When I asked Seher to iron my dresses, she said she couldn't because she had to accompany the hanîmefendi to the doctor's office in town. They left on the first ferry this morning.'

'Why is she being so secretive?' Hakiye demanded.

'You know Mother,' said Aliye. 'She'd never tell us anything that would upset us.'

'Then it must be serious!' Nissa exclaimed, looking worried.

'Don't get excited, all of you,' urged Mizou. 'It's probably only a routine examination.'

'If that's all it is, she would have told us. I don't like it at all,' Nissa said, shaking her head, and buried herself in her sketch.

When about an hour later the telephone rang, they all jumped, but, as custom demanded, they let Hakiye, the eldest, answer it. The call was from the doctor, a close family friend.

'Thank Allah you called!' said Hakiye. 'What's going on? Why did Mother come to see you?' Without waiting for the doctor's reply, she continued, 'We have been worried sick. She told us nothing.'

'Ask him what is wrong with her,' cried Aliye from across the room.

'Tell him we want to know exactly,' added Ayşe.

'And tell him not to hide anything from us,' said Nissa firmly. 'We have a right to know.'

'Quiet!' Hakiye demanded, receiver in hand. 'Give me a chance to find out.'

Hakiye listened intently for some time; then suddenly her face turned ashen. 'Operated!' she gasped. 'What do you mean, operated?' The sisters held their breath. 'Cancer!' cried Hakiye in a voice choked with fear, and the three sisters, like a Greek chorus, repeated,

'Cancer!' 'Cancer!' 'Cancer!' in disbelief. Then they shrieked with horror and burst into loud cries and sobs, crowding around Hakiye.

'Please,' Hakiye implored, 'calm down. Be quiet. I can't hear the man.'

The sisters hushed, and for a long time Hakiye listened to the doctor's report. Then she put down the receiver and turned to the others, who were huddled, motionless.

'The first thing the doctor wants us to know is that Mother is all right and is resting comfortably in the Şişli hospital.'

'Thank Allah,' moaned Ayşe.

'But why did he operate so quickly? What was the rush?' demanded Nissa.

'A couple of days ago,' Hakiye explained, 'while Mother was washing in the *hammam*, she felt a lump in her right breast. Without telling anyone, she called Dr Aziz and made an appointment to see him today. When he examined her, he was alarmed at the size of the lump and suggested that she be operated on immediately.'

'But why this very day?' exclaimed Aliye. 'Without telling any of us? I think it's terrible!'

'That's the way Mother wanted it,' Hakiye assured them. 'She insisted that the doctor perform the operation and then inform the family.'

'Poor Mother! What she must have gone through!' said the sisters, for once stunned into speechlessness.

After a long pause, Aliye burst out, 'The doctor had no right to operate without letting us know. Perhaps she didn't need the operation at all. He had no right to operate without a second opinion, without telling us!'

'Oh, Aliye, shut up!' said Hakiye. 'He's the best doctor in Istanbul and a devoted friend of Mother's. Do you think he'd do anything to harm her? Now all of you please quieten down and think rationally. What's done is done, and we hope it is for the best. I will take the last ferry to town tonight and stay in the apartment. Early tomorrow I'll go to the hospital with Mother's things.' The others said they would follow the next morning.

At the hospital, they found my grandmother resting comfortably and in good spirits, and this calmed their fears. With the shock and the danger apparently past, Grandmother's room became a gathering place. Every day it was crowded with family and friends, who brought flowers, sweets, cologne, even home-made soups. There were so many visitors that they often had to stand in the hall, and the nurses' desperate efforts to maintain hospital decorum were in vain.

Then, about ten days after her operation, Grandmother contracted the dreaded complication: pneumonia. As her condition grew rapidly worse, the doctors forbade any visitors but her daughters, who took turns sleeping in her room and drove all the doctors and nurses to distraction with their constant comments. questions and suggestions. Each knew best what should be done! They argued and fought with the medical staff and with one another over the patient's treatment.

Realizing the gravity of the situation, Grandmother's brother Mithat notified Uncle Cevat in Bodrum. Cevat had been at sea for three days with the sponge divers, about whom he was writing a series of short stories and articles. As the small fishing boat pulled into anchorage at Bodrum, a child ran from the café. 'Fisherman, Fisherman! There is a telegram for you,' he shouted. (Since Cevat had become known as the 'Fisherman of Halicarnassus' the locals called him 'Fisherman'.) Cevat was not alarmed. As he did not have a phone, anyone who needed to contact him sent a telegram, which in those days was cheap and the best means of communication. Before going home, he stopped in the café on the waterfront to have a glass of tea with the fishermen returning with their morning catch.

After sauntering through the narrow streets, he reached his house, where he found his wife Hatice hanging out the wash. The moment she saw him, she reached into her bosom. 'Here,' she said, 'this arrived yesterday,' and she handed him a telegram: 'YOUR MOTHER SERIOUSLY ILL IN ŞİŞLİ HOSPITAL. MITHAT.'

Cevat felt as if a bolt of lightning had struck him. 'Mother is ill,' he told Hatice, and ran to his room. From the wooden trunk on the floor he took out the only suit he had, a navy gaberdine shiny with use, and hastily packed a few toilet articles, some underwear, and a bunch of writing pads into a small, battered leather suitcase, then ran to the village square to catch the bus. When, after a long, hot, dusty bus ride, he finally reached Istanbul, he went straight to the hospital, where he was told by the doctor that his mother was failing rapidly. Upon opening the door of the hospital room, he found his four sisters and Mizou at Grandmother's bedside, looking pale and spent, holding back their tears and mumbling prayers. His mother's eyes were closed, her face flushed and her breathing laboured.

Ayşe and Hakiye had neither seen nor talked to Cevat since the killing of their father twenty-four years before. Stunned at the sight of him, they backed into the far corner of the room, but Nissa and Aliye ran over and, embracing him, said warmly, 'Welcome, *ağabey*, we are glad you came.'

Mizou shook his hand politely. 'Welcome, you look tired. It must have been a long journey.'

Then Cevat sat on Grandmother's bed, taking both her hands in his. 'I've come, Mother,' he said in his booming voice. 'I've brought you the smell of the Aegean and greetings from Neptune.'

Grandmother opened her eyes, a faint smile crossing her lips. 'Thank you, my son,' she whispered with difficulty. Cevat pressed her hands against his chest.

'We should leave,' Ayşe whispered to Hakiye, and the two elder sisters quietly slipped out of the room.

All that night, as Grandmother sank toward death, Cevat held her in his arms, entreating her to stay. Even when she breathed her last and died in his arms, he leaned over, desperately giving her mouth-to-mouth respiration until the doctor pulled him away from her body.

Early the next day, the sisters accompanied their mother's bier back to the island on a chartered launch. As they sat in the tiny lounge, weeping and pale, they looked fragile, like wounded birds. Always solicitous of one another, each was more concerned about the other's grief than her own. Hakiye tried not to show how sad she felt in order not to upset Ayşe. Aliye held back her hysteria, trying not to grieve her sisters more. They watched one another for signs of weakening, so that the other three could support the weak one. All of them worried about their brother, Suat, who had been appointed, that summer of 1938, as Turkey's special commissioner to the New York World Fair. At the time of the tragedy, of which he was of course ignorant, Suat was at sea, returning from America.

'He will never forgive himself for not being here,' exclaimed Ayşe. 'He was so devoted to Mother.'

Mizou interrupted. 'I, for one, am relieved he is not here. His mother's death is enough to destroy him, not to mention having to face Cevat and relive once again that awful night at the farm. He would have gone to pieces.'

The mention of their elder brother was all they needed.

Emin Pasha

Cevat Pasha, Grand Vizier of the Ottoman Empire

Ismet, the Cretan wife of Shakir Pasha and Nimet, the
Circassian wife of Cevat Pasha

Shakir Pasha with his favourite daughter Ayşe whom he
called 'my princess'

L to R Nissa, Aliye and Ayşe, Istanbul 1923

Hakiye and her daughter Fureya, Istanbul 1915

Suat, Syida and Geraldine, c.1926

Muhitten Lala

Izzet–Melih Devrim, c.1920's

L to R Nissa, Ismet, Hakiye, Syida, Ayşe, Aliye and little
Geraldine in front, c. 1920's

The Shakirs, c.1927, *L to R* back row, Emin Pasha, Syida,
Aniesi, Ayşe, Ismet, Nissa, Hakiye, Izzet;
front row, unknown child, Geraldine, Mutara and Fureya

Nissa at a ball of the painting school, Istanbul 1921

Nissa, Shirin and Raad, Berlin 1938

Shirin, Fureya and Nissa setting out on a trip to Cologne, 1937

Nissa and Emir Zeid, Berlin 1938

Shirin, Nissa, Emir Zeid and Raad, Baghdad 1938

Shirin, Baghdad 1943

In front of King Ghazi's plane the Blue Bird, Baghdad 1938.
L to R Shirin, the royal sherifas and emiras, Melek wife of Emir Abdullilah, Abdiye, Jelila, Bedia, daughters of King Ali and sisters of Queen Aliya of Iraq, Emira Saliha older sister of Emir Zeid, Nissa, Emir Cemil's wife, Sherifa Fatima, Queen Nefisa wife of King Ali, Queen Aliya of Iraq, Queen Zein of Jordan, Sherifa Azza, Emira Rajiha daughter of King Faisal I, Sherifa Nafia sister of Queen Zein, in front Sherif Nasser

Nejad, Rome 1949

Shirin, 1951

Queen Elizabeth coming to visit Nissa's first exhibition in
London at the St George's Gallery, 1946

Nissa, London c.1950

Çevat with Yaşar Kemal

Suat in his last years in Side, late 1960s

Nissa in her bedroom, Amman 1987

'I wish he hadn't come,' said Ayşe in a strangled voice. 'Seeing him upsets me so. I will never forgive him for what he did.'

'I certainly agree, but I can see why he wanted to be at her bedside in the hospital,' Hakiye said reasonably, 'after all she did for him. Of course he had to be with her when she died. But *now* let him go home and leave us alone!'

'But, after all, *abla*s, he is her son,' said Nissa, irritated.

'And he's our brother,' added Aliye.

'Well, I'm grateful that Cevat buries himself at Bodrum where we don't have to see him. I wish he would just stay there and never come to our house again,' declared Ayşe.

'On the contrary, I wish he were not so far away,' said Aliye. 'Such a brilliant, cultured man! So interesting! I could learn so much from him. He is like Karamazov. Uncle Charles says that patricide is common, since every young man, at some point or another, wants to kill his father.'

'Don't be grotesque, Aliye,' scolded Nissa. 'This is not the time for Uncle Charles's Freudian theories. You really are impossible.'

Silence descended on the sisters as they finished their journey.

When the launch arrived at the ferry landing in Büyükada, the weeping Lala and a host of islanders carried the coffin from the waterfront up to the house. Placing the coffin on a table in the coolness and gloom of the formal living room, they carefully draped over it a green velvet cloth with a border of gold thread tracing holy texts from the Qur'an. As the news spread, one by one came the *hoja*s and finally the *imam*. Sitting in a circle around the coffin, they read from the Qur'an and chanted prayers for the salvation of Grandmother's soul. We children were made to sit there for a while, but we could stand the gloom and sadness only a few minutes and soon fled.

In accordance with Islamic custom, burial had to take place as soon as possible. Consequently, the house quickly became a beehive of activity, swarming with mourners, for Grandmother in her unobtrusive way had helped many poor people. They all came, some on ferries from town and others from the island itself. After standing briefly beside the coffin, the visitors were shown upstairs into the family living room where refreshments were served. Little trays with used coffee cups and tea glasses lay about everywhere waiting to be cleared. In the kitchen the cooks clattered about, preparing enough food and *halvah* for all who had come to mourn, and upstairs, maids with piles of quilts in their arms made up beds for the many relatives and close friends who intended to spend the night.

So as not to embarrass his family and to avoid the stares and whispers that he knew he could expect from the guests, Cevat waited until late that night to come to Büyükada. Escorted by Mithat, he was shown to the upstairs living room where Nissa, Aliye and Mizou were sitting alone, while Hakiye and Ayşe prayed with the mourners downstairs. When Cevat saw the closed door to his mother's room, he stood in front of it for a long moment and then, turning the doorknob, walked into the immaculate, chapel-like room. Nothing had been moved. On the sofa were his mother's round, old-fashioned eyeglasses and her Qur'an, and at the bedside was a vase full of jasmine. The big brass bed had been beautifully made with an array of white lace pillows. Cevat crossed the room and lay on her bed under the white netting. What memories and painful regrets he must have felt! After a few moments he rose and marched resolutely out to the living room.

On the third floor, I lay in bed, feeling guilty that I had not yet cried for the grandmother I had so loved. Excited by the events taking place around me all that day, I had actually enjoyed the drama, and that realization bothered me. Suddenly, over the faint chanting that rose from the ground floor, I heard a vibrant, booming, masculine voice, unlike any other I had ever heard. 'Oh,' I thought, 'that must be him. He has finally arrived.' Earlier I had heard that Uncle Cevat had been at Grandmother's death bed and planned to come to the funeral, and I had looked forward to meeting my mysterious uncle.

Jumping out of bed and running to the head of the stairs, I listened intently to the strange, dominant voice declaiming on subjects I could not comprehend.

'. . . Homer was an Anatolian and belongs as much to us as to the Greeks. The Trojans were as much the heroes of the *Iliad* as the Achaeans, the mainland Greeks.'

I could not make out the other voices over Cevat's booming sound.

'Do you know what Bernard Shaw said, my dear Nissa? "Every man over forty is a scoundrel." How old are you now, my dear? I've been a scoundrel for years. What a genius that Shaw is! The greatest of our century.'

Aliye's voice followed, then Mother's.

Then the masculine boom again: 'Well, he foresaw so much. I mean, his best work was in the nineties and shortly thereafter. *Man and Superman* was produced in 1903, remember. There he foresees all the trouble we're having now. We're just lucky the atom hasn't yet been split. A madman in power could split the atom and doom us all without so much as a by-your-leave. Mark my words: the most important event of the century will be the splitting of the atom.'

Consumed by curiosity, I tiptoed downstairs to the landing outside the living room, where the door stood open. Pacing up and down was a tall, wiry man, very erect, talking at the top of his voice and gesticulating with both arms. He had a round, well-shaped head, a protruding forehead, a mane of curly black hair around a bald pate, and big, dark brown eyes like overboiled chestnuts. His tanned face was deeply lined and weathered. The corners of his mouth, in contrast to his tragic eyes, were perpetually turned up in a smile.

As I paused in the doorway, he turned and boomed, 'Who are you?'

'I'm Shirin,' I answered.

'She's my daughter,' Mother added.

'*Merhaba*, Shirin,' he said as he raised his arm in a Roman salute. 'Come here, child, let me look at you. So tall! It's good to be tall. You can look over people's heads, even beyond them. Think of spending your life looking at belly-buttons and chests!'

As I drew near, he came forward, seized me about the waist, picked me up effortlessly, and kissed me heartily on both cheeks. 'I am your Uncle Cevat,' he said.

Much impressed by my uncle, I thought him a hero and did not want to believe that those horrible rumours about him were true. His vitality and dynamism made everyone else look sleepy, even Mother.

The next morning, the procession formed in the garden, and the men took turns carrying the plain wooden coffin up the hill. As it swayed out of the red gate on its journey to the Muslim cemetery which Grandfather had had built and where he was buried, the crowds fell in behind it on foot, the mourners moving slowly in the crush. Now the village was left behind; now the last houses fell away; now we were climbing up the steep white path between the fields.

Although, in Islamic countries governed by Sharia law, women are not allowed to go to funerals, we Muslims in secularized Turkey do attend them. At my grandmother's funeral Mother, Aunt Aliye and I were side by side; Nejad was at the front, ready for his stint among the coffin bearers. At a bend in the path we could see Cevat still up ahead and shouldering his burden, although all the other bearers had yielded to replacements. When we arrived at the open grave, there he stood, sweat streaming from his face, tears spouting from his eyes. If he had been allowed, he would gladly have carried the body up in his arms by himself.

When we returned to the house, all passion spent, trembling with exhaustion and grief, the family gathered once more with our closest friends and relatives, and, as usually happened, tears and laughter mingled.

I slipped out into the garden, went straight to where Grandmother's favourite pots of flowers were lined up, picked a handful of jasmine and pressed the flowers against my nostrils. Suddenly the strong fragrance had Grandmother at my elbow. Tears sprang. I had joined the mourners.

After Grandmother's death the Büyükada house was never the same. She had been the loving force that had kept the family together.

14

Baghdad – 1938

Two weeks after the funeral, Mother, Raad, his nurse Schwester Edith and I boarded the Taurus Express for a three-day trip across the plains of Anatolia and the Taurus Mountains to Baghdad, where we were to join Emir Zeid.

The mention of Iraq's fairy-tale capital evoked in my mind fantasies of Aladdin and his magic lamp, Ali Baba and the forty thieves, Scheherazade dancing in transparent harem trousers, and all the pornographic prints I had peeked at in my father's unexpurgated edition of *The Thousand and One Nights*. Mother, for her part, with her penchant for antiquity, was looking forward to discovering the cradle of Western civilization and visiting its sites.

As we boarded the train on the Asiatic shore of the Bosphorus, the family saw us off *en masse*. When the shrill whistle announced the imminent departure of the train, Nejad, who was staying behind, wrapped himself around Mother and would not let go. His fifteen-year-old defences crumbled; tears flowed, and his deep, coughing sobs drowned out the chatter of farewells. Mother was disturbed, because she had lectured Nejad for hours on the logic of his continuing school in Istanbul and thought that he had reconciled himself to the idea.

'Nejad, pull yourself together. You are upsetting me,' she said, trying to break free of his grip.

The Shakirs immediately came to the rescue and pried Nejad away. 'We will take care of you, you have us,' they assured him as they eased him down the stairs and on to the platform.

These heart-wrenching scenes upset me. 'Why do we always have to say goodbye?' I thought. 'Our life seems to be a series of farewells. Why can't we live in a house with our parents, like other children, without these constant separations?' Feeling sorry for Nejad and myself, I too burst into tears. As the train pulled away from the station, I leaned out of the window as far as I could to get a last glimpse of all those I loved, clustered on the platform waving their white handkerchiefs. From a distance the Shakirs looked like a field of daisies swaying in the breeze. As the engine, huffing and puffing, rounded a curve, they were blown out of sight.

Our first stop early the next morning was to be Ankara, where I expected to see my father who, having had no choice, had left his beloved Istanbul in order to accept the government's only offer – to become director of the Anatolian News Agency, the semi-official news bureau in Ankara. He also taught French literature at the War Academy and made translations for various embassies. These different jobs enabled him to maintain his lifestyle, down to his custom-made Sulka pyjamas. Father was never one to shrink from work and did not consider it demeaning to go to the embassies at night in his fur-lined coat and homburg and work like a clerk, translating documents for a pittance.

As the train pulled into the station I saw him waiting on the platform, looking as dapper as ever, two neatly wrapped sweet boxes dangling from his kid-gloved finger. Mother had decided to stay in her compartment, for she feared the sight of Izzet would stir up painful memories. Holding him in her arms, Raad's tall, blonde, good-looking nurse, Schwester Edith, and I stepped down from the train. Father kissed me heartily on both cheeks and patted Raad on the head. 'What an adorable little boy!' he exclaimed, smiling. 'He looks just like Emir Zeid.' Then, looking toward the train, he asked, 'How is your mother?'

'She's fine,' I replied, embarrassed that she was making such a point of avoiding him.

When the time came to depart, Father held me in his arms for a long while. He had tears in his eyes. 'Write to me,' he urged. 'Write to me as often as you can, all about your impressions and experiences in Baghdad. I will keep your letters, and some day you can read them and recall how it really was in Iraq.' I had shed all my tears for Nejad, and the Shakirs, and I had none left for my father. I kissed him calmly on both cheeks, said, 'I promise I will write,' and boarded the train.

Three days later we arrived in Mosul, an oil-rich city in northern Iraq very close to the Turkish border, where the railway line ended. Originally it had been Germany's dream to extend the railway line from Mosul to Baghdad and from there all the way to Basra, thus linking Berlin via the Orient and Taurus Expresses with the Persian Gulf. As early as the 1880s, the sultan had given the kaiser permission to do just that, but the British, sensing the threat that this route posed to the Suez Canal, had intervened and blocked the extension of the railway beyond Mosul.

As soon as the train stopped at the end of the line, Emir Zeid boarded it, followed by an Arab chauffeur wearing a white *keffiyeh* and carrying a flat package. When Emir Zeid entered our compartment, Mother threw herself into his arms. 'Zeid, my love, if you only knew how much I have missed you!' she said and burst into tears. After Grandmother's death, tears came easily to her.

'I am so sorry, so very sorry about your mother,' he said, hugging her closely. 'And it all happened so suddenly! I deeply regret not having been at your side during those difficult days.'

Then Emir Zeid noticed me standing by the door. He lowered his head so I could kiss him on the pate and said, 'It's good to see you, Shirin, my girl.' He then took Raad from Schwester Edith's arms and bounced him up and down. 'My, how he has grown in three months!' he remarked. 'He is so heavy.'

'I call him my little Buddha,' I added, bringing a smile to their faces.

At this point the chauffeur handed Emir Zeid the package, which he gave to Mother. 'My sister Saliha wanted you to have this.' Mother thought it was a welcome gift from her sister-in-law – a piece of silk material, a brocade, perhaps an embroidery – but when she opened it she found a thick, black-silk, ankle-length cape with a hood. As she lifted it, a long black georgette veil slipped to the floor.

'Saliha sent you your first *abayeh*,' said Emir Zeid, picking up the veil from the floor. He was somewhat embarrassed that Nissa, even before leaving the train, had to don this restrictive costume, but how could Emir Zeid's wife be seen in public without an *abayeh*? Stepping out into the aisle, he added, 'Shirin can help you put it on.'

We struggled with this black contraption – Which side was up and which side down? Which side had to be held on the crown of the head – and finally discovered that the veil had to fit snugly under the hood part so that it could hang straight down to the waist. As I watched Mother try to handle the cumbersome *abayeh* down the steps of the railway car, I thought to myself, 'Thank Allah I am not old enough to have to don the *abayeh* and look like a witch.'

Like most sophisticated ladies of Istanbul, Nissa had shed the veil in 1919 – long before Atatürk publicly ridiculed it. Ironically, she now faced having to wear a much more restrictive mode of covering, but she accepted the *abayeh* as a necessity of her new status. '*Il faut faire ce qu'on doit faire,*' she said.

Before we drove on to Baghdad, Zeid had arranged for us to spend the night in the mayor's house in Mosul. When we arrived, a host of servants served us tea in a charming garden on the Tigris River. It was a balmy September afternoon, and the air was fragrant with the scent of the multi-petalled, peony-like roses in full bloom. Mosul has two springs, and we were experiencing the second.

At dinner-time, a meticulously set table with an array of foods covering it appeared, and the respectful servants tended to our needs.

'Where are our hosts?' asked Mother, surprised that they had not yet appeared.

'They are entertaining us from behind the scenes,' Zeid replied. 'We are still a restricted, segregated society. A woman cannot mix with men, unless they are members of her family.'

'Then I am not going to meet any men socially unless they are your relatives?' Mother asked, somewhat surprised.

'Yes,' said Zeid. 'I am sorry, but that is the custom.'

'I did not realize it was so strict,' commented Mother, then shrugged philosophically, accepting with good humour what was inevitable.

Early the next morning, the six of us – Emir Zeid, Mother, Raad, Schwester Edith, the chauffeur and I – piled into the blue Nash that King Ghazi, Emir Zeid's nephew, had given him. Mother conscientiously wore her *abayeh*, even though no one but a few Bedouins would see her on the trip. As we drove through long stretches of desert, the *abayeh* soon turned to tan, and to my delight Schwester Edith's immaculately starched uniform and nurse's cap were covered with dust, which she tried unsuccessfully to brush off.

Suddenly we were startled to see, in the middle of the desert around Kerkuk, hundreds of huge, surrealistic contraptions, some shooting flames into the sky. Emir Zeid told us that these were oil rigs. 'Thank Allah, Iraq has huge oil reserves; that is a great blessing for the country,' he remarked. After the Great War there was a long and bitter dispute over Mosul with the Turks, who were aware, like the British, of its subterranean wealth. And at the Lausanne

Conference in 1922, it was awarded to Iraq at the insistence of the British, who were administering Iraq as a mandate.

'The Turks never got over losing Mosul and all its oil,' commented Mother with irritation in her voice. 'Obviously the British had the clout.'

'They were the victors, and to them went the spoils,' Zeid said reasonably.

'Still, it was unfair. That Lausanne Treaty was a death sentence for Turkey.' Zeid did not pursue the matter any further.

Upon entering Baghdad, dusty and tired as we all were, we drove straight to Qasr al-Zuhur, the Palace of Flowers, where the royal family had gathered to greet us. This was a singular honour for Emir Zeid on the occasion of his wife's first visit to his country. The royal family had heard many tales about Nissa and were eagerly waiting to meet her.

The dusty car was waved through a pair of wide wrought-iron gates by guards dressed in crisp khaki uniforms and *keffiyeh*s and proceeded up a long driveway lined with palm trees and rose-beds. Ahead loomed a large, rose-coloured stone villa of unidentifiable architectural style. Its two storeys consisted of many different wings decorated with balconies, the whole structure dominated by two graceful towers which raised blue-tiled roofs to the glaring sky. The front door, surmounted by the Hashemite coat of arms, could be seen behind a semi-circle of Corinthian columns of white marble which supported the roof of the portico.

This was the residence of twenty-seven-year-old King Ghazi, his three-year-old son, Faisal, and his wife, Queen Aliya, who was also his first cousin, the daughter of Ali, briefly king of the Hijaz and the eldest of Zeid's three brothers. At the age of twenty-one, Ghazi had succeeded his illustrious father, King Faisal I of Iraq. As Emir Zeid had been extremely close to his brother and had not had children of his own until recently, he loved Ghazi as his own son, and the latter was devoted to his Uncle Zeid.

As our car drew up at the entrance, a handsome mulatto major-domo stepped forward to usher us inside. After refreshing ourselves and removing the desert dust, we followed the majordomo down a long hall of pink marble, through a door at the other end and down a few steps into a garden.

I stood blinking in the sudden brightness. My first impression was of a profusion of roses and other flowers, which released a delicious aroma into the air, and my second was of the number of faces turned expectantly toward us. Emir Zeid stepped forward and warmly greeted a young man with a pleasant face. This, I guessed, must be King Ghazi. Like most of the Hashemites, he was short, and he had a simple, boyish quality and a warm, engaging smile. His wife-cousin, Queen Aliya, was taller than he, a lovely, girlish figure with a broad, open face and large, round, intelligent eyes. She was simply dressed and wore no make-up. Her three sisters were also present – the eldest a plain old maid, the two younger sisters petite and dainty, dressed in crisp linen suits, their hair coiffed, their smiling lips bright, and their eyes highlighted with eye-shadow. Like a couple of birds, they twittered in unison. The Queen's mother, a fair-skinned, devout old lady, was the only one wearing a white kerchief covering her head. Then there was a slight woman with dark hair, an enormous, beak-like nose, and a thin, oval face with sharp, darting eyes. She was Emir Zeid's elder sister, Princess Saliha, from Sherif Hussein's Circassian second wife.

After the introductions, followed by tea, King Ghazi asked Mother if there was anything he could do for her. Aware that the young king was a natural sportsman who loved high-powered sports cars and piloted his own plane, she replied, 'I would very much like to fly over Baghdad and see the city from above.' Delighted, he promised to take her up as soon as possible in his new plane, the *Blue Bird*.

The official visit over, we left for the newly built stone house that Emir Zeid had rented in a new section of the city called Veziriyah. He had furnished it to the best of his ability with the few antique pieces that had come via Berlin from Büyükdere and with basic items such as beds, tables and chairs, which he had purchased. Without any redeeming features, the house sat like a square grey stone box in the middle of nowhere, surrounded by desert, on which were scattered a few other new stone houses, mud huts, Bedouin tents and herds of goats. Like all the houses in Baghdad, it had a flat roof where we would sleep during the unbearably hot weather and a cellar where we would live during the heat of day. Later, when Mother discovered the infinitely charming old houses on the banks of the Tigris River, with their cool inner courtyards shaded by huge date palms, their overhanging balconies and latticed windows, their wind-scoops on the roofs to trap the breezes and circulate them through the house, she wished that Emir Zeid had not succumbed to the lure of the modern.

A few days after our arrival, Mother received her invitation to fly with the king. On the appointed afternoon, wearing a long black satin skirt with a matching top, she drove with me to Qasr al-Zuhur, but we found the palace deserted and all the doors locked. After our chauffeur had knocked for a long time, the mulatto majordomo answered and told him that we were expected at the royal hangar where the plane was kept. Since this was at some distance from the palace, we arrived very late, to find the king and all the ladies of the royal family, in their linen suits and print dresses, waiting for us. They were amazed to see Mother step out of the car looking as if she were going to a black-tie dinner, but, forewarned of her eccentricities, they managed to hide their surprise.

A table had been set with lemonade and soft drinks, and the Armenian royal photographer, Arshak, certain that he would never again have so many of the princesses together with the queen, lined us all up in front of the *Blue Bird*. As I look at that picture now, I realize that it is historic.

The king flew himself, with Mother sitting in the co-pilot's seat, and myself and the youngest of the queen's sisters as passengers. This was the first time Mother and I had ever been in an aeroplane, and we were thrilled. As we flew over the city, King Ghazi pointed out the sights, the most impressive being the gold-capped domes of the Kazimayn Mosque, one of the most important shrines in the Muslim world.

'There is the Bilat, the official palace,' said he, pointing to a big, white-domed structure set in a garden criss-crossed with long, palm-lined lanes. 'My office,' he added smiling.

We looked down on the main street, Haroun al-Rashid, busy with cars, horse-drawn carriages and crowds of people, and on the King Faisal Bridge. Baghdad, seen from above, with the Tigris flowing through its centre, its long rows of tall date palms and the turquoise-tiled domes of its many mosques, was a very attractive sight. In the days that followed, however, it turned out to be a drab, dusty, backward city lashed by desert winds. Many of its roads were unpaved. Most of its buildings were plain, square constructions of yellow and grey stone, while others were no more than mud huts.

The country was in turmoil, and Emir Zeid was actively helping to establish a new and stable government. Political crisis had caused the Cabinet to fall, and, except for the civil service, there was no functioning government. Emir Zeid, the trusted loyal uncle of King

Ghazi, loved and respected by everyone, was ready and willing to help his country, and during our first weeks in Baghdad we found him completely preoccupied with his mission. At the house, cars came and went in the night, and secret meetings were held in his ground-floor office until the early hours of the morning. Prospective Cabinet members visited, and Nouri Pasha, one of Iraq's great political figures, was a frequent caller. In the end, Emir Zeid's political wisdom, dedication and unique ability to bring people together resulted in Nouri Pasha becoming prime minister. It then fell to Nouri to form a new government; but in so doing he neglected to create an official position for Emir Zeid.

Mother, furious that Emir Zeid had been ignored after all his arduous work and his influence in putting Nouri Pasha into office, protested, 'What about you? You have no position, no title. Nouri Pasha could at least have given you a titular position in his new government.'

Zeid shrugged off her complaint with his usual complacency. 'I did not ask for any position. I don't need a title. I am what I am.'

'I wish he were more ambitious,' Mother complained to me later. 'He is always on the giving side and never demands anything for himself. People take advantage of him.'

Mother was wise enough not to reiterate her indignation to Zeid, for she realized it was pointless to try to change him. Instead, venting her frustration elsewhere, she plunged with a vengeance into decorating the house. For the next few months transforming the cold stone edifice into a home became her *raison d'être*. She sent for bolts of silk and velvet materials from Florence and ordered curtains and upholstered furniture. Several carpenters were set to making tables and cabinets and bookcases and shelves. Thrown around in profusion were Bukhara rugs, brocade covers and her numerous collections. Finally life was pumped into the bleak structure and it became an attractive home, with vases of roses giving off their unique scent in every corner.

Grey uniforms with gold buttons were made for the staff, and one evening, when all was done, they lined up white-gloved at the door to receive the entire royal family for a sumptuous dinner reception given to justify Mother's reputation as a great hostess. After her guests arrived, she tried desperately to mix men and women in order to create a warm, party-like atmosphere, but the long tradition of segregation caused them immediately to separate like oil and water into two groups. The men sat in one corner of the room drinking whisky, smoking, discussing politics and telling jokes, while the women sat stiffly in the middle of the room and talked of nothing but their own and their children's health. As smoking and the crossing of legs were considered disrespectful in front of elders, the younger ladies refrained from doing either; nor did they instigate conversation, merely answering briefly and politely the questions directed at them by the elder ladies.

Mother was working very hard to put the ladies at ease by telling them amusing anecdotes and stories, but despite all her efforts they could not relax and continued to sit frozen, bolt upright as if they had swallowed sticks. As the youngest member of the gathering, I sat in a corner of the large living room with the Queen's teenage sisters, princesses Badia and Jalile, and regaled them with stories of Berlin, my childhood, and the colourful Shakirs. Unlike their elders, they smiled and giggled, though they tried to hide their enjoyment by covering their mouths with their hands.

When Mother discovered that there was a good French convent school in Baghdad, she at once enrolled me as a day student. The pale-faced nuns who sailed silently around like angels in their big, floppy white headdresses were very different from the 'Heil Hitler!'-bellowing male teachers I had had in Berlin! The quiet atmosphere of the school – we were not allowed to talk during meals, in the corridors, or in embroidery class – was as soothing as the smell of incense that pervaded the rooms. I was filled with reverence, and understood why Mother had so loved her convent.

One day Mother announced, 'Tomorrow you will skip school. Reza Pahlavi, the crown prince of Iran, is coming to Baghdad on his way to Cairo, where he will pick up his bride, Princess Fawziyah, the sister of King Farouk of Egypt, and escort her to Teheran. King Ghazi has asked Zeid to meet him. We will go to watch the parade.'

The next day at the head of a motorcade the twenty-one-year-old crown prince and Emir Zeid drove through the city in the official cream-coloured touring car emblazoned with the Hashemite royal coat of arms. The streets were decorated with Iranian and Iraqi flags. We had been invited by a prominent merchant to view the procession from a covered balcony on his building on the main street, Haroun al-Rashid. The merchant had taken care to make us comfortable by furnishing overstuffed leather chairs, while his wife and daughters attended to us in person, serving Arabic coffee, tea and lemonade.

Two-and-a-half-year-old Raad, attired in full Arab dress for the occasion, *keffiyeh* and all, looked like a little Arab doll a tourist might purchase in a souvenir shop.

On both sides of the street crowds had gathered to view the cortège and see the crown prince of Iran. A woman in the crowd, looking up at the balcony where we were seated, noticed Raad on the lap of Schwester Edith, surrounded by ladies wearing *abayehs*. She started to wave and point at Raad, whom Schwester Edith persuaded to wave back. Slowly more and more people looked up, nudging each other, pointing and waving. The crowd thought the little boy was their Crown Prince Faisal, who was only nine months older than Raad. Thus started a demonstration of love and affection for the little prince, with people cheering and screaming, 'Long live, long live. Allah protect you.' Those waiting in the street thought they had been given a bonus – two crown princes in one day!

'They are cheering him,' Mother said, exhilarated by the show of affection for her son. 'Look how they are cheering Raad.' When someone dared to suggest that the crowd had mistaken Raad for Faisal, the crown prince, Mother denied it heatedly. 'No, you are mistaken. They are applauding Raad. Don't you hear them chanting, "Raad, Raad"?' Mother was quite capable of imagining anything she wished.

As his car passed below our balcony, the crowd cheering and waving, Zeid looked up and smiled and, in response to our waves, touched the side of his cap. Seated next to him, Crown Prince Pahlavi was extremely handsome in his impeccable uniform and peaked military cap; as I watched him, I hoped secretly that my parents would one day marry me off to such a prince. Fortunately, they did not.

Once the procession had passed, we tried to leave, but the crowd, anxious for a closer look at Raad, or Faisal, surrounded us and started to pull at Raad's clothing. Literally mobbed, we barely escaped with the aid of the police, who were called to our rescue and led us to our car. Even when we were safely inside the car, throngs of people pressed against the windows for a last, close view of the little prince.

As usual, Mother had overextended herself and exhausted her energy decorating the house and preparing for her first big party. Once the challenge was over, she collapsed into bed and retreated into her own world. Looking like a beautiful lily-pad floating on a sea of shade-on-shade, peach-coloured satin pillows, in her hand-embroidered nightgowns, she spent her time reading, writing in her diaries, sketching and painting, and listening to Dvořák's violin concertos and Tchaikovsky's *Pathétique*.

During her years with Father, she had hobnobbed with writers and intellectuals in Istanbul and the Paris salons, and in Berlin she had led a colourful and active social life. She was accustomed to her emotional, expressive, creative family.

Now, in this restricted, segregated society where women were uneducated and could do little but tend to their families, shop and call on each other, she tried to fill the void in her life by giving herself more and more to her art. Although she had prepared a room in the house as a studio, she rarely went there. Instead, she worked in her bed, which was her refuge.

Bedouin women were her favourite subject, and she painted and sketched them in all shapes and poses. Early in the mornings they came from the flat red horizon like a swarm of bats, their arms outstretched to balance the weight of the burdens they carried on their heads, pitchers of milk and pots of yoghurt stacked one on another, their black *abayehs* flapping on both sides like wings. They were immobile to the waist, all movement centred on the rotating motion of their hips and the quick steps of their bare feet as they carried their wares to the market.

Another of Mother's favourite subjects was the statuesque and handsome Armenian maid, who looked like a Vigeland statue carved out of granite. Some of these sketches were framed and hung all over the house, except in the formal salon where Emir Zeid received his male callers.

As servants, Emir Zeid had hired Armenians from northern Iraq who spoke Turkish, knowing that Mother liked and felt comfortable with them, since Armenians had always been part of our household in Istanbul. He also remembered how devoted I had been to Miss Tina. And, of course, neither Mother nor I spoke Arabic; no provision had been made for either of us to learn that extremely difficult language. We got by with Turkish or English, except when certain Iraqi ladies who spoke neither came to call; then we resorted to smiles and sign language and felt like fools.

Mother also found refuge in frequent excursions to ancient sites such as Babylon and Ninevah. By far the most dramatic was our pilgrimages to the holy city of Kerbala, five hours by car from Baghdad. To Shiite Muslims, Kerbala is second only to Mecca, and for this visit, although I was only twelve, I had to wear an *abayeh* and a *peçe*.

Since the chauffeur parked the car some distance away, Mother and I entered the city on foot. There were thousands of people dressed in black as if at a mammoth funeral, and donkeys and mules loaded with corpses and boxes of bones which funeral parties had brought to bury as close to the shrine as possible. Many old and sick, hobbling on their canes and crutches, had come to die in the city near their martyr. All this seen through a black veil made it particularly oppressive. As we walked toward the huge, gold-domed shrine in which Imam Hussein's tomb is located, we had to fight our way through the mob.

Inside the mosque, the tomb itself was like a big, ornate, silver bird-cage. Clustered around it were people praying, and some women were kissing the silver bars of the cage. We noticed that the silver, like the marble steps, was deeply worn. As Mother caressed one of the bars, she said, 'Look how the silver has acquired a satin-like patina from the millions of lips that have kissed it. It is so pleasing to the touch.' In the presence of the martyr, both Mother and I felt a surge of deep religious reverence. She was so affected by everything she had seen in Kerbala that for days after our return to Baghdad it was the subject of her numerous sketches, all in black china ink and black gouache, without a drop of colour.

Once Mother had visited all the historical sites in Iraq, and without much else to do, she began to spend more and more time in bed, scarcely leaving her room. The bed, always her refuge, now became the throne whence she ruled the household, demanding to know everything that went on and every word uttered under its roof. At luncheon, Emir Zeid and I ate hurriedly in the dining room and rushed immediately to Mother's bedside. In the evenings, a small table was set for us in her room; she did not like to be left alone.

Although she was only thirty-seven years old, a series of afflictions plagued her. She suffered from shortness of breath, chest pains, fainting spells, depression and catatonia. These outward manifestations of her malaise were magnified when she got upset or found herself in a situation that displeased her. We often suffered from her shifts into moods of depression which, though so bright and intelligent about many things, she never tried to understand or control. They simply swept over her, and we were left adrift in their wake, though expected to adapt and sympathize. Thus, Mother's health and mood became the barometer of the household and determined the quality of the day for its inhabitants. When I returned from school, the first thing I did was to ask our old Armenian butler, 'How is my mother doing?'

When Artin smiled and said, 'Her Highness is good today, good, good,' I would run up the stairs and into her room to be greeted with a big smile, a hug, and many kisses. Then I would settle by her bed and tell her all about school and the nuns. Mother liked hearing every detail.

But when Artin looked sorrowful and shook his head, I would creep up and peek into Mother's room. More than once, when I saw her lying in bed, short of breath, white, and moaning as if gravely ill and on the brink of death, I'd run to my bedroom, throw myself on the bed, and sob, 'Please, Allah. Please let her not die. You can make her well. Please, let her recover.'

And, as if Allah had heard my prayers, recover she did! Trying to shake off her depression, she would struggle out of bed and say, 'Come on, Shirin, let's go shopping. I need to get out. Perhaps it will do me good.' Then off we would go to the *souk*, the fascinating bazaar with its labyrinth of shops and hordes of hustling and bustling people. The din of artisans beating designs into copper and the laments of Arab singers, blasting from the radios of cafés, where men sat on divans smoking their water-pipes, echoed in the arched domes of the *souk*. Vendors carrying on their heads huge wooden trays laden with bright green, shiny romaine lettuce wove and dodged their way through the throng, and little boys dashed in and out of doorless shops, swinging brass trays on which rested tiny coffee- and tea-cups.

On these occasions Mother shopped with abandon, not because she needed anything, but because she found shopping therapeutic. However, she had difficulty handling the veil while shopping; we were both fascinated to see how dextrously the local women manoeuvred theirs. When they looked over merchandise or counted money, some flipped it back and forth over their heads, others pulled it to the side as if it were a curtain, and the most modest ones pulled it down only as far as their noses, revealing one eye like cyclopses.

When Mother had finished her shopping, she would hail a carriage and we would ride home – clip-clop, clip-clop – just as we had in Büyükada.

Eventually, however, Mother became unable to leave her room at all. As her mysterious illness and depression worsened, she became irritable and demanding, and everyone in her periphery had to watch what they said, for a misplaced word or action could bring on her fury. Mother was very much like the sea. She could be as docile and peaceful as a sunny cove, yet in a moment turn into a typhoon. Like light pleasure-boats in a storm, the servants, I, and sometimes even Emir Zeid would be caught up in her fury, not knowing exactly what had triggered it.

Doctors came and went, but none seemed able to diagnose her symptoms. Zeid was at a loss. He finally called in Professor Hans Hoff, a famous Viennese psychiatrist who had fled the Nazis just before the *Anschluss*. When he arrived, I was present, as usual, to help out. Instead of a sickly patient, he found a handsome woman in a pink chiffon nightgown, sitting up in bed, surrounded by satin pillows and bouquets of flowers. Her hair was neatly coiffed and crowned with a pink satin bow; her cheeks were highlighted with rouge; and her luminous green eyes were heavily made up with kohl and mascara. Sketches, watercolours, oil paintings, some framed and hanging on the walls, some on the floor, others in piles on tables and chairs, were everywhere in the room.

'Welcome,' said Mother, extending a manicured hand, which Professor Hoff gallantly kissed.

Looking around the room, he asked at once, 'Did you do these paintings?'

'Yes,' Mother replied. 'I am a painter, but I don't feel like painting any more.'

The professor eased himself into the armchair by the bed and let Mother talk of her numerous ailments and her state of mind. After a long recitation of her ills, she concluded, 'I don't feel like doing anything. I just want to lie here with my eyes closed. I don't even want to see the sun.'

'I think the best thing for you would be a complete change of atmosphere,' said Dr Hoff. 'Is there any place in particular you would like to go?'

Mother thought for a moment; then, as if remembering some far-away place, 'Paris. Yes, Paris. I'd like to go to Paris,' she said.

'Then go,' urged the doctor. 'A change will do you good. Pack up and leave as soon as possible; and, above all, continue to paint. You have great talent, and you should keep working. Work will save you.' How right he was! Painting saw Mother through a long life in spite of continual bad health.

That afternoon Professor Hoff told Emir Zeid that Mother was suffering from depression and needed a complete change. (In those days, this was the accepted remedy.) He recommended that she go to Paris. Faced with the prospect of having to oversee the house and two children alone, Emir Zeid merely shrugged and said, philosophically, '*başa gelen çekilir*,' repeating a Turkish saying: That which befalls you, you endure. And without delay he contacted the Iraqi legation in Paris to make arrangements for Mother's trip.

A few days later, with six suitcases and two hatboxes, Mother left for Paris and checked into the Ritz. She then called in a prominent French heart specialist who, upon examining her and listening to her complaints, announced, 'It sounds as if you have angina.' The doctor ordered that an electrocardiogram be made, but much to Nissa's disappointment the test proved negative. She had embraced the idea of having angina, for it would have explained all her symptoms, helped her understand her illness, and justified her flight from Baghdad.

The Iraqi minister in Paris, who felt personally responsible after Emir Zeid's phone-call, invited Nissa to Maxim's with a congenial group of people. At dinner he said, 'My dear princess, there is nothing wrong with you. The test proves it,' and, raising his glass of champagne, he toasted her: 'To your good health.' This upset Nissa. Obviously no one believed she was sick; they thought she was a hypochondriac. Well, she would prove them wrong! The next day she left the hotel, checked into the American Hospital in Paris and summoned Aliye, who immediately left Istanbul and Uncle Charles, and hurried to her sister's bedside.

On the night of 4 April 1939, while I was engrossed in *Gone With the Wind*, which Mother had left behind, the telephone rang shrilly in the marble hall outside my bedroom. It was past midnight, and all the servants had gone to bed. I heard Emir Zeid's bedroom door open and his slippered feet shuffle to the phone. Jumping out of bed, I opened the door a crack and listened. Emir Zeid spoke hurried words in Arabic. 'Has anything happened to Mother?' I wondered, for I could tell from his voice that something was terribly wrong.

Emir Zeid hung up, turned sharply to go to his room, and saw me standing at my door.

'Shirinaki, what are you doing up so late?' he asked. Then, without waiting for my reply, he added, 'The call was from the palace. There has been an accident, and the king is involved. I am going there right away.'

A few minutes later I heard the scrunching of tires over the newly gravelled driveway. Hugging my book for comfort, I hid under the covers, for the cold of the big white marble hall seemed to creep into my room under the door. In time I dozed off, only to be awakened by the noise of the returning car. Beyond the window I could see the red dawn on the flat horizon. I threw on a robe and ran to the landing. Emir Zeid stood at the bottom of the stairs, looking like a shapeless grey rag; the outline of his body and features seemed blurred.

'Ghazi is dead,' he said flatly. 'He was in his new car, racing down the palace drive at high speed to the bungalow at Harthiya. He lost control and crashed into an electric pole, which was uprooted and fell on his head. Ghazi was already dead when I got to the palace.' Laboriously, Zeid climbed the stairs.

'But why was he going to the bungalow at that time of night?' I asked, mystified.

'He had just had a stag party for a few friends and decided to end the evening with the showing of a film in the palace theatre. Unfortunately, the film happened to be at the bungalow. Why didn't he send someone to fetch it? Why did he have to drive himself at that time of the night? His driver was actually in the car with him, but Ghazi chose to drive.' Emir Zeid shook his head. 'What a terrible thing to happen! What a tragedy!' As he spoke, two tears trickled down his pale cheeks. It was the first and last time that I ever saw him cry.

Later that morning, Princess Saliha picked me up in her car and gave me an *abayeh* to wear, and then we drove to Qasr al-Zuhur. In the lower living room, women in black, some of them professional mourners, were huddled, crying and wailing.

Princess Saliha and I were escorted upstairs to the queen's private quarters, where the queen's mother, three sisters and other royal princesses were gathered in the little living room, all looking pale and stunned. Queen Aliya entered from her bedroom and respectfully bent down to kiss Princess Saliha's hand and put it on her forehead. She kissed me on my cheek.

I had read that a person's hair could turn white with grief, but I had not believed it. Now, in shock, I saw that it was true. The young queen's hair had turned grey in the few hours since the death of her beloved husband. On the floor in the anteroom, the fragile, asthmatic Crown Prince Faisal, then almost four, was playing with a red fire engine, his English nanny at his side.

During the minority of King Faisal II, the logical step was for Emir Zeid to be named regent. The oldest member of the family, he had fought in the Arab revolt alongside his brothers, he was familiar with Iraqi politics, and he had already served several times as regent of Iraq during King Faisal I's absences. Moreover, he was popular with the people, and even with the Kurds in the north. The charismatic Kurdish leader Barzani, who respected and liked Zeid for his humane treatment of the Kurds and his adroit handling of their requests in the early days of the kingdom, had named Zeid the 'Emir of Mosul'.

For these reasons, most Iraqis wanted Emir Zeid, as had King Ghazi himself. In an article in the magazine *Afaaq Arabiye* in August 1987, Sait Hakki, former treasurer of the Royal Palace, wrote that he was in the room when King Ghazi, in the presence of Nouri Pasha and Prince Abdulillah, stated, 'If anything should happen to me, my uncle Emir Zeid should become regent during my son's minority.'

Queen Aliya, however, afraid of losing her power, wished her younger brother, Prince Abdullilah, to be regent, and on the night of the accident tried to elicit from her dying husband a statement to this effect. Sir Henry Sinderson, the King's physician, who attended him at his death bed, wrote in his book *Ten Thousand and One Nights*:

Queen Aliya remained very calm and asked to be told the truth. 'I want to know,' she begged, 'because if Ghazi is to die a regent must be appointed.' She had already guessed that the injuries were mortal, and when I admitted their severity she asked me to give him an injection in the hope that he would survive sufficiently to say that he wished Abdullilah to be invested with sovereign authority during Faisal's minority. I did as I was asked, but it was a vain hope.

Having failed in this attempt, the queen then managed to persuade King Ghazi's sister, Princess Rajiha, to testify that she had overheard her brother say, 'If anything happens to me, let Abdullilah become the regent.'

The Cabinet accepted Princess Rajiha's statement, and Nouri Pasha, the power behind the throne, acquiesced, probably figuring he could manipulate Prince Abdullilah more easily than he could Emir Zeid. At twenty-six, the prince was a charming and attractive graduate of Victoria College in Egypt, an accomplished horseman, an anglophile, and not much more. In addition, the British were pleased with this choice, for they had been suspicious of all the attention Nissa had received from the Nazi leaders in Berlin. With the backing of all these parties, the completely inexperienced young Prince Abdullilah was approved that morning as regent of Iraq.

When Nissa, who had a capacity for unusually profound feelings, heard the tragic news in Paris, she was desolate and grieved over the young king's death and for his family; but when she learned that Emir Zeid had not been named regent, she was angered at the slight and at this denial of his rightful position.

'It is because of me,' she cried to Aliye, beating her breast. 'They don't want *me*. The queen and princesses are intimidated by me. They don't want me to be the regent's wife. They have nothing against their uncle – who wouldn't love Zeid? It is *me* they fear.' She was probably right.

Although Emir Zeid was too proud to admit it, his family's unfair rejection of him as regent hurt him deeply. Ghazi was gone. Nissa was in Paris. There was no reason for him to remain in Baghdad. Therefore, as soon as my school term was over in late May, he put me, Raad and Schwester Edith on the train to Istanbul and undertook the difficult task of closing the house, letting the staff go and disposing of the furnishings.

When we arrived at the Haydarpaşa Station after the three-day journey, we were met by Nejad and the Shakirs and taken straight to the island. This time I found things drastically changed at the Büyükada house. After Grandmother's death, as the eldest of the family, Uncle Emin and Aunt Hakiye had taken over the household management, ordering the meals and seeing to the accounts. Dissatisfied with this arrangement, Aunt Ayşe had decided to have her own cook provide food for her family, and they ate their meals at a small round table in the garden apart from the rest. This separation destroyed the togetherness of the big table, which had been the throbbing heart of the family.

15

World War II

Mother returned from Paris in July, apparently recovered from her ailments, and soon after Emir Zeid joined us from Baghdad.

On 1 September 1939, as we were having lunch at the Büyükada house, news of Hitler's invasion of Poland reached us.

'This time I hope our leaders will not make the same mistake that was made in 1914 by entering the war,' said Uncle Emin, 'but if we do join, I hope it will be on the Allied side.' Everyone listened intently to the old general's opinion.

That same afternoon, as Mother and Aunt Ayşe sat near the jasmine bushes, Aunt Ayşe said, 'Now that you have given up the Baghdad house and Europe is at war, you will probably settle here in Istanbul.'

'We have no other choice,' replied Nissa listlessly, 'but I certainly have no intention of opening the house in Büyükdere. We'll wait and see what happens next; things are changing so fast.' Then, remembering that Ayşe's flat in the Shakir Pasha apartment block was available, she asked, 'Why don't I rent your flat, Ayşe *abla*?'

After Ahmet's harrowing war-time experiences and his stressful internment on Malta, followed by his escape to Samsun, he had decided to give up public service and become a private citizen. A Samsun tobacco merchant named Cohen persuaded him to go into the tobacco business, and together they had decided to build a cigarette factory in Argentina. Ahmet, taking his family, had sailed to Buenos Aires, but a few years later, because of unfair competition from the government-owned tobacco monopoly, the business failed, and they had returned to Turkey. With only his army pension to live on, they had been obliged to move to a less expensive area on the Asiatic shore and rent Ayşe's apartment.

'Before anything else,' replied Aunt Ayşe to Mother's question, 'enrol Shirin at the American Girls' College which, as you know, is the girls' section of Robert College. Then she won't lose a semester. Nermidil has been attending it for a year, and we all think it is a great school.'

As Ayşe was an *abla*, she felt she had the right to advise Nissa, although she knew her younger sister rarely listened to anybody. But this time, to Ayşe's surprise, Nissa was grateful for the advice and acted promptly on it. She ordered a dark blue gaberdine uniform with half a dozen white cotton blouses for me, purchased bedding and underwear, had name-tags sewn on them, and sent me off to school just as Warsaw was being reduced to rubble by German bombs.

Moving into Ayşe's apartment, Nissa furnished it haphazardly with some of the contents of the Büyükdere villa left behind when they had departed for Berlin. She hired a staff, including a Bolu cook, a White Russian butler who had been a Tsarist cavalry officer and who charmed everyone, and an Armenian maid. Raad and his new Greek governess (to my delight, Schwester Edith, whom I disliked intensely, had returned to Germany) had a room. So did Emir Zeid and I, and Nejad visited on weekends from the Galatasaray Lycée, where he was a boarder.

With the best of intentions, Nissa set out to live as a 'normal family'. However, life in Istanbul seemed humdrum. The social scene bored her, and her former friends no longer interested her; everything was *déjà vu*. Moreover, the constant comings and goings of the Shakirs, including Grandmother's two brothers, who had rooms in the building, annoyed her. Feeling trapped and imposed upon by her family, Nissa again took to her bed, as she had done in Baghdad. Once more the doctors attributed her depression to some vague form of neurasthenia. In those days chemical disorders were unheard of, and psychiatry was still looked upon with suspicion. When Nissa's family and friends made the mistake of saying, 'Nothing is the matter with you. It's only nerves,' she got worse. Their lack of understanding aggravated her condition, and she lay in bed unable to function, 'waiting for Godot'.

As ill-health would give her a reason and, above all, the justification to extricate herself from a situation she found unbearable, Nissa nurtured her illness and became chronically sick, as she had in Baghdad. Chest pains, fainting spells, depression and extreme nervousness plagued her. Barely six months after moving into Ayşe's apartment, convinced that a total change of atmosphere was her only chance, she fled again, this time to a place she had never been before, to Budapest, to the famous spa at the St Gellert Hotel. As always, Emir Zeid let her do as she pleased.

Once again, Aunt Aliye moved in with us to play mother. Since Grandmother's death she had been living with Suat and Mizou on the top floor, and therefore all she had to do was put her bits and pieces into boxes and come down to the first floor. Aunt Aliye's room always looked as if a cyclone had hit it. Out of open bureau drawers hung all kinds of clothing, and on top of tables already cluttered with bric-à-brac were strewn books, magazines and music sheets. Out of this chaos she would emerge around noon, all painted up and dressed in a flouncy skirt, as if she were about to join a carnival. When she went to visit Berger she would pack into her big, black-leather bag a jar of home-made rose-petal jam, a bottle of lemon cologne, some French pâté or a bottle of the good cognac Suat gave her. As everyone in the family knew that any gift they made her would end up with Berger, they gave her presents which he would enjoy.

Immediately upon the collapse of France in 1940, afraid that Hitler would turn toward Eastern Europe, Emir Zeid telegraphed Nissa in Budapest and, for once, ordered her to return home. She arrived on the train, looking pale and listless. The spa had not improved her condition.

After her arrival we moved for the summer to the Büyükada house. My only vivid memory of that summer of 1940 is of Mother lying pale and ill in her bedroom or on a chaise longue in the garden, painting sporadically. Then, in the autumn, to the family's bewilderment, Mother, who was still battling with her demons, decided to return to Budapest. I cannot understand how Emir Zeid allowed her to do so. However, when Mother wanted to do something, she had an uncanny ability to get her way, reasoning, arguing, cajoling, pleading, threatening, until she made him give in. 'You are impossible, Fahrelnissa. You really are impossible,' I heard him say many times; but I believe he let her do as she pleased because it was easier to give in than to oppose her. Moreover, he did not know how else to handle her, particularly in the state she was then in.

This time Mother returned to Budapest determined to concentrate on painting, convinced that only that would save her. She rented a flat, bought new paints and canvases and set out to live the life of an artist. Finally, away from all family obligations, she would give herself totally to her art. Working furiously, she painted a series of oils depicting the life of the city – a group of people on the steps of a church, children ice-skating at a rink, men sitting in cafés. Each canvas was a justification of her new existence. Yet things did not work out as she had hoped. Except when she was painting and caught up in the euphoria of accomplishment, she felt lonely and depressed. Most of all, guilt plagued her. What was she doing alone in a foreign country in the middle of a war? How could she desert her husband and children? 'Whenever I saw children on the street,' she once told me, 'I thought of Raad, you and Nejad and wept openly.' Soon, the physical ailments which were the external manifestations of her inner malaise reappeared, and she could no longer paint or function.

Realizing she was in a bad way, she left her apartment and entered the Siesta Sanatorium in Budapest. When, years later, she told me how she had checked into the sanatorium, she laughed at herself.

'I was dressed to the hilt and was wearing a hat with the longest pheasant feather you have ever seen. My six suitcases, easel, paintbox and canvases were lined up in the reception hall. "I would like to see my room," I said to the nurse seated at the desk, as if I were checking into a hotel. You should have seen her expression. "What is this madwoman doing here?" she probably thought.'

At the sanatorium Mother's depression increased, and when the doctor said, 'There really is nothing we can do for you here,' she took that as a final judgment on her condition and decided to end her torment for good. She swallowed a handful of Phanadorm sleeping pills and, seated in an armchair waiting to die, wrote a letter and testament to Emir Zeid:

Forgive me, Zeid. Please forgive me, but I cannot stand the pain and suffering any more. I had to do it. I feel particularly sorry for little Raad. Take good care of him. To Shirin go all my jewels; to Nejad, my jade collection; and my fur coat to my sister Ayşe . . .

Before she had time to finish the letter, the sleeping pills took effect, and she lost consciousness. Thank God, a nurse found her lying on the floor in the nick of time and summoned the doctor, who had her stomach pumped out. Later that afternoon, when she woke, she discovered that her face was all scratched. The doctor told her, 'You thrashed about violently and pulled at your face with your fingernails. You have gone through a great ordeal, but rest now, and soon everything will be all right.'

The Hungarian doctor at once called Emir Zeid in Istanbul, told him of the attempted suicide, and advised him to come and get Mother. 'She needs to be near her family. Anyhow, there is really nothing wrong with her physically. Her problems are psychological, and there is nothing we can do for her here.'

Instead of going himself to fetch Mother, which would have been expected, Emir Zeid sent Aunt Mizou. I think that, like many people, he did not understand what Mother had gone through and regarded her attempted suicide as another manifestation of her erratic behaviour; by not going himself, he showed his disapproval. Only much later did he realize that she had suffered from clinical depression.

I was not told about the suicide attempt at the time. All I knew was that Mother arrived with Mizou and a load of paintings. Instead of returning to our apartment, she checked into the Tokatliyan Hotel in Pera, where she took a large suite overlooking the main street with an extra bedroom 'for the children to spend the night in at times'. When in one of our last conversations I asked Mother why she went to a hotel when she had a home, she replied, 'I know it sounds inconceivable, but when the train pulled into the Sirkeci Station and I saw all the family lined up waiting for me on the platform, I broke into a sweat. The idea of returning to the Shakir Pasha apartment, to be engulfed by them, terrified me. I begged Zeid not to make me return to the apartment, to the life from which I had fled, but instead to go to a hotel where I could recuperate quietly, away from family obligations. Thank Allah, Zeid was understanding. What a wonderful man he was!'

Our apartment was dismantled, the furniture sent back to Büyükdere, and the staff let go. Aunt Aliye picked up her boxes and moved back upstairs to Uncle Suat's. Raad and his governess were given a room there too. Raad, then five years old, was delighted with the move, for in Uncle Suat's second son, Toto (nickname for Tarik), he had a constant playmate. For me, home became a room in an aunt's flat, a room in the Tokatliyan Hotel and a tram between there and school. After weekends during which I never knew what to expect, the security and ordered structure of the American Girls'

College was like a big, warm, mohair blanket in which I wrapped myself.

Soon news reached Zeid that there had been a pro-Nazi coup in Baghdad. Ever since the end of World War I, Arabs had harboured serious grievances against their war-time allies, who they felt had double-crossed them. In Iraq, anti-British sentiment had come to a head in 1939 when King Ghazi had died, many Iraqis, probably wrongly, blaming the accident which killed him on the British. The Arabs have a proverb: 'The enemy of my enemy is my friend.' To the anti-British Arabs, therefore, Germany was their friend. Besides, they admired strong leadership, militarism and extreme nationalism, and by 1941 were impressed by Nazi victories and power. They were led by Husseini, the grand mufti of Jerusalem, who had fled Palestine to Baghdad, and by Reshid Ali, the prime minister of Iraq. When the British ousted Reshid Ali for his pro-Nazi activities, he and a group of colonels staged a coup against his pro-British successor, Nouri Pasha, and the regent, Emir Abdullilah. Although the six-year-old king himself was not threatened, Nouri Pasha and Emir Abdullilah had to flee Baghdad.

Anxious to gain legitimacy for his new regime, and knowing that the popular Emir Zeid had been slighted by being denied the regency when King Ghazi died, Reshid Ali decided now to offer him the position and sent a special messenger to him in Istanbul. However, when Emir Zeid heard Reshid Ali's proposition, he was shocked and flatly refused.

'How could Reshid Ali even think that I would accept such a position? How could he think I would join forces with them? Does he expect me to be a traitor to my own family? Besides, Reshid Ali won't last more than three weeks, if that long,' he told Uncle Suat.

As usual, he was right. Barely a month later, the British, with the help of King Abdullah and Jordan's Arab Legion, defeated the rebels. Emir Abdullilah and Nouri Pasha returned to Baghdad and order was restored. Once the coup had been defeated, Emir Zeid went to Baghdad to give the royal family his moral support and found both Emir Abdullilah and Nouri Pasha grateful that he had not lent his weight to the rebels.

Mother soon tired of living alone in the hotel and, again wanting family around her, moved in with Uncle Suat and Aunt Mizou. This time I ended up on a studio couch in her room, and although this was a far from perfect arrangement, I did not mind it at all, since I loved my uncle and aunt and it was fun to be living together again as we had in the Büyükada house, although the quarters were much closer. This time Mother seemed happy to be surrounded by family. How quickly her needs and moods changed!

Thanks to its neutrality and strategic position, Istanbul quickly became a centre of espionage and intrigue, and an important listening post for both the Allies and the Axis countries. The bar of the Tokatliyan Hotel was a gathering place for both spies and foreign correspondents, Axis and Allied agents sitting at adjoining tables, sipping their drinks while pretending the others did not exist. Emir Zeid, back from Baghdad, liked to sit in the bar, have a scotch and chat with his English and American drinking chums. His best friend was a grey-haired, ruddy-faced, outspoken American named John Way, who worked for the Socony-Vacuum Oil Company and who, I think, was an OSS agent, like his boss Archibald Walker. It is ironical that Zeid's two best friends in life were American – John Way and Israel Treiman, a St Louis lawyer whom he knew at Oxford – yet he died never having set foot in the United States.

Unknown to most members of the Shakir Pasha family, my Uncle Suat was working for MIT, the Turkish intelligence service. His primary job was to collect information from his sources and pass it on to the Turkish authorities, who more likely than not would relay it to the Allies. One of Suat's main contacts was a young man named Wilhelm Hamburger, a twenty-five-year-old from a family of wealth and breeding. While earning a doctorate on the Middle East at university in Vienna, he had joined a fascist student group and was then sent by the Abwehr, the German intelligence service, to Istanbul with the cover of a hemp buyer. Gregarious, charming and attractive, with a cherubic face, he obtained entrance to Istanbul society through Suat and was invited everywhere. While Suat was a necessary channel to the Turkish authorities for Willi, as he was known, Willi was an important contact for Suat. In addition to that, the two developed an extremely close personal relationship, so much so that Willi was constantly in and out of Suat's Shakir Pasha apartment. At the time, Willi was so much a part of the household that I came to know him as 'Uncle Willi'. As he was an irresistible, extremely polite and courteous young man, all the Shakirs, although pro-Ally, liked him. Under Suat's influence, and with his encouragement, Willi gradually started to falter in his loyalty to the Nazi regime.

In early 1944 Uncle Suat pulled a coup by saving his friend Willi Hamburger from arrest by the Germans and helping him to defect to the Allies. One of the other Abwehr operatives in Turkey had defected, and an enraged Hitler ordered all the agents back to Berlin. One morning two Gestapo officers knocked at Willi's door and told him, 'You are under arrest and will be put on the next train to Germany.' Willi calmly told them that he should phone his Turkish contact so that the latter would not be suspicious at his sudden disappearance. With their permission, Willi phoned Uncle Suat and said, 'I am going to Vienna for a week to see my family and will be back soon. Tell our friends to "Tell it to the Marines".' This was one of Suat's frequent expressions, which he had learned during his travels in America and which meant, 'Don't believe a word I say'.

When Suat heard Willi's message, he at once knew that something was very much amiss and called the British Secret Service. Meanwhile, Willi stalled, waiting for Suat to call back, gathering his clothes and packing slowly, even bargaining with the two German agents over the sale of his radio. When at last the phone rang, he immediately picked up the receiver. It was Suat, who told him, 'A car is waiting for you at the door. Make a dash for it.' Before the two agents knew what was happening, Willi had put down the receiver and was out through the door. He jumped into the car waiting for him and was driven to the British Consulate. Within twenty-four hours he was smuggled out of Turkey and into Cairo, where he gave the British much valuable information.

When my husband Bob and I went to Vienna in the mid–1980s to visit my cousin Erdem, the Turkish ambassador there, we saw Uncle Willi, a businessman who now uses a different surname. He came to the embassy, big bouquet of flowers in hand, with his much younger Hungarian wife. I noticed that he had had a face-lift, for his once round blue eyes were rather Chinese-looking, and he seemed much younger than his seventy years. We talked at length of the old days in Istanbul, and he was anxious to know how Suat was and what had happened to the different members of my family. 'You know, Suat saved my life,' he said. 'I owe him my life.' He then told us how in the summer of 1941 he had gone as a representative of the German–Syrian Military Mission to offer Emir Zeid the kingdom of Syria.

This was the first I had heard of that meeting. Once Germany had conquered France, it found itself in control of the French colonies, including Syria and Lebanon, and decided that Emir Zeid, a Hashemite who had entered Damascus triumphantly with his brother Faisal in 1918, a brother to King Abdullah of Jordan and great-uncle of little King Faisal II of Iraq, would be the perfect choice for king of Syria, under German control. The Berlin authorities had sent Willi to approach Emir Zeid because they were aware that he knew him. Willi told us how, on that particular day, he had gone to call on Emir Zeid in the Büyükdere villa with a big box of chocolates for Mother and how, after tea, when he had broached the sensitive subject of Syria to Emir Zeid, the latter had laughed out loud at the preposterous offer and had flatly turned it down.

In doing so, Emir Zeid had proved himself once more to be politically astute, for within a month of Willi's visit the British and French had captured Syria and Lebanon and had later declared them to be independent nations.

In the summer of 1941 Mother had chosen not to go to the house on the island. The last time she had been there, she had missed her mother's harmonious presence and had been displeased by the new set-up. Instead, she reopened the Büyükdere villa on the Bosphorus and converted part of the stables into a studio. As she did not want to be disturbed, she had the telephone removed. Anyone who wanted to reach us had to send a telegram, which the postman had to carry up the hill. (The exhausted man always received a good tip.) Away from everyone and everything, Mother concentrated on her painting.

The villa was even more isolated from town than usual, for the war-time shortage of petrol meant we no longer had a car. Instead, Mother had bought a carriage pulled by a single horse and driven by a bow-legged Armenian coachman. With the little carriage we often visited Uncle Suat and Aunt Mizou, who, that summer, instead of going to the island as usual, had rented a house in Tarabya, the next village, where the German Embassy had its summer residence in a beautiful wooded park overlooking the Bosphorus. By living in Tarabya, Uncle Suat could befriend Ambassador von Papen and the other German diplomats and keep a watchful eye on their comings and goings.

Many times one's destiny is affected by a series of events that take place in another person's life. In Mother's case, it happened to be my half-sister Remide who, after the death of her consumptive lover, had married Fikret Adil, a prominent art critic and newspaper columnist. Father, who liked and approved of his new son-in-law, forgave Remide her previous indiscretions and took her back into the fold. Fikret Adil's home was frequented by intellectuals, artists and writers of the day. Father, who enjoyed this atmosphere, was a constant caller, and during this period both Nejad, by now an art student at the Academy, and I saw a good deal of our half-sister.

At this time Remide was teaching English and French at a girls' school. She was a redhead with a perfectly shaped body and a good deal of sex appeal. Having taken after her mother and our father, she was a natural flirt and had numerous liaisons with her husband's friends. She finally ran off with one. Although I was never close to my half-sister and did not appreciate her abrasiveness, I admired her intelligence and the fact that, to her dying day, she worked and earned a living and was therefore financially independent of her husbands, of which I think there were six in all.

Since my parents' divorce, Mother had kept up relations with her ex-stepdaughter, who had grown to appreciate her after having made her life so miserable as a child. When in the late summer of 1941 Remide and her critic-husband came to the Büyükdere house to visit, Fikret Adil saw for the first time Mother's paintings, which covered the walls of the living room and were piled up in the stable-studio. He was flabbergasted. How had he not known of the existence of such a painter?

'This is marvellous work,' he exclaimed. 'You must have the art world see your paintings. You must come out of your closet.'

Fikret Adil was the key that opened the door to a world Mother had not known existed for her in Turkey. Through him she met the leading painters of the day, most of whom were teachers of art at the Academy of Fine Arts, which she had attended. She also met the leading poets, writers and intellectuals of Istanbul. She had known my father's friends, of course, but this was a new generation. To these artists, Mother was a rare find. They loved her work, her extraordinary personality and her generous hospitality. The first time she invited a group of artists to the Büyükdere villa, they were overcome with the view, but most of all with her paintings. At the picnic under the pine trees, they sat on oriental rugs, drank wine and watched a whole lamb being roasted on a spit. This was true paradise!

To her delight, Mother was invited to join and exhibit her paintings with the 'D Group', an association of Turkey's leading painters, which had great influence on modern Turkish painting and contributed to the creation of a national school of art. In the catalogue of an exhibition of modern Turkish art held in Edinburgh in 1957, Derek Patmore writes:

> The painters forming D Group, which held a number of exhibitions in Turkey, aimed at keeping contemporary Turkish painting in the great classical tradition whilst not sacrificing the lessons learnt from abstract painting and cubism. They also sought inspiration from the colours, patterns and designs to be found in the peasant arts of Anatolia ... At the same time a few painters ... discovered inspiration in the old Turkish miniatures, and others were influenced by the beautiful calligraphic writing which was such a feature of Ottoman art ... Whatever the cause there is no doubt the Turks have approached the problems posed by abstract art with considerable success. Fahr-el-Nissa Zeid has evolved a technique which gives abstract painting almost the jewelled effect of medieval stained glass ...

Now that Mother was recognized as a painter, she had a *raison d'être*, and her health immediately improved. Full of enthusiasm, she decided to really settle in Istanbul and be a part of its art scene. She rented a twelve-room apartment in Maçka, a fashionable residential section of town, in a building owned by a famous Greek banking family, the Ralli. Down the hill from the Ralli, she also leased a small ground-floor apartment which she made her studio, to which she went every day to paint.

Talking of this period, Mother has said, 'Oh, how happy I was, painting away in my little studio on Kiraz Sokak [Cherry Street], which really was no more than three miserable little rooms!'

In this little studio she worked non-stop and filled the place with canvases of all sizes. A seven-foot painting she was working on had to be stretched between two rooms. In this painting she depicted the three phases of existence, birth, life and death. It was one of the few surrealist paintings she ever made. At noon, when she saw our cook coming down the hill with her lunch-box, she was as happy as a child. 'That food tasted better than any I have ever eaten before or since,' she told me.

In the new, spacious Ralli apartment, Mother also held weekly salons for her artist friends and the writers and intellectuals of the time. Disregarding the elegant armchairs, the guests sat on the floor on cushions. Poets recited their latest poetry; philosophers spouted truisms; and invariably I was asked to declaim a passage as the evil queen Clytemnestra, a part I had recently performed in school, wearing over my white and gold Grecian costume Mother's red velvet Schiaparelli cape. This school production of Sophocles' *Electra*, for which Nejad had designed the set, had been so well received that we were asked to give a benefit performance in the horseshoe-shaped City Theatre in town. I remember caressing the mirror of my dressing room, not knowing that one day I would return to it as a leading actress.

Although war was raging all around us, my immediate family had finally settled down into a pleasant and satisfactory routine. Mother was jubilantly painting away, exhibiting with the D Group and hold-ing salons. As for me, I was totally fulfilled in school – an active member of the debating and drama societies, president of my class and of the student union, and captain of the volley-ball team. Working under Léopold Levy, a French painter very much influenced by Cézanne, Nejad loved his art education at the Academy. Aunt Aliye, who had been given a room in our apartment, enjoyed living with the sister she so adored while she continued her visits to Berger. Zeid followed the war news closely and attended the Tokatliyan bar where he talked politics and picked up a great deal of information. We had an excellent Bolu cook, who had already worked for Aunt Hakiye and thus was devoted to the family, an agreeable butler whom Mother had bribed away from the Tokatliyan Hotel, and a smiling and bustling Greek maid. Raad's governess, also a Greek, was an amusing woman who told fortunes with a deck of cards.

Uncle Kılıç no longer a deputy in Parliament, had lost his clout following Atatürk's death in 1938, and he and Cousin Fureya were living all the year round in a large wooden house in an estate on the Asiatic side of the Bosphorus. Uncle Kılıç liked company, and his house was always bustling with family and guests.

Enterprising Uncle Ahmet had parcelled out into lots the many acres which surrounded his little wooden house on the Asiatic shore and was selling them for a profit. This was the first of many real-estate ventures which eventually made him a very rich man.

In late 1942, as I was happily living my life, the wing of war brushed me and shook me out of my complacency. Joachim Cyliax, my Bavarian schoolmate in Berlin, had sent me many love letters after my departure. When the war started, his letters were heavily censored. One of them was so sliced away that it looked like a paper cut-out, and I wondered why the German censors even bothered to send it to me. One day in school I saw on the blackboard outside the principal's office, 'Shirin Devrim, come to the office.' When Miss Nellie Summers summoned you, you trembled, for she was a most formidable woman.

As I entered Miss Summers's office, I noticed on her desk two opened letters from Joachim. Picking them up, she thrust them into my face and scolded, 'These letters are shocking. Love letters at your age! And coming from Germany in the middle of a war! I shall send these on to your mother with a note.' When Mother received the letters, she paid no attention, and I wrote to Joachim asking him to send letters from then on to the apartment and not to the school.

Early in 1942 I had received a letter from Germany with a different handwriting on the envelope. Upon opening it, I discovered that it was from Joachim's elder sister, Ursula, who said that her brother had been drafted into the army when he turned eighteen and was fighting for the Fatherland in (censored) and that he was happy to be geographically closer to me in (censored). She added, 'He wants you to know that your letters mean a great deal to him, and you should continue to write to him here at his home address, although he will not be able to answer you directly for some time.'

One weekend, when I was home from school, Mother asked me to go out to buy something for her and told me to get the money from her purse. When I searched for her wallet in the black suede pouch which was always crammed with a multitude of things, I came across a crumpled black-bordered envelope addressed to me, which had been opened. Why, I wondered, did everyone open my letters? When I picked it up, a small photograph of Joachim fell out. He looked very handsome in his uniform with peaked hat. The photo was warmly dedicated to me. When I unfolded the letter, a sentence in bold black print jumped off the page: 'Joachim *ist gefallen in Stalingrad.*' The impact was immediate. The news struck me violently in the solar plexus, and I started to cry and vomit. I spent the weekend locked up in my dark room thinking of my young friend and his terrible destiny.

One other time we were touched directly by the war was the night Uncle Emin called and said, 'I have it from high authority that a German attack is imminent.' As Emir Zeid was in Baghdad, Mother, thinking a hill-top in the country would be safer than the city, decided then and there to move the entire household to the Büyükdere villa, which had been closed since the end of summer. Hurriedly, we packed a few clothes while the servants filled hampers with provisions, and in the middle of that cold, blustery, winter night we drove to the villa.

While we were settling in and the servants were making up the beds and lighting the stoves, I heard angry voices in Mother's room and went to see what was happening. Mother and Nejad were in the middle of a violent argument. Nejad, who was holding up a stool as if he were about to throw it at her, shouted sarcastically, 'Why is it that you always know best?' This detonated an immediate explosion. Mother picked up the chair next to her and threw it at Nejad, screaming at him, 'How dare you lecture me on what is right and what is wrong! Instead of helping me, as a son should, you stand there and tell me I was wrong to have brought you all here. If you don't like it, leave the house. Get out right now!'

Red-faced and in tears, Nejad mumbled an apology and ran out of the room, and Mother, exhausted by the nerve-racking events of the night, collapsed on her bed. This fight was the worst of the many arguments between Mother and Nejad that were to follow in later years. Little Raad had followed me into the room, saw Mother throw the chair and, terrorized, screamed his lungs out. To this day he remembers how frightened he was on that dark, cold, winter night on top of the hill, with chairs being flung and screams piercing the air.

The next day we were told that Uncle Emin's warning had been a false alarm, and, shaken by the events of the night, we returned to the city.

16

Baghdad Twice Revisited

In the spring of 1944, just as I was about to start rehearsing for our school play, Mother announced to my dismay that we were leaving for Baghdad. The regent Emir Abdullilah and his sister, the queen mother, as a gesture of rapprochement toward their uncle, had invited Mother and Emir Zeid officially. Wishing to have me at her side as companion and confidante, Mother had decided, without consulting me, that I should go with them.

It had been six years since we had lived in Baghdad. Our last stay had ended tragically, with Mother's sickness and sudden departure for Paris and King Ghazi's death. I wondered how *this* Baghdad visit would play itself out.

In Baghdad we were put up at the Qasr al-Abiad, the White Palace, the official guest house, which was nothing more than a semi-circular structure with a series of rooms topped by a dome, set in a large rose garden. Knowing what Baghdad life would be like, Mother had decided, in advance of the visit, to spend her time making a series of 'Baghdad sketches' for her forthcoming exhibition in Istanbul. Once she had called on the royal ladies and received them in return, she retired to her room, sending out the official word that the Baghdad air did not suit the princess, who was not feeling well and therefore could not receive visitors. Thus she escaped the onslaught of women who otherwise would have come calling on her.

As women in Iraq were not allowed to attend official functions and mixed social gatherings, calling on one another was the ladies' main entertainment. Each one set aside a special day, usually once a week, for her *kabul*, and the ladies made the rounds of these gatherings, often going to two or three a day. At these stultifying affairs, they sat in a circle, sipped lemonade or coffee, talked to the ladies seated next to them – for general conversation was not possible with people coming and going constantly – and then left. For Mother and me, who did not even speak Arabic, these were torturous affairs.

In her bedroom, which was always full of roses and fresh-cut spring flowers, Mother listened to music and wrote her diaries. When I read them, I found, intermingled with descriptions of events, exquisite watercolour sketches of various bouquets and roses in every stage of bloom. This was her flower period. One morning Lady Cornwallis, wife of the British ambassador, sent Mother a bucket of spring flowers she had picked in her garden. Inspired by the beauty of this fresh, colourful arrangement, Mother made a particularly lovely, three-foot-wide sketch of it in china ink and watercolours, had it framed and sent it to Lady Cornwallis as a 'thank-you' gift. It was such a beautiful picture that I remember to this day thinking, 'The flowers will fade in a day or so, but their likeness, which is more beautiful than nature itself, will live for ever.'

As I was eighteen, I now had to wear the veil. After the carefree, teenage existence I had led in Istanbul, with mixed tea parties where we danced 'cheek to cheek', the restricted life in Baghdad should have bothered me; but like Mother I said, '*Il faut faire ce qu'il faut faire*' and created a whole world to my liking.

Early every morning I went horseback riding, wearing a khaki riding habit with jodhpurs similar to a cavalry officer's and a pair of custom-made English riding boots given my by the regent, Emir Abdullilah. Before leaving the house I covered myself with the black *abayeh* and the *peçe*. In this freakish outfit I was driven to the royal stables. There I flung aside the *abayeh* and *peçe*, jumped on a chestnut filly and galloped off, open-faced and short-sleeved, followed by the regent's aide-de-camp and an army riding instructor. The few Bedouins we met in the desert took me for an English girl, for whom such a costume was perfectly acceptable.

Later, after breakfast, my English tutor would arrive. He often had me paraphrase speeches from Shakespeare's plays and sonnets, and made me appreciate and understand the beauty and nuances of the English language. Much later in life, when I directed and acted in many Shakespearean plays, I was grateful for this basic training.

Then, almost every day I would go to the Qasr Rihab, Palace of Welcome, a big, square, unattractive yellow structure with a roof terrace, to have lunch with my great friends, the princesses Bedia and Jelila, who lived there with their mother and their elder brother, the regent, who was at that time divorced from his first wife, an Egyptian. At lunch I always found myself seated next to the handsome prince and quickly became infatuated with him.

Emir Abdullilah, then thirty-one, proud to be the tallest Hashemite alive, had very fair skin, luminous hazel eyes, and light, wavy, chestnut hair. His pointed nose and upwardly slanted eyes and eyebrows gave him a constantly surprised expression. Always immaculately dressed in London-tailored suits and shirts with jewelled cufflinks, a dark red carnation in his lapel, he was the perfect picture of the English dandy. As I thought I was in love with him and that he and his family wanted me to be his next bride, every invitation to the palace, every attention on the part of the royal ladies or the regent, took on special significance.

Since I was constantly seen in the company of the palace ladies, everyone in Baghdad started to speculate that I was indeed going to become the regent's next wife, and ambassadors' wives began to curtsy to me as if I were royalty. This, of course, fanned my fantasy. Mother also was carried away by the idea of my marrying the regent, and with her vivid imagination and enthusiasm already saw me in bridal dress. Every afternoon, when she took tea in the rose garden, she waited eagerly for my report on the doings at Qasr Rihab, wanting to hear every detail – how the emir had smiled when he saw me, what he had said and how I had replied. Although purely a fantasy, my 'romance' became the focus of our life. It served me well in one respect, however, for she let me go and be with the royal ladies whenever they invited me and did not demand that I stay with her to keep her company.

Unlike my mother, Emir Zeid was not at all amused by the gossip about the prince and me and was annoyed with her for encouraging it. He thought we were nurturing the romance simply for lack of other entertainment and was convinced that my teenage crush would end as soon as we left Baghdad. But, more important, he did not want such a marriage to take place, for he was convinced that it could not last and would only complicate family relationships.

One May morning Mother announced from her bed that Emir Zeid's elder brother, King Abdullah of Jordan, was coming to Baghdad and that Emir Zeid was planning to give a stag dinner in his honour in the garden. On the appointed day, she asked me, 'Please, Shirin, see to it that everything is in order, and check each place setting. I don't trust these Bedouin servants.'

It was to be Mother's first meeting with her famous brother-in-law. As she was not feeling well, she received him in bed, wearing a long-sleeved, pink satin bed jacket and surrounded by vases of roses. The king swept in like a ball of light. Dressed in a white, raw-silk Arab gown and white turban, with a magnificent gold belt and dagger, he looked the perfect image of an 'Arabian Nights' caliph. Short and portly, he had a pleasant round face, an immaculately trimmed beard and a warm, winning smile. As he approached the bed, Mother leaned forward so that he could kiss her on both cheeks.

'Please, sire, forgive me for receiving you from my bed,' she said, and then, putting her hand over her heart, she added, looking pained, 'I have angina.'

The king was solicitous. 'May Allah protect you, my dear. You are much too young to be suffering and in bed.' Then, noticing a watercolour of a rose pinned on the wall above her bed table where one in a bud vase stood, he added, 'What a beautiful rose you have painted, more beautiful than the original!' Mother was delighted.

When this courteous exchange was over, I stepped forward, kissed the king's hand, and placed it on my forehead. 'Young lady,' he scolded, patting me on the cheek, 'do not appear in front of the male servants with bare arms again.' At first I did not know what he was talking about. The king then explained that he had arrived earlier than expected and, so as not to disturb the household, had quietly gone to the small balcony in front of the dome to wait for the appointed time. From there he had seen me arranging the flowers on the banquet table, while the many male servants hired for the occasion swarmed over the garden. As always in the presence of strange men, I had covered my hair with a scarf, but I had overlooked my short-sleeved dress. I accepted the king's criticism gracefully, for it was the pious Muslim attitude. But deep down I was grateful to be living in Turkey, where such dress was not required.

Then, like a magician, from somewhere in his robes, King Abdullah produced a gold watch with rubies marking the numerals and placed it on my wrist. Again from somewhere in his robes he brought out a gold pin with little diamonds and pinned it on Mother's bed jacket. Just then Emir Zeid came into the room to escort his brother to the garden, where the guests, including the regent and the premier, Nouri Pasha, and many other dignitaries were waiting.

That was the first and last time Mother and I saw the king,

who was tragically assassinated in 1951 at the Al Aqsa Mosque in Jerusalem.

Early in June, when the summer heat descended (and the Baghdad heat is the worst I have experienced), Mother was glad to have an excuse to return to Istanbul. The White Palace was not air-conditioned and did not even have a roof terrace on which to sleep, as most houses did in Baghdad. The visit had lasted three months, and enough was enough. As for me, although in some ways I hated to leave Baghdad and my prince, I too welcomed the cool breezes of the Bosphorus.

Once we arrived in Büyükdere, Mother was delighted to return to her stable-studio and to paint and to entertain her artist friends. As for me, having just read *Wuthering Heights*, at first I roamed the thick walls of the estate while the wind howled, and cried, 'Heathcliffe, Heathcliffe, where are you?' all the while thinking of the emir. But once the swimming parties and the dancing began and the summer season was in full swing, his image gradually faded. Emir Zeid had been right. My love for the prince had only been a teenage crush.

That winter, after we returned to the apartment in town, Mother continued to paint diligently in her little studio down the hill in Cherry Street and, once a week, held her salons. I did not return to the American Girls' College, for I did not want to be a class behind my friends. A stupid decision. Mother, who had seen a couple of paintings I had done as a pastime that summer, decided that I had 'great talent' and sent me to the Academy of Fine Arts to study with her favourite colleague and close friend, the renowned painter Bedri Rahmi. Although I had no desire to become an artist, for lack of a better idea, I acquiesced, hoping that the course of events would interfere and change my destiny. In a very roundabout way, President Roosevelt did just that.

In the spring of 1945 the American president invited the regent of Iraq to pay an official visit to the United States. Delighted, Emir Abdullilah asked Emir Zeid to take over the regency during his absence, and Emir Zeid accepted. As their brother would be away, Princesses Jelila and Bedia invited me to stay with them at the Qasr Rihab in Baghdad.

Although this time Mother had absolutely no intention of going to Baghdad, for she was much too busy with preparations for her first one-man show, she was amenable to my leaving the Academy of Fine Arts and going to stay with the regent's family. Their invitation re-awakened our fantasies, and we interpreted it as a demonstration of the royal family's continued interest in me as a prospective bride.

Queen Mother Alia also took this opportunity to invite Raad, then aged nine, to stay at the Qasr al-Zuhur with his friend and cousin, little King Faisal.

Mother was delighted. With all three of us in Baghdad, she could concentrate on her art without family obligations. She could savour every minute of her freedom and spend her time painting, entertaining her artist friends and planning her show.

When I arrived in Baghdad, the whole royal family received me with open arms, and the princesses welcomed me as a long-lost sister. Naturally I was delighted to see Emir Abdullilah again, but he, excited to be going to the United States for the first time, spoke of nothing but his forthcoming trip. But on 12 April 1945, as preparations for his departure were underway, President Roosevelt died, and the trip was postponed for a month. The delay meant that I would be living in the same house as the regent, which had not been planned and, in that restricted Muslim society, was rather awkward. There was plenty of grist for the gossip mill of the *kabuls*. As I was under the same roof, I saw him constantly, and our close contact rekindled and increased the infatuation I had had for him the year before. I became totally caught up in his comings and goings, and he became the focus of my life. My diary is full of nauseating, sentimental entries about him, which I cannot bring myself to quote.

In late May, a rare silver bird landed at the Baghdad Military Airport. It was a Skymaster of the US president's Flight, which had come to take Emir Abdullilah and his party to Washington. The plane was on its way home from Moscow, where it had carried Mr Molotov, the Soviet foreign minister, from San Francisco after he had attended the United Nations Charter Conference.

At Emir Abdullilah's suggestion, the princesses and I went to see this exceptional plane. When we boarded it, we were impressed by its luxurious fittings and elegantly designed interior. It had two beds, separated from the main cabin, which contained sixteen comfortable, reclining armchairs. Sitting in one, I closed my eyes and imagined that I was flying to the United States. Since I had gone to an American school everything about the States attracted me.

About a week after the regent's departure, Emir Zeid, who had been living since our arrival in the Bilat, the building which housed the royal offices, came to dinner at Qasr Rihab. As we were sitting in the garden beforehand, Emir Zeid drinking his whisky while we girls sipped our ice-cold, freshly squeezed lemonade, I happened to mention my longing to go to America. To my surprise, Emir Zeid at once took me seriously and asked, 'Would you really like to go to the States?' 'Oh, yes,' I replied. 'I want that more than anything, to continue my studies there, to go to college. Ever since I went to the American school, I hoped that once I graduated you would send me to college in the States.'

Emir Zeid realized that my having been taken out of school to go to Baghdad the year before had unfairly interrupted my education and that my attending the Academy of Fine Arts had been only a stopgap measure encouraged by Mother. Knowing that I was in limbo, he decided then and there to give my life a new direction. Above all, his main objective, I now know, was to get me away from Emir Abdullilah. The next morning Emir Zeid contacted the American Embassy, which promptly arranged my admission to Barnard College. The only question remaining was when I would be able to start, as the war in the Pacific meant that there was no transportation from either Baghdad or Istanbul to America.

So far, Mother had not been informed of any of these plans, for I wanted to ask her permission personally. Since she was totally unpredictable, it was impossible even to speculate how she would react. What if she said no?

17

Exodus

When I returned to Istanbul, leaving Emir Zeid and Raad behind, I found Mother in the best of spirits. Her exhibition had been a stupendous success, a social and artistic event, and she had received accolades. She was ecstatic. Many years later, in an interview, talking of her first one-man show, she said, 'My little studio was crammed with paintings I had made in every size. There was no room to move or even to breathe; I felt constricted and confined. Some of the paintings were finished. Some were not, and I could not bring myself to complete them. I was at a total standstill, and I did not know where to go from there. I was not even sure the paintings were any good. Perhaps what I had painted was pure rubbish. How was I to tell?

'Then one day the art critic Fikret Adil came to the studio. When he saw the number of paintings there, he suggested I have a one-man show. "An artist needs to exhibit," he said. "You need reaction, feedback, criticism, and an exhibition will help you to better understand your work."

' "But where am I to hold it?" I asked. "There are no galleries in Istanbul." [Now there are thirty.] He suggested that I hold it in the gallery of the Academy of Fine Arts, where I had already exhibited with the D Group. Suddenly I had a divine inspiration. "Why don't I have the exhibition in my home?" I asked.

'Fikret Adil scoffed at the idea: "Are you mad?"

' "Why not?" I asked.

' "First of all," he said, "your apartment is in a residential section of the town at the last tram stop. It isn't even on the ground floor. No one will come."

'I surprised myself then, for I answered, "If the work is good,

161

people will come, and I will continue to paint. If it is not, I will know it and stop painting." What could he say?

'I had a hundred and seventy paintings ready to exhibit. Keeping only the chandeliers, I emptied four big reception rooms, sent all the furniture to storage, and organized the entire exhibition to the last detail myself, as if I had been doing it all my life. As I didn't want people to say that Fahrünnisa Zeid was only an amateur, I priced my paintings and put them up for sale. That shocked many of my old society friends, as did the nudes I displayed, but I didn't care.

'The opening day, at four o'clock I was dressed and ready in my bedroom. When I took a last look at myself in the mirror, I saw I was white with fear. To my reflection in the mirror I said, "You are going public. Be prepared to be torn apart." Then I recalled a line from Molière: "*Tu l'a voulu*, Georges Dandin, *et tu l'a eu*." [You asked for it, and you got it.]

'Leaving the safety of my bedroom, I entered the exhibition rooms which, to my relief, were already full of people. It was the most exciting day of my life. Fikret Adil proved wrong, for big crowds attended my show, including classes of schoolchildren, accompanied by their teachers. Most of all, I enjoyed escorting the children around and instructing them about my art.'

After the exhibition, since we had been away in Baghdad, Mother had not bothered to open the Büyükdere house for the summer. She went instead to the lovely clapboard Tokatliyan Hotel on the bay at Tarabya, where she chartered a *kayık* every day and went swimming in the Bosphorus as she so enjoyed. Whenever she wished, she could visit Uncle Suat and Aunt Mizou, who had again rented a summer home in Tarabya. Therefore, upon my return to Istanbul, I went to see my Mother at her hotel.

After she told me at great length all the details of her exhibition and showed me the many photographs taken before, during and after the show, she gave me her full attention.

'Now tell me all about Baghdad. Did anything interesting happen with the emir? What are the latest developments?'

'Nothing particular happened,' I replied. 'I don't think the emir is interested in me as a woman. He likes me as a cousin. That's all.'

She was disappointed. However, the moment I told her that what I really wanted more than to marry the emir was to go to college in America, and that Emir Zeid was willing to make the arrangements if (I emphasized the *if*) she approved, she forgot all about the royal marriage and reacted positively to my new plan. One of Mother's assets was that she never dwelt on a subject, especially if it was unpleasant, and could instantly shift gears and change her frame of mind. Instead of seeing me as an Arabian Nights princess, she suddenly pictured me as a modern, twentieth-century career woman.

'Concentrate on your studies, and become someone,' she said with enthusiasm. 'Have a career. If a woman is unhappy with her husband, she should be able to give him a kick, walk out, and earn her own living.'

As she had not been able to do this herself, she wanted me to be economically independent. I took her advice, became an actress and walked out on three husbands within ten years.

Back at the Ralli apartment that September, I was awakened one morning by the booming of a twenty-one gun salute coming from the Bosphorus. I knew immediately that Emir Abdullilah and his party had arrived. After a four-month visit to the United States and Europe, they had boarded *HMS Ajax* in Naples for the trip to Istanbul. The *Ajax* was a British cruiser which had taken part in the first naval action of the war, the battle of the River Plate in 1939. After a brief official stay in Istanbul, the emir planned to return to Baghdad by the Taurus Express. When he arrived there, Emir Zeid would be relieved of his duties as acting regent and would be free to return to his family in Istanbul.

I ran into Mother's room as she was having breakfast in bed, as she had done all her life. 'They're here,' I said excitedly. 'They have arrived. It is going to be great to see the emir again. I wonder what he thought of America. What shall I wear to the mayor's luncheon?'

'Put on your pink print dress with the carnations,' Mother replied as she bit into a piece of toast, 'and tell Mehmet [the butler] to make sure that all the silver in the drawing room is polished and that the rooms are well aired. I am sure that Emir Abdullilah will call on me at his earliest convenience.'

When the emir arrived in a motorcade followed by Turkish security guards, a sight uncommon in a residential area, the passers-by, curious to know who the important person was, gathered in front of our apartment. They soon enough found out, and the news spread all over Istanbul like a prairie fire. The emir's visit to Mother and me resulted in endless speculation which, this time, had Istanbul tongues wagging, and at all the balls and parties celebrating his arrival I received much more attention than I ever had before.

Emir Abdullilah was as glad to see us as we were to see him. We kissed and embraced and welcomed him with joy. After handing a beautiful gift to each of us, he told us briefly about his extended US tour, how impressed he had been with the magnitude and the beauty of the country and its limitless resources. Finally, after he had drunk his Turkish coffee, he sat back and, with a gleam in his eye, said, 'I have great news for you. Uncle Zeid has been appointed our first ambassador to the Court of St James.'

'What superb news!' Mother exclaimed, jumping up and embracing Emir Abdullilah.

This was not as much of a surprise to her as it was to me. After her great success in Istanbul, wanting to exhibit in Europe and make an international name for herself, she had written to Emir Zeid in Baghdad and suggested that, now that the war had ended, they move back to Europe. Already tired of the limited local art scene and the petty jealousies and rivalries of her painter group, she wanted to leave Istanbul, but being the ambassador's wife in London was a bonus she had not expected. She knew the London embassy was of the utmost importance to Iraq, which had stronger political and economic ties with England than with any other country. This was to be the first embassy established anywhere by the Royal Kingdom of Iraq, and Emir Zeid was going to be its first ambassador. (Until then Iraq had had only legations.) Mother was pleased for Emir Zeid as well as for herself.

At the mayor's luncheon the following day, I was seated next to Emir Abdullilah. Wondering how he would react, I told him of my plan to attend college in America. With a puzzled, disturbed expression, he asked, 'Why would you want to go to the United States, particularly now that your parents are going to London? You would get just as good, if not a better, education in England.'

In light of the regent's reaction, I started to worry that perhaps Mother would feel the same way and take me with her to London instead of sending me to the States. Fortunately, however, she was so engrossed with her forthcoming move, which she regarded as a double challenge – she would not be going only as an ambassador's wife, but also as a painter in a major European capital, where she saw herself holding exhibitions and making an international name for herself – that she did not even consider taking me with her.

Although the American consul-general in Istanbul assured me that I was at the top of their priority list and would be among the first to leave, transportation became available too late for me to make the first semester at Barnard. Finally, in late February 1946, a call from the consulate informed me that a liberty ship which was arriving from Varna in Romania would be leaving for New York in three days.

'Will you be ready to leave at such short notice?' they asked.

'Yes, I will,' I answered joyfully. 'I have been packed for months.'

As soon as I put down the receiver, I told everyone the good news and then telephoned my mother, who had gone to the hospital to have her tonsils removed, which had been bothering her all winter. When I went to bid her goodbye, she rose from her bed and saw me off at the door to her room.

'Go, my child,' she said, hugging me closely. 'Go open your wings and fly on your own. Soar to great heights. Near me, you will always be a bird in the nest under my wings.'

As the liberty ship on which I was to travel was anchored in the bay, the Shakirs chartered a motorboat to see me off. After a quick inspection of the little ship and the presentation of *bon-voyage* gifts and much hugging and kissing, they left. When their motorboat receded to a point where I could no longer see the handkerchiefs being waved, Nejad took off his big winter coat and waved it. As they neared the dock, Nejad's coat became a black speck against Istanbul's spectacular skyline with its domes and minarets, which I was not to see again for eight long years.

The sea voyage to New York took thirty-two days. We encountered many storms and, as the ship had no ballast, we pitched and rolled like a pea in a witch's cauldron. Early on the morning of 27 March the ship slid into New York harbour. Manhattan, with its skyscrapers poking through low-flying pink clouds, looked like the City of Oz wrapped in cotton candyfloss.

Shortly after my departure, Mother and Emir Zeid left for London, where they were to live for many more years than they could possibly have foreseen. Without parental approval, Nejad quit the Istanbul Academy of Fine Arts and went to Paris to live the life of an artist on the Left Bank. From then on Mother, Nejad and I lived in different countries and had totally different lives. Mother and I, however, were able to retain a close relationship, for we kept a voluminous correspondence for the next forty-five years and visited each other whenever we could in many cities throughout the world.

18

Reunions in London

After a year of studying international affairs at Barnard and enjoying everything New York City had to offer, mostly its theatre life, I went to London for my summer holiday. My parents were living at the Iraqi Embassy (formerly Legation) at 22 Queen's Gate, near the Albert Hall, and they were delighted to have me spend my entire holiday with them. Mother had great plans for me. She would take me to the queen's garden party, to the Wimbledon tennis matches, the Ascot races and to Stratford to see Shakespeare.

As Mother felt the small room on the third floor was not adequate, she had a bed put in her own room for me so that she could have me at her side all the time. We stayed up and talked for long hours into the night. She told me her impressions of the British and of her life in London, and I regaled her with New York anecdotes.

My parents were much busier in London than they had been in Berlin. For one thing, the diplomatic corps was twice as large as it had been in the German capital, as after the war many new nations had been created. Every day there were three to four 'National Days' to attend at foreign embassies. Moreover, the staff of the Iraqi Embassy was ten times as large as the one in Berlin had been. In spite of all her diplomatic obligations, however, Mother allotted more time to painting than she had in Berlin. Whenever she had a free morning or afternoon, she would go to her studio on the third floor, which had been a maid's room, and work. On Sundays she locked herself in the studio all day and painted non-stop. Mr Hooper, the butler, was afraid to knock on the door to announce lunch. When he hesitantly did, she would look at him blankly as if he were a Martian. What was this creature doing there? How dare he disturb her? 'Don't you see I am painting?' she'd say. 'What do I care about food? Leave me alone.' Once she even threw a brush full of paint at him. When Mother donned her artist's smock, she became a totally different person. Her concentration was absolute, and no interruptions were allowed. Mr Hooper soon learned to take her lunch up on a tray and leave it quietly in front of her door.

When Mrs Jaray, the Viennese owner of the St George's Gallery in London, came to the embassy and saw Nissa's work, she was so impressed that she promptly invited her to show the paintings in her gallery. Mother's first art exhibition in London became a diplomatic as well as a social event. 'The Painter Princess' one newspaper started to call her. Another wrote, 'The painter Fahrelnissa Zeid [by then she had arabicized her name] is none other than the Iraqi ambassador's wife.' The queen herself attended this exhibition, and the press photo of Nissa greeting her in front of the gallery was prominently displayed in her room. In a later exhibition the queen liked one of Nissa's large paintings called *Kent Caverns* so much that she had it made into a Davencote tapestry which now hangs in the museum in Edinburgh, Scotland.

As if London and its social and artistic activities were not enough, Nissa took every opportunity to visit Paris, for it was still her favourite city, and she felt more at home with the French language and culture. In Paris she bought clothes, visited Nejad, who was working as a painter on the Left Bank, and participated in the Paris art scene. At an exhibition of Turkish painters at the Cernuschi Museum in 1946, Parisians saw her work for the first time. The French art critic Jean Guichard-Meili singled out two of her works in the weekly *Temps présent* of 6 December, 1946:

> Two canvases of Princess Fahrelnissa Zeid, *The Golden Horn* and *Figure of a Woman*, are of exceptional richness and sensitivity, authentically oriental in their magical colour. These two paintings evoke a Matisse and a Dufy. Their exoticism, instead of being acquired, is the expression of an interior nature of a people where passion is a strength and colour a language of the millennia.

As 6 December happened to be her forty-fifth birthday, Nissa, overjoyed, exclaimed, 'This is the best birthday gift I have ever received.'

My father, Izzet-Melih, was by now retired from the Anatolian News Agency and after a long liaison had married Fatma, a vivacious, petite lady, and was living once more in Istanbul. Hearing that I would be in London for my summer holiday, he decided to go to Paris where he hoped to meet me.

When I told Mother cautiously that Father had invited me to spend a week with him in Paris, she flew, as I had expected, into a rage: 'If your father wants to see you, let him bring you over from the United States. No, you are not going to Paris. I want you here with me. You are away enough as it is!' A few days later, however, she gave in: 'All right. Go to Paris, but not for more than a week. There's a reception I want you to attend.' Handing me a pocketful of francs and a list of purchases which would take up at least half my time there, she sent me off by boat train.

Finally I was going to see the city in which I had been conceived and which meant so much to both my parents. Paris was everything I expected, even more. Father and I were both delighted to be reunited. It was touching to know how much he loved me; all he ever demanded of me was my company. Even when I was a little child, he used to sit me on the toilet seat while he shaved, which took a long time, for the process was elaborate with many latherings ending with several lotions and hot compresses. Sitting with me at a café in Paris, I knew he was happy.

Nejad had a typical studio on the Left Bank at the Cité Falquière (now torn down). When Father and I visited him there, after serving us tea, he would display, one by one, his latest paintings. As examples of the post-war art movement, L'Ecole de Paris, his work looked as good as any I had seen in galleries and museums. On one visit to Nejad's studio I met Miss Alice Toklas, Gertrude Stein's constant companion, who was fond of my brother, one of her protégés, and had come with her dog Basket to see his latest work. Through Alice Toklas, Nejad had met many personalities of the time, like the painter Sonya Delaunay, Madame Kandinsky, and the American composer Virgil Thomson, and in a short time had made a place for himself in the Paris art scene. A few days after we met, little mustachioed Miss Toklas invited me to tea at the famous apartment she had shared with Gertrude Stein, and I was overwhelmed to see the Picassos, Braques, Légers and Picabias that covered the walls. I remember as if it were yesterday the huge portrait Picasso had made of Stein in 1905, which faced me as I sat and gorged myself on Alice Toklas's brownies. That day, fortunately, they were not laced with hashish!

(In a cookbook Toklas wrote, she gives recipes for chocolate brownies laced with hashish.)

It was my good luck that cousin Fureya, whom I loved like an older sister, and her husband Kılıç Ali were staying at the Plaza Athenée where they entertained me many times. My darling Uncle Suat was also in Paris on some kind of business. While lunching with him one day at Fouquet's, I noticed that he looked pale and drawn. His *joie de vivre* seemed to have disappeared. When we left the restaurant, right in the middle of the Champs Elysées, he suddenly exploded, 'Shangrila, I am going out of my mind. You know how devoted I am to your Aunt Mizou; yet I cannot live without Yvette.' Two years before, he had fallen madly in love with Yvette and had been carring on a passionate love affair ever since. All of us and half of Istanbul knew of this liaison and felt sorry for Mizou, who suffered in silence.

I had met Yvette when I was ten, in the Cumhuriyet apartment, for she lived below us with her parents, the Matalons, a prosperous Sephardic Jewish family whom I often visited. Then in her late teens, Yvette was a quiet, demure young girl with black hair pulled back tightly in a bun, who attended Mother's nuns' school as a day student. Many years later, to my utter surprise, Yvette surfaced as Uncle Suat's mistress – a bleached blonde with short, unruly hair and lips covered with overflowing bright red lipstick. When she went out on Uncle Suat's motorboat she wore the miniest of bikinis. I could not believe it was the same girl. She had been married to a Jewish businessman whom Suat had befriended. The two couples were inseparable, and, as in many such delicate situations, the two spouses looked the other way while Suat and Yvette carried on their affair.

That day in front of Fouquet's, sensing that my uncle was in pain and did not quite know what to do or how to get out of his predicament, as if I knew such things, I advised, 'You yourself have told me that passion is a disease. Why don't you divorce Aunt Mizou, marry Yvette and get her out of your system like a fever? Then you can return to Aunt Mizou, who I am sure will be waiting for you. She knows as well as we all do that you could never leave her for good. You would die of guilt, and she would probably kill herself.'

My advice had some effect, for on his return to Turkey Suat candidly told Mizou of his predicament: he was possessed, he could not help himself, of course he loved Mizou and always would, but his passion for Yvette was destroying him, he could not work, eat or sleep. Amidst tears and recriminations, Mizou understood. She was the loving, suffering wife who would faithfully stand by and wait for his passion to run its course, as she knew it would some day.

Back in London I went to the theatre as often as I could and was especially impressed with the ensemble acting, which I found superior to that of the New York theatre. A performance of *The Cherry Orchard* at the Old Vic, where Dame Edith Evans played Madame Ranevskaya and Sir Cedric Hardwick her brother Gaev, was the turning point of my life. This production affected me so much that I knew I wanted to be an actress, and that night I decided that I would become one. When I told Mother about my new-found passion and that I wanted to leave Barnard and my government studies and transfer to a drama school, she advised me not to make such a rash decision. 'Return to Barnard now, and we'll see how you feel later,' she advised me. 'Give yourself time to formulate your life.'

In September Emir Zeid saw me off at Southampton on the *Queen Mary*. Since the Iraqi delegation to the United Nations was also travelling on the ship to attend the General Assembly, Emir Zeid told them to 'look after me'. That trip was full of celebrities. Sixteen-year-old Elizabeth Taylor, in Christian Dior new-look dresses, twirled around the dance floor every night with a blond South American. Some others on the ship were Merle Oberon, Cary Grant, Betsy Drake, Robert Coote and Robert Ryan. Everywhere I went I was followed by one or more of the Iraqi delegates, who had taken Emir Zeid's advice to heart. Even while I was instructing Merle Oberon how to swim the crawl in the big indoor pool, I noticed one of them hanging over the railing, watching. Since I sat at the captain's table, usually wearing Arab or Turkish kaftans, always attended by one of the Iraqi delegates, everyone thought I was some exotic Arab princess. When Robert Ryan asked me, 'Can't one ever see you alone on this ship?' I simply replied, 'Oh, no, those men are my bodyguards.' I played the part I had been cast in; yet all I was was a college girl returning to school.

Back at Barnard that autumn, I joined the school's drama club and also performed across the street with the Columbia University Players. Slowly, slowly, like a magnet, the theatre pulled me away from my government studies. One can row against the current just so long. I applied to the Yale Drama School, and once I was accepted, I phoned Mother and told her about my decision. 'If that is what you really want, go ahead,' she said.

Mother was a difficult woman who at times could be impossible. But strangely enough, when it came to major decisions in my life, she never objected and let me do as I chose. As long as I was happy and successful, she was content.

The next time I went to London, this time for Christmas, I found Mother and Nejad, who had come from Paris, waiting for me at the airport. Wrapped in a voluminous mink coat and wearing a mink hat with a jewelled pin fastened on one side like a cockade, Mother looked like a Russian tsarina. I threw myself into their arms, shrieking with such abandon that the reserved British looked askance at us.

As we drove from the airport to the new Iraqi Embassy, I noticed a lot of construction work going on. The debris of bombed-out buildings I had seen on my first visit to London a year and a half before had been cleared, and new buildings were rising all over the city.

As the 22 Queen's Gate Residence had proved much too small to house the embassy staff and to be also a residence for the ambassador, Mother had found, and the Iraqi government had purchased, a beautiful Georgian mansion next to the Russian Embassy in Kensington Palace Gardens, a tree-lined private road with gates and gatekeepers on both the Kensington High Street and Notting Hill Gate entrances. This was now the residence and 22 Queen's Gate remained as the chancellery.

When our limousine entered the gravelled circular driveway, I saw Mr Hooper, our butler, in striped trousers, cutaway coat and white gloves, standing outside the open front doors of the embassy. Mother's orders were that no guest should have to ring the bell. How the poor man managed not to catch pneumonia I will never know. We climbed a few marble steps flanked by columns and entered a marble hall with ornate gilt mouldings.

Hearing the sound of our arrival, Aunt Aliye flew out of the little sitting room off the hall. I had not seen her since that cold February morning almost three years before when I had sailed out of Istanbul, and was amazed at how much she had changed. She looked thin and pale and frightened as she clung to me in the hall. Clearly, the sudden death of Charles Berger little more than a year ago had taken its toll.

'Shirinaki, Shirinaki,' she said, her huge lavender eyes filling with tears, 'so much has happened since I saw you last, so much!'

After a liaison which had lasted twenty-three years, Charles Berger had finally decided that the time had come for him to relinquish his artistic freedom and marry Aliye. To please the family he had converted to Islam, and he and Aliye had gone to live on Büyükada in a little pink house high up the hill. In a letter Aunt Aliye had written me at Yale, this is how she spoke of her short-lived marriage:

The view here is breathtaking, so beautiful one cannot even sleep. And that marvellous clean smell of the pines! In the early morning the dew glitters on the pine needles like diamonds, and your Uncle Charles, inspired by the beauty and the solitude of the groves, plays his violin while he strolls through the woods. It is absolute heaven! I am afraid it is too good to last.

One morning, six months after their marriage, they were planning to catch the ferry for an appointment in town. As usual Aunt Aliye tarried, and since they were late they had to run all the way down the hill. When they arrived at the ferry landing, Berger was breathless. Clutching his chest and looking at the departing ferry, he exclaimed, 'Oh, we've missed the boat,' and slumped into a chair at one of the cafés, victim of a massive heart attack. A few minutes later he died in Aliye's arms.

Villagers carried him up the hill to the Shakir Pasha house. As it was late September, the house was shut and padlocked for the winter. Frail little Aunt Aliye seized the padlock on the iron gate and with some superhuman force broke the chain in two. Berger's body was laid on the stiff mother-of-pearl inlaid sofa in the lower living room.

That evening Mrs Ahmet Emin Yalman, a close family friend living on the island, whose husband was the owner and editor of the daily newspaper *Vatan*, heard the news and rushed to the house. Many years later I asked her to write down exactly what happened that night. This is the account she gave:

The big old house was dark. They obviously had forgotten to pay the electricity bill. The lower living room, the one with the grotto, was lit only by candles, there were candles everywhere. Berger's body was lying on the sofa in the middle of the room. In his white silk shirt strewn with jasmines, his long white fingers drooping over the edge, he looked like some martyred saint. All night Aliye knelt beside him, and every few seconds she put a little mirror to his lips in the hope it would cloud with his breath. Of course it never did.

One by one, members of the family arrived from town. Since there was no electricity to make the bell sound, they abruptly appeared at the door and were faced with the scene I just described. At one point, to add to the confusion, a Catholic priest from the church next door appeared. This was a great embarrassment, for he had to be told that Berger had become a Muslim and would be buried as one. When the *imam* from the mosque across the street arrived, he asked to see the documents pertaining to the conversion before he would allow Berger to be buried in the Muslim graveyard on top of the hill. Lala offered to go to Hakiye's apartment, where the documents were kept, and bring them back. He caught the last boat to town and returned on the first ferry the next morning.

As arrangements for the funeral were being made, Aliye had to be persuaded that her husband of six months was actually dead. Fureya, who at the time was suffering from consumption and lived in the pine groves near the sanatorium, after staying with Aliye for most of the night, had come to my house for a short rest and a little breakfast. At sunrise, when we returned, we met Aliye running out of the house toward the old well, determined to throw herself in. She had finally accepted the fact that Charles Berger was dead. Fureya and I ran after her and, at the well, grabbed her skirt and pulled her away, forcing her indoors where the doctor gave her a sedative. After that, she went through the funeral ceremony without emotion.

The moment Nissa heard the news, convinced that she alone could save Aliye, she took the first plane to Istanbul and returned to London with her half-dead little sister. Nissa prepared a room for Aliye on the third floor of the embassy near her studio and nursed her like a sick child. She had to be watched day and night. Slowly, very slowly, Aliye began to mend and finally, looking like a ghost, rose from the bed. She was a difficult guest, however, for she constantly lamented and started to drink heavily.

The day of my arrival, after Aunt Aliye had greeted me in the hall, Mother took me by the hand and, saying, 'Come, let me show you what a beautiful new embassy we have,' led me into an enormous formal drawing room which looked, because of its size and opulence, like a ballroom. Marble Corinthian columns with gilded capitals stood at both ends, and two enormous chandeliers lit the room.

As we stepped down into a glassed-in porch, through the draperies of a large archway, to my surprise Aunt Hakiye rose and came forward to embrace me. 'What a wonderful coincidence for us to meet in London!' she exclaimed.

Hakiye had stopped to see her sisters in London after visiting Fureya, who was recuperating from consumption at a sanatorium in Leysin, Switzerland. Since Hakiye could not have afforded on a general's pension to go to Switzerland and stay with her sick daughter for a long time, she had persuaded the family to auction most of the antique furniture and art effects contained in the Büyükada house. Because they all loved Fureya and recognized Hakiye's need, the family had reluctantly agreed to this move. Soon after that, however, because no one felt like living in the depleted house, it was rented.

The walls of the embassy porch were covered with Mother's paintings, many of which I knew well. (I referred to them as my sisters and brothers.) A comfortable set of wicker furniture was placed around a colourful kilim. On one end table next to the sofa stood a sculpture by Henry Moore and on the other one by César, and in the centre of the room hung a large wooden mobile by Lynn Chadwick, whom Mother knew well. As she had done in Istanbul, in London too Mother held salons for her artist and writer friends. At one I met Chadwick and César, as well as the sculptor Armitridge, the art critic Penrose, the writer John Haywood in a wheelchair, the critic Maurice Collis, the poet Kathleen Raine, and that marvellous actress Louise Rainer, whom the world had admired in Pearl Buck's *The Good Earth*.

When Aliye and Nejad joined us on the porch, we crowded around a turquoise-coloured, ceramic-tiled coffee table which Fureya had recently made. Mother had visited her at the Swiss sanatorium several times and had taken clay and urged her to work with it as therapy. Her thoughtful action had awakened a dormant talent in Fureya, who found ceramics not only therapeutic but also totally engrossing. She attended classes in Leysin and, during her convalescence, learned the art of ceramic-making.

'Shirinaki, you look so slim and sophisticated in that black suit and all that perfectly applied make-up,' commented Mother as she reached for a glass of the sherry Mr Hooper was serving. Since Mother had put on a lot of weight herself and was quite portly, she was particularly aware of my new figure. 'Now tell us all about America,' she continued.

'Suat loved America,' interjected Aunt Aliye. 'Do you too? Did you by any chance see Syida, Suat's American wife?'

Before I had a chance to answer their questions, Aunt Hakiye, as if demanding an accounting, asked, 'Why ever did you leave Barnard College? I thought you intended to study international affairs and wanted to become a diplomat or go into politics. "I want to be a deputy in Parliament," you once told me. Now I hear you are going to some theatre school and want to become an actress.'

'I think that's wonderful,' butted in Aunt Aliye, who detected a slight tone of criticism in her elder sister's voice. 'I cannot wait to see Shirin on stage again, for I still remember how impressed I was when she played Clytemnestra in school.'

Mother agreed. 'I for one never was for Shirin entering diplomacy or politics. Politics is a dirty game, not for a woman. When she called me from New York and told me she wanted to study drama, I was glad she had changed her mind. Besides, when she was born, Count Bonarelli predicted that she would become an actress. It is her destiny.'

Nejad, who had already adopted the Frenchman's superior attitude toward Americans, asked Mother, 'As long as Shirin is studying drama, why doesn't she do it in London where there are better theatre schools? Why not the Royal Academy of Dramatic Art?'

I could have killed him. What if Mother agreed with Nejad and said, 'Yes, he is right. You should transfer to the Royal Academy and live in London with us. Why stay in America all alone?'

Although it was logical for her to agree with Nejad, she chose not to. At this period Mother was leading a rich, active, creative life, and there was no room in it for me. All her needs apparently fulfilled, she seemed to have come into her own. Although her health had improved immeasurably, she constantly overtaxed herself. Every time she returned to the embassy after a full day of luncheons, exhibitions and receptions, she would throw off her clothes, almost in a faint, and collapse into bed.

As I now look back, I am convinced that Mother had

hypoglycaemia, which was never diagnosed. Her constant craving for sugar – her room was full of boxes of sweets, which she consumed ravenously – her fatigue, her depressions, her fainting spells, all point to this disease. Later in her life this condition reversed itself, and she became a diabetic.

Between Mother's constant activities and her exhaustion, she had neither the time nor the need for me. Moreover, I was no longer a child, and she probably preferred not to have competition from a twenty-two-year-old budding actress. She liked to be the queen bee. And so, to my relief, she did not respond to the suggestion that I study in London.

At that moment Emir Zeid, looking very fit and more self-assured than I had ever seen him, walked on to the verandah. I jumped up and ran to meet him. When I kissed him on the pate, I noticed a faint aroma of good pipe tobacco and lemon cologne, just as when I had first kissed him at the Büyükada house. How good it was to be home!

Just then, in a stentorian voice, Mr Hooper announced, 'Your Royal Highnesses, luncheon is served,' and, Mother leading the way, we all walked into the dining room, which had a very restful atmosphere – cream coloured walls with beautiful mouldings and grey-blue satin curtains which matched the leather seats of the Chippendale chairs.

After a delicious luncheon we took coffee in the little sitting room. Emir Zeid excused himself and returned to his office. When Aunt Aliye asked Mr Hooper in a small voice for a cognac, I could see clearly that Mother was annoyed.

'How are Aunt Ayşe and Uncle Suat and poor Aunt Mizou doing?' I asked, anxious for their news.

Aunt Hakiye volunteered and with a look of superior distaste said, 'Ahmet Bey obviously has a knack for business. He is getting richer by the day, buying and selling property. Now Ayşe lives in a pink stone house overlooking the Marmara Sea in Moda, for her old wooden house was torn down and its land cut up into lots and sold for great profit. That section of town is getting to be very popular. Nermidil is going to Istanbul University and wants to become a chemist. And Erdem is in Ankara attending the *Mülkiye* [the College of Political and Administrative Sciences]. I'm sure he will make a very good diplomat.'

'He should have become a musician. He plays the violin beautifully,' interrupted Aunt Aliye.

'Don't be silly, Aliye,' said Mother. 'He can be a diplomat and continue to play the violin. Look at me. I manage to paint and do my diplomatic duties as well. Where there is a will, there is always a way.'

'And Uncle Suat?' I asked cautiously. 'How is he doing with his new wife?'

Aunt Hakiye's face turned the colour of camel-hair. 'Don't even mention the words "new wife". Mizou is his wife and will always remain his wife.'

'I am totally on your side, *abla*. Mizou is and always will be my sister-in-law,' Mother agreed.

'How can you say these things?' said Aliye, her voice rising. 'Suat married Yvette, and she is now his wife, whether you both like it or not.'

'They are going to have one of their fights,' I thought. 'I wish I hadn't brought up the subject.'

'Suat is still very much in love with Yvette,' said Aliye, 'but he goes to see Mizou regularly. Meanwhile with her two boys she lives quietly in her apartment and waits. Poor Suat, torn between his passion for Yvette and his deep devotion to Mizou!'

'Instead of sympathizing with Suat, you should feel sorry for Mizou,' Hakiye scolded. She then rose from her chair. 'We cannot just sit here and talk all day. I have some shopping to do at Harrods,' she said, and left the room.

At that we all dispersed in different directions. I went up to my room to unpack.

That night, as Mother and I sat up in her bedroom, as we always did when I went to visit her, talking into the early hours of the morning, she confessed, 'Aliye drinks much too much. I don't know what to do with her. It's getting to be very embarrassing. She hides the empty bottles under her bed, and the maids find them. What will they think? After all, this is an embassy! Moreover, I am worried that she is becoming an alcoholic. I tried to save her by bringing her here after the tragedy, but it looks as if she is going to drink herself to death.'

'It won't be easy for her to get over Uncle Charles,' I said.

'I'll tell you how she will get over his loss! She must give herself totally to her work.'

'What kind of work are you talking about, Mother?' I asked, intrigued.

'I knew that work would be her only salvation; so one morning I stood her before an easel and stuck a paintbrush in her hand. 'Paint!' I ordered, and Aliye painted. Later I decided that etching would be more salutary, because it demands more physical effort to drive the tool into the sheet of copper. To inspire her, I suggested that the etchings she would make be used as illustrations for the book of Charles Berger's poems which she intends to publish. This has caught Aliye's fancy, and she has responded. I only hope she will drown her sorrows with work instead of the bottle. That will save her.'

In an article named 'An Artist: Aliye Berger' in the June 1963 issue of *The Golden Horn*, Godfrey Goodwin writes:

When her heart was in disarray, her sister, Princess Fahrelnissa Zeid, drove her to study engraving . . . Had she painted then, the confusion and indiscipline that is her outward aspect would have resulted in chaos . . . It takes metal to control one of these people . . . Engraving was at once a release from grief and the discovery of an inevitable destiny. For it was after Charles Berger's death that her passionate love was transformed into creative power.

Having found a good teacher, John Wright, Aliye studied etching and worked very hard in London for two years, during which Mother and Emir Zeid put up with her. 'As I worked,' she wrote to me in America, 'I felt I was being re-attached to life.' Her first etchings of tenderly lit gardens with blossoming trees were reminiscent of Samuel Palmer, and among those trees continually appeared and re-appeared the ghost-like figure of Berger.

But grief could not continue for ever at such heat. Gradually the Berger-figure faded in the garden, and domes and minarets began to appear in Aliye's etchings, reflecting a growing homesickness for Istanbul. In 1950 she returned home with 140 etchings and opened up Berger's old apartment. A year later she had her first one-man show, and her etchings proved to be quite popular, for, as Goodwin says, 'they were so romantic that they even depicted moonlight. What saved them from being banal were the ease and skill with which she drew.'

Three days after my arrival in London, Mother and Aliye had a terrible fight. The maid had again found numerous empty brandy bottles under Aliye's bed, and, when Mother confronted her, she followed her protestations of innocence with a remark that infuriated Mother: 'But Nissa, you are being so bourgeois. Who cares what the maid thinks?' Mother slapped Aliye, pulled her hair and hit her on the head with her two fists.

'Don't, Nissa. Please don't,' Aliye kept crying. 'It hurts.'

I watched, frozen. There was nothing I could do, for when Mother was angry she was like a violent storm and would smash anything in her way.

After that incident, Aliye did not leave her room for two days; and Mother, deeply remorseful, sent up well-prepared trays of all the delicacies which would please her, with little bouquets of her favourite flowers, and even a bottle of Napoleon brandy. When Mother realized she had gone overboard, she always made amends with special attention and gifts, and as everyone knew she was basically a good-hearted, generous and loving person, they forgave her her violent outbursts.

Except for that unpleasant event, my holiday was idyllic. Nejad and I visited the museums, where he lectured me on art, and I went to the theatre as often as I could. The highlight of my visit was Mother's exhibition at the Gimpel Fils Gallery. I was impressed to see how many new paintings she had made since I had last been in London, only a year and a half before, and how different in style they were from her previous impressionist canvases. The new ones were non-figurative, patches of vivid colours separated by black lines like sunlight cut up by the mullions of a latticed window.

Thirteen-year-old King Faisal II, who was attending Harrow at the time, was at the opening of the exhibition. Knowing that he was interested in art, Mother took him by the arm and led him around the hall, pointing out to him what she had tried to accomplish and the different techniques and brushstrokes she had used. When Faisal saw me at the gallery, he invited me to visit him at his school. With an armful of sweets and biscuits, I went to Harrow and was amused to see the students wearing striped trousers and tail-coats, topped incongruously by stiff straw hats. To me they looked like a flock of penguins. When the king took me to his room, he proudly demonstrated how his narrow, iron Murphy bed could be pulled down from the wall. Upon seeing that the bed almost filled the entire room, I exclaimed, 'But Faisal, you are a king. Can't they give you a better, a larger room?' Looking up at me with his big, docile, brown eyes, he replied, 'My dear Shirin, this builds character.'

On New Year's Eve, we dined at the embassy *en famille*, drank a lot of champagne and enjoyed the special feast our French chef had prepared. At bedtime I followed Mother upstairs, for I was anxious to share with her my secret. In the privacy of her bedroom, I declared, 'I'm in love. I'm in love. I have really fallen in love for the first time in my life, and he absolutely adores me.'

'How exciting! Who is the man?' she asked.

'His name is Wesley Lau. He's a classmate of mine at Yale, but unlike me he is majoring in play-writing. Tall and blond, he is extremely handsome and looks like Gary Cooper. He is four years older than I am, for he is a veteran, that is, he was in the American army during the war,' and, knowing that the next statement would please her, I added, 'He is an intellectual, and he's extremely well read.'

'Lau. That is an odd name; it sounds Chinese.'

'No. Of German extraction, he comes from Sheboygan, Wisconsin.' Then, dreading that Mother would ask what his father did, I added, 'His parents are simple, unsophisticated people.'

She asked the question anyway. 'What does his father do?'

How was I going to tell her in this opulent ambience that his father was an uneducated fireman? 'His father is a municipal employee,' I said, gulping. 'Wesley comes from a relatively poor family, and he's attending Yale under the GI Bill.'

Mother did not seem to be particularly interested in these details. Here I was tripping all over myself trying to make Wesley look good in her eyes, but all that mattered to her was that I was in love and happy to be so.

'To fall in love is the most wonderful thing that can happen to a person,' she said. 'To love and to be loved in return, that is all that really matters. You are a lucky girl, Shirinaki.'

'Yes, Mother,' I chanted, relieved and grateful. 'I am a lucky girl,' and, hugging her, 'I love you, Mother,' I said. 'Happy New Year! Happy 1949!'

19

Marriage

The day after my twenty-third birthday, on 4 March 1949, I married Wesley Lau in the New Haven City Hall. The short ceremony was attended by a few of our schoolfriends; no member of either family was present.

That evening, to celebrate our marriage, we gave a party for our classmates and teachers in a Gothic reception room Yale University loaned us for the occasion, and after a one-night honeymoon in a nearby inn we went to classes holding hands and books.

A month later Mother decided to make her first trip to the United States to meet her new son-in-law. She had two other objectives, to arrange for an exhibition of her painting at the Hugo Gallery in New York, and to be fitted for a hearing aid.

A week before our Easter vacation she arrived in New Haven. We put her up in a boarding house across the street from our basement apartment near the university. 'I feel like a student,' she said, delighted with the arrangements. When she entered our two-room basement apartment, she exclaimed, looking around, 'What a charming place! You seem to have everything you need. How did you do it so quickly?' and, 'So many books!'

'They belong to Wes,' I said with pride as I helped her remove her mink coat, while Wes placed her alligator Gladstone bag on the floor.

After dinner Mother watched me wash the dishes in the little sink in the corner of our bedroom, 'Oh,' she exclaimed, 'how fascinating! Those dirty dishes go into a mountain of airy, white bubbles and come out shiny clean.' She then sat on the couch in the living room and, like a magician, started to remove gift after gift from the Gladstone bag in front of her.

'Here, this is for you,' she said, handing Wes a beautifully wrapped package containing an alligator wallet and matching cigarette case with corners and initials in 18-carat gold. Wes, who had never received such an elegant gift, was overwhelmed.

'This is also for you,' Mother said, handing him a magnificent antique stick-pin in the shape of a diamond-studded acorn with a large and perfect pearl. 'It belonged to Zeid's father, and we want you to have it.'

'When will Wesley ever wear such a thing?' I thought to myself. 'She should have kept it for Raad.'

For me she brought a whole '*parure*' of jewellery that had belonged to her – a large bow-shaped gold pin with rubies and diamonds, a beautifully crafted gold bracelet-watch, also with diamonds and rubies, and a matching pair of earrings. (All of these were eventually pawned and sold.) From the Gladstone bag next emerged a bolt of brocade and a linen tablecloth for twelve, with napkins embroidered with Mother's initials and the Hashemite crown.

Although I realized the material and sentimental value of these 'royal gifts', I wished that they had been more practical. But how could I expect Mother to be anything but herself, impractical, extravagant and magnanimous?

In New Haven Mother was like Alice in Wonderland. Everything enchanted her. When we took her to lunch at the Commons, a baronial oak-panelled Gothic hall which served 1000 freshmen and drama students as a dining hall, she was so impressed with the décor and ambience that instead of eating she sketched Wes and me against this extraordinary background. That sketch, framed, still hangs today in the study of my Princeton home.

During Mother's visit the drama school was putting on its main stage a spectacular production of Goethe's *Faust*. Everyone, teachers and students, in one way or another, had been involved in the production except for Wes and me, who had been excused by the dean because of our marriage. With its spectacular sets and magnificent lighting, the production caused great interest in theatrical circles and was photographed for *Life* magazine. Mother was so overwhelmed by the visual elements that she spent the whole evening sketching. I don't think she heard a word that was said on the stage.

When I had her attend a run-through of Camus's *Caligula*, where I was playing the female lead, Casonia, she was amazed to discover that I was a real actress. She had seen me perform only once before, in a high-school production back in Istanbul. I played the scene in which Caligula strangles Casonia with all the realism I could muster, and when I heard Mother gasp I was thrilled.

The morning we were to leave for New York, where we were to spend our Easter vacation as Mother's guests, Mother was in our apartment watching me strip the bed, empty the hamper and put all the laundry into a bundle and hoist it on my back. 'I've got to take this to the Chinese laundry down the street,' I said. 'I'll be right back.'

When later I became a renowned actress, Mother said to me, 'That morning in New Haven, when I looked up from your basement apartment and saw your long legs walking down the street, with you carrying that bundle of washing on your back, your head held high like a queen, I said to myself, "This girl of mine is going to go far in life." '

What impressed Mother most about New York was its sky.

'There is no night, no darkness in this city. The buildings go into the sky, and their lights mingle with the stars. One feels surrounded and never lonely,' she commented.

From her Plaza Hotel room, which faced north, she made a Dufy-like watercolour of Central Park. Wes asked her why she had painted the clouds yellow and she replied, matter-of-factly, 'Because the taxis are yellow.'

We took Mother to see all the sights, from the Empire State Building to the Versailles Night Club where Edith Piaf was singing. She had several meetings with Mr Iolas, the Greek owner of the Hugo Gallery in New York, and made all the arrangements for her exhibition in the autumn. I was to follow up on all the details and represent her at the opening.

Mother had achieved her three objectives – a hearing aid, a New York exhibition of her work, and meeting my new husband, whom she described as 'absolutely charming'.

Wes, in turn, found Mother both fascinating and imposing. After her departure and our return to New Haven, he observed, 'She certainly is an extraordinary lady, a great personality, but very strong-willed, not a person you would like to cross. You know, baby, with such a mother I would have expected you to be a shy, introverted, insecure wallflower; yet in many ways you are like her. I was surprised, though, to see how much you want and *need* to please her. She actually intimidates you.'

'That's an exaggeration,' I said defensively.

That June, Wes and I went off to the Court Theater in Beloit, Wisconsin, where we both made our professional débuts. On our way to Beloit, we stopped in Sheboygan, Wisconsin, for me finally to meet my in-laws. When we arrived Mr Lau was on duty at the fire station, and we went directly there to see him. As I stood on the main floor of the firehouse, suddenly a round hatch opened in the ceiling above me, and down the brass pole slid a puffy-faced, ox-like man. 'Hello, Dad,' said Wesley, shaking his big red hand. 'Hello, Dad,' I echoed and gave him a hug, thinking what a unique way this was to meet my new father-in-law.

The Laus lived in a typical small, clapboard worker's home with a little back yard where we had several cook-outs with Wes's parents and his sister and brother-in-law, a car salesman.

The opening play of the season at the Court Theater was *Gaslight*, and Wes and I played Mr and Mrs Manningham. (Ingrid Bergman and Charles Boyer had played these parts in the film version, and Angela Lansbury the Irish maid.) My cousin Erdem, who had been sent on his first diplomatic post to Chicago as Turkish vice-consul, drove up to see the production and was impressed by the way the play had been staged in the round. 'Shirin,' he said in the green room after the show, 'when you held that razor up to your husband's face, pretending to be crazy, I really believed you were.'

When we graduated a year later, we moved to New York and lived in a one-room apartment with a Dutch door in a mews in Greenwich Village. Wesley made the rounds of the casting agents while I modelled and helped pay for our living expenses. Wes eventually broke into television and began getting parts on TV. One show paid him as much as I made in a month of modelling. We lived frugally, like all starving artists, and were perfectly happy.

Five years into our marriage we decided to have a baby, and once pregnant I started to prepare for the arrival of the child. We wall-papered the alcove of our little apartment where we planned to put the crib, and I set out to knit blue bonnets and booties. Since I wanted a boy I prayed, 'Please, Allah, give me a son, and let him have blue, blue eyes and blond, blond hair like his father.' Unfortunately, my pregnancy had problems. Early into it, my gynaecologist advised bed rest as much as possible, but as we needed the money I continued to model.

Just about that time my father came to New York. He was travelling as newspaper correspondent with the president of Turkey, Celal

Bayar, who was on an official visit and tour of the United States. The owner of the daily paper, *Yeni Sabah*, for which Father wrote a column, had asked him to cover the president's trip to the US. Although he had never been a correspondent, Father had accepted simply to see me, for it had been almost seven years since we had last met in Paris. When I saw him, I was shocked to notice how much he had aged in that time. His former brisk stride had turned into a slow shuffle.

In his honour I gave several parties in my one room to introduce him to my friends, went shopping for him and showed him the sights of New York. The effort did not help my condition. When he left, I started bleeding heavily, and the gynaecologist ordered strict bed rest. I left my modelling job and lay in bed reading Dr Spock's book.

On the day I had to sign for my unemployment cheque, I became seriously ill. We needed the money, but I was afraid to leave my bed. I asked Wes what I should do, hoping that he would prevent me from going and say, 'You just stay put. I'll sell something. I'll steal if necessary, but just don't move!' But to my disappointment, as always, he chose not to take the responsibility and said instead, 'Do as you please, baby.'

I rose from bed, dressed, took the subway, climbed a steep flight of stairs and signed for my $30 unemployment cheque. That night I started having violent cramps, and the next morning I was rushed to the hospital, where, after a whole day of terrible pain, I miscarried. The four-and-a-half-month-old foetus slipped out of me, and when my doctor's partner, whom I had never seen before, finally arrived, she removed it from between my legs. As she did so, the sac burst, and when I cried, 'Let me see it,' the thoughtless doctor held up the perfectly shaped foetus for me to see. I screamed and sobbed. When I learned it was a boy, I felt as if something had exploded in me and as though I were dying. I immediately called Wes, whom I had sent home to pick up a few things. 'Our son is dead,' I choked, 'gone down some drain.' I sobbed hysterically.

My pain and anguish at the loss of the child brought on a deep depression, and I began to blame Wes for the tragedy. If I had not got up, if I had not climbed those stairs, if he had prevented me from going out, I kept thinking, I would not have lost the baby. Now I realize the miscarriage was the result of my having RH-negative blood, but in 1954 medical science was not conscious of the importance of blood types in pregnancies. My doctor had not even given me a blood test! 'It was a bad baby,' they said heartlessly at the time, dismissing it.

The death of the baby led to the end of my marriage. Until then I had not felt the need to return to Turkey or to be with my family. Now all I could think of was going home. Father sent me a ticket on a Turkish freighter, and Wes encouraged me to go. 'It will do you good to be with your folks and back home. Don't worry about me. I'll take care of myself. I'll write to you every day.'

The voyage took three weeks, and the clean sea air and the rest helped me mend both physically and psychologically. Early one June morning we sailed into Istanbul harbour, and the sight of the skyline with its domes and minarets in the morning mist brought a flood of tears to my homesick eyes.

As the ship anchored in the bay to await its turn to dock and unload, my family came alongside in a motorboat belonging to the harbourmaster, a Galatasaray classmate of Father's. There they all were, smiling and waving up at me – Father and my new stepmother Fatma, my half-sister Remide and her fourth husband, a quiet intellectual banker, Aunt Hakiye and little Aunt Aliye, and darling Uncle Suat with Aunt Mizou at his side. His marriage to Yvette had lasted a little more than a year, and he had returned to Mizou. From then on they did not bother to get remarried but lived together until the end.

Once ashore, I was delighted to hear that my stepmother had invited all the Shakirs to lunch. 'How did you know that red mullet is my favourite?' I asked her as I looked at the fish on my plate. 'Your father told me,' she replied, staring at him with adoring eyes.

'Welcome home, my daughter,' said Father, raising his wine glass. 'It's good to have you back.'

'Welcome,' said the Shakirs, lifting their glasses. 'Welcome, Shirinaki.'

Oh, how good it was to be back home!

'Shangrila, Shangrila . . .' sang Uncle Suat.

That summer I could not go to the Büyükada house, for it was rented. I was horrified to hear that the tenant had, without the family's permission, cut the trees and converted the garden into an amusement park with volleyball courts, ping-pong tables, bumper cars and a small ferris wheel for children. Everyone blamed Uncle

Ahmet for having found this hateful man. Instead of going to the island, therefore, I went to live with Father and Fatma in her mother's summer home, a little jewel of an Edwardian house with masses of shade-on-shade hydrangeas, located in a big park on the Asiatic side of the city.

From my one-room New York apartment and life as a model in the garment district, where my cigar-chomping, vulgar bosses treated me like a brainless body, I was catapulted into a fairy-tale existence in Istanbul. I had not known that life could be so wonderful, and I had not expected such a homecoming. I found myself the centre of attention of a new family, adored, pampered, doted on by an entire household.

I was given the guest room on the main floor, overlooking the wisteria path and fruit orchards at the back of the house. That first night, as I lay in the massive mahogany bed between cool linen sheets, the scent of the magnolia trees outside the room seeping in through the green shutters, I could not help comparing this scene with my one-room apartment in Greenwich Village.

As Fatma's only purpose in life was to please my father, she tried her best to be a good mother. She made me clothes, embroidered handkerchiefs for me, ironed my dresses which she laid out on my bed like a French maid, and even polished my shoes. She always made sure the vases in my room were filled with fresh flowers from the garden and saw to it that the toast on my breakfast tray was warm and crisp – things my own mother had never done for me.

My mother was concerned only with our artistic, intellectual and moral development and did not bother with the basics of mother-hood. Therefore I revelled in the new kind of mothering Fatma gave me. I recognized that I would have been spoiled rotten and unintellectually oriented had I been her daughter, and I was grateful to be my mother's. However, I loved Fatma for what she was and appreciated enormously the care she gave me.

That magical summer my family and friends outdid themselves with their attentions. They entertained me in their homes, gave parties in my honour and took me to lunch and dinner in the famous fish restaurants along the Bosphorus. Aunt Hakiye took me to the Bazaar, for she was familiar with the ins and outs of that labyrinth. She often went there in search of antique belt buckles, which she used as clasps on purses she made out of old Turkish embroideries. She was a pioneer. Her creations were unique, for at that time no one had thought to make use of the magnificent old embroideries found all over the country. At tea parties for her friends she displayed and sold these unusual purses and used the money to travel to Anatolian villages where she found, often in old hope chests, these unique pieces of art. Hakiye's three sisters, as well as her daughter, were artists, and this was her way of creating something.

After these forays Aunt Hakiye and I would lunch in the Spice Bazaar and then we'd call on my cousin Fureya, who, having returned from Switzerland cured of her consumption, had become a ceramist. Ever gracious, Fureya, wearing a pair of cotton trousers and a loose shirt, received us in her studio in the rear of her big apartment where she had installed a huge kiln imported from Paris. This 1000-pound monster had been hauled into the apartment through a window removed for the occasion. While I sipped Turkish coffee in colourful ceramic cups she had made, I feasted my eyes on her other works which covered the walls. Each time I visited, there was a new piece of ceramic to admire, for Fureya worked incessantly, experimenting with different techniques and forms.

Since she had discovered her vocation at the sanatorium in Leysin, Fureya had become a totally different woman. She had metamorphosed from a chic society matron to a serious artist. As her values changed, so did her lifestyle and friends. Her husband Kılıç was not pleased with the turn of events, for he wanted her to be the charming hostess, giving dinner parties followed by card games, as she had done before this 'clay madness' (as he called it) had hit her. Neither did he appreciate her locking herself up in the studio and working all day, nor did he enjoy her new artist friends. That summer I was conscious of a lot of tension between those two. A few months later, after nineteen years of marriage, Uncle Kılıç departed one day, leaving on his desk a short farewell note. Fureya auctioned all her possessions and moved to the ground floor of the Shakir Pasha apartment where she set up a ceramics studio. From then on she worked tirelessly and supported herself. She had many exhibitions in Turkey and Europe, winning several international prizes and becoming the leading ceramist of Turkey.

When I went to town, I also visited Aunt Aliye, who still lived and worked in Berger's old apartment, which she had converted into an unbelievable studio-home reminiscent of Christian Berard's set for the *Madwoman of Chaillot*. People dropped in on her at all hours for a glass of yellow vodka which she made, as Godfrey Goodwin says, 'in her fantastic kitchen with its falling roof, sorcerer's tins and jars and emotionally disturbed pigeons'.

After I had knocked on her door several times, for the bell never worked, Auntie would appear, as always heavily made up, her hair awry, chaotically put together in bits and pieces of clothing. 'Come in, Shirinaki, my darling child,' she'd say, leading me into the living room, 'and meet our great poet/prize-winning author.' At Aunt Aliye's, besides prominent artists, I met many aspiring ones, as well as several Robert College faculty members, who found her fascinating and appreciated her zany and bohemian ways. Some of them, like Goodwin and Sumner-Boyd, who were English teachers and writers themselves, often wrote about Aliye.

In his book *Strolling Through Istanbul*, published in 1974, Hilary Sumner-Boyd writes:

> Aliye's place has been the madcap centre of the local artistic scene, and her incredible apartment is forever cluttered with the unpublished authors, the unheard playwrights, and the unhung painters of Beyoğlu. There are those of us who would have Aliye's apartment declared a national monument, where she would reign for ever as Queen of old Pera.

Once we reached the living room, with the help of one of her guests Aunt Aliye would pour me a glass of yellow vodka from a five-gallon bottle which sat on a wooden crate next to Berger's piano. The bottle was covered wtih flower and animal cut-outs and had a shocking-pink taffeta bow at its neck. Over the piano hung a full-length portrait of Berger, playing his Stradivarius.

Overflowing ashtrays and half-empty beer and brandy bottles stood everywhere. As always, Aunt Aliye smoked and drank too much and lived in disarray, never letting the clock govern her actions. Neighbours across the courtyard reported seeing her in her small kitchen at three o'clock in the morning in the flimsiest of nightgowns, a bottle in one hand, the other cranking out etchings on an old-fashioned iron press that reminded me of the black scorpions I had seen in Baghdad.

She had always lived in complete confusion, but now that she was an established artist, particularly one who had been praised by leading European art critics, she did so with even more abandon than before. In the winter of 1954, shortly before my visit, the Yapı Kredi Bankası, as a public-relations effort, had sponsored an art competition to be judged by three luminaries of the art world, Sir Herbert Read, Lionel Venturi and Paul Fierens. Having decided to participate, Aliye purchased a large canvas, brushes and oilpaints. The painting, her first, which depicts a huge sun, swirling in thick ropes of paint, galloping across a landscape that is breaking up in demonic fury, won first prize. This created a furore in the art world. The established painters of Istanbul were incensed. They felt cheated and ridiculed by the judges. Although they accepted Aliye as a good etcher, they did not consider her, rightly so, a painter. This extraordinary story added to her earlier notoriety, and made her even more of an institution.

That summer, I also visited my dear Uncle Suat, who at the time was working for a wealthy Black Sea shipping magnate. When he worked for someone, Suat became his employer's personal friend, companion, confidant, drinking partner and advisor, particularly on matters of etiquette and on how to enjoy one's life to the fullest. His employers became so attached and dependent on him that they demanded his constant company, usurping his personal time. In Vienna Willi Hamburger, the ex-Abwehr agent who had known Suat so well, told me, 'Suat was an exceptional man, for he gave so much of himself to other people and cared so deeply and had so much empathy for his friends, making their problems his. They often took advantage of him and abused his generosity. Even when they underpaid him for his services, he was too much of a gentleman to point it out. He gave much more than he ever received.'

As Aunt Ayşe had been saddened by not being able to use the old house in Büyükada, Uncle Ahmet had found her an ugly stone house directly on the sea, not far from the Büyükada ferry landing, which he had bought as a bargain. For me the house had only two assets. First, we could swim from its pier. Second, to reach it, one walked along a lovely, tree-shaded street through a charming market, lined on both sides with artistic displays of fruit and vegetables. Glad that I still had a foothold on the island, I of course visited Aunt Ayşe for a few days and, although Erdem was at that time still in Chicago, I saw Nermidil, who was now married to an engineering professor and had an adorable little son. I so wished that mine had survived.

That summer, although I was married, men fell all over me and the gossip columnists had a hot new subject to write about. In her flowery style, Adelet Cimcoz, the Louella Parsons of Turkey, said, 'A comet has appeared in our skies, and her tail brushes everyone with star dust.' When, at a formal dinner dance at the Moda Club, I took off my silver sandals and tossed them into the Marmara Sea to dance barefoot, she called me 'the barefoot contessa'. Never had I felt so sought after, so appreciated, indulged, fêted and celebrated.

In this fairy-tale I was living, there had to be a 'prince charming', and he arrived one hot July evening, a dark, husky Turk, a good-looking bachelor in his early forties who was brought by a friend to a supper I gave.

The 'prince' tried several times to dance with me, but other men kept cutting in, and he did not have a chance. As he stood at the edge of the dance floor, I could feel his frustration, for his dark, brooding eyes never left me the entire evening.

When the party was about to end and most of the guests were departing, he came over to me and said, 'Why don't you and the rest of your friends come to my house on the Marmara for a moon-light swim and a nightcap?'

Everyone liked his suggestion and cheered. As we made our way to the garden gate where the cars were parked, the 'prince' grabbed my hand and pulled me into his Jaguar convertible, and, before anyone else had a chance to get into the car, he sped away. With the other cars following at a distance, we drove to a hill-top called Çamlıca, a place famous for its extraordinary panoramic views of Istanbul and the straits. When I saw the Bosphorus shimmering like a silver ribbon under the full moon and the city, with its domes and minarets like a black cut-out silhouetted against the sky, I cried dramatically, 'This view is breathtaking. I want to die right here and now to eternalize this moment.'

Reaching out and pulling me roughly into his arms, the 'prince' kissed me so fervently that I had to push him away in order to breathe. 'I am sorry,' he said. 'I could not help myself.'

'By the way,' I asked, looking up at his big, black, smouldering eyes, 'what is your name?'

'My name is Şehsuvar,' he replied.

'Şehsuvar,' I mused. 'What an unusual name! What does it mean?'

'Commander of the Cavalry,' he replied, flashing a smile and revealing a beautiful set of teeth.

'But who *are* you?' I asked, intrigued. 'What do you do?'

'I am an electrical engineer and contractor. I bring electricity to the Anatolian villages.'

'You must feel like a magician when the villagers see their bulbs light up for the first time.'

'Yes,' he replied, 'it is a rewarding experience. You should see how they clap and cheer.'

When Şehsuvar drove me home after a long evening of swimming in the Marmara and drinking on his moonlit terrace, I found Father waiting up for me. He was furious, and scolded me as if I were a teenager returning from her first date.

That summer, unknown to Father, I managed to see Şehsuvar a few more times. Fatma encouraged these secret rendezvous, knowing how happy Father would be if I lived in Istanbul and hoping that Şehsuvar would sweep me off my feet so that I'd leave Wesley and America, marry Şehsuvar and settle back there.

By mid-August, alas, it was time for me to leave for London, where Mother wanted me to spend a couple of weeks with her before returning to New York. Although I wished I could tell her that I wanted to stay in Istanbul, I dared not, as she would never have forgiven me. The idyll was over, and reality stared me in the face like a bleak lunar landscape. So, tearing myself away, I left. As the ship sailed out of Istanbul, I longed for all I was leaving behind.

My visit with Mother was most unsatisfactory. At first, as always, she was delighted to see me and to hear all the news of the family. As I kept telling her about the summer and all its pleasures, however, in spite of my efforts she became aware that I would rather have been in my stepmother's country house than with her. She felt piqued, annoyed and somewhat jealous. This spoiled our time together, and I felt that she was relieved to see me go.

Back in New York, all I could think of was finding a way to return to Turkey. The taste of the past summer lingered on my palate, and I wanted more of the same. This time, however, I felt that if I went I would not return, and that frightened me. Did I really want to leave Wes? Did I want to live with my father in Turkey? Did I want to give up my aspirations to be an actress in the United States? A holiday was one thing; changing one's life totally was another. Trying to sort out my conflicting emotions, I even consulted a psychiatrist, who was of no help. Wes knew I was in a dilemma but did not try to influence me one way or another. That was his way of dealing with the situation.

After wavering all winter, I finally decided not to go to Istanbul, and, to prove that I was serious, I went to look for a modelling position. The first job I applied to, on Seventh Avenue, had already been filled; for the second I was a bit too tall. At the third wholesale house a salesman handed me a dress. 'Put this on,' he said and, pointing at the showroom added, 'and model it for the boss.' As I entered, I saw a small, stocky, grey-haired man seated in the middle of the large, mirrored room, having his shoes shined and reading a tabloid, a cigar held between his stubby fingers. He did not acknowledge my presence. I walked up and stood directly in front of him. After what seemed an eternity, he slowly lifted his head from the paper, took a quick look at the lower part of my body, and mumbled, 'Hips are too wide.' Then, without ever looking me in the face, he dismissed me with a wave of the hand as if he were chasing away a fly.

I felt squashed like a bug underfoot. Tears welled in my eyes and, running to the dressing room, I ripped off the dress, threw on my clothes and walked out, slamming the door behind me. The rude behaviour of one man at that particular time in my life was the drop that made my cup overflow. It is frightening to realize that an important turn in one's life can be triggered by such a trivial occurrence. I often wonder what would have happened if I had succeeded in getting one of those jobs.

That night I announced to Wes that I needed to go back to Turkey. 'I warn you, darling,' I told him, 'this time I may not return.'

'If that is what you need, go ahead,' said Wes, ignoring my threat. 'I'll get a job in summer stock, and we'll be together again in September.' Then, hugging me, he added, 'You know I love you baby. I'll always be here for you.'

Why did he have to be so understanding? Why could he not put his foot down and refuse to let me go? Why couldn't he tell me to go to hell?

20

Too Many Cooks

Once back in Istanbul, I was again showered with affection and attention. Şehsuvar's jubilant welcome surprised me, for I had thought that our brief affair of the previous year had simply been a summer escapade. Since we had not corresponded, I was unaware that I had made such an impression on him. As for me, I was drawn to him even more than the summer before. His hold on me was electric. The moment he touched me, as if charged, my whole body vibrated. This must be a '*question de peau*', I thought, remembering my father's belief in the erotic significance of skins. With a complete disregard of decorum, we embarked on an intense affair.

Tongues wagged, and people speculated. 'Obviously Shirin returned to Istanbul for Şehsuvar,' they said, 'but will he marry her?' 'Will she, on the other hand, leave America and her handsome, "film-star" husband for him?'

Looking discreetly the other way, Father pretended that nothing was happening, but my stepmother Fatma cheered me on. When she decided that the time was ripe and the moon was full, she gave a candlelight dinner in the garden of her lovely country home, to which she invited Şehsuvar and his divorced older sister Reyan, to whom he was devoted. It was the first time they were received by my family. Şehsuvar arrived with a magnificent gift for me – two large butterfly-shaped, diamond-studded, red enamel pins. Everyone knew that no Turkish man would give a woman that kind of valuable gift in front of her family unless he intended to marry her. Therefore we regarded the butterflies as an unspoken proposal.

Since my arrival in Istanbul, I had tried to explain in my many letters to Wes that for me our marriage was over and that I intended to stay in Turkey for good – in my country, with my family, my people. Wes refused to believe me. He convinced himself that I was going through a 'phase' and would get over it. When I begged him on the phone to give me a divorce, he still would not agree. Finally I had to be blunt and hurtful.

'I am in love with another man,' I cried into the phone. 'I want to marry him. Please give me a divorce.'

There was a long silence, and Wes hung up. Feeling his pain, I started to sob. My father, who was in the room, asked, amazed, 'Why are you sobbing, my daughter? *You* chose to leave him.' I cried harder. 'Women,' he muttered, shaking his beautiful mane of white hair. 'I thought I understood them.'

Once Wes gave me a statement of 'no contest', I hired a lawyer and, as there were no children and no financial considerations, we were promptly divorced in a Turkish court.

In January 1956, Şehsuvar and I were married in a civil ceremony and immediately left on our honeymoon, which ended up as a series of family visits. Our first stop was London, where Emir Zeid entertained us lavishly at the embassy. We then went to Paris so that Mother could meet my new husband. She was staying temporarily at her studio-apartment on the Rue de Grenelle and had just had a very successful exhibition at the Dina Vierny Gallery with the artists Poliakoff and Pichette. At the Paris studio she gave a little dinner for us, with food ordered from Fauchon, to which she reluctantly invited Nejad and his new Polish wife. Since mother and son were no longer on good terms, our little family get-together was strained. Moreover, I could tell that Mother did not take to Şehsuvar. He was not her type – a wealthy businessman, not an intellectual and not '*cultivé*'. I could not wait for the evening to end. From Paris we travelled to Florence to visit Şehsuvar's niece Esra, who was studying art history there, and when we returned to Istanbul we settled into his bachelor pad.

Despite the contractor's promises, the large stone house Şehsuvar and his sister Reyan were having built on the Marmara Sea had not yet been completed, and we had to spend our first summer in its two-bedroom, one-bathroom guest cottage. That would not have been a problem except for the fact that Esra, who had come from Florence for her summer holiday, and her ten-year-old brother Mehmet occupied the second room. As the house and property belonged equally to Şehsuvar and his sister, Reyan felt at liberty to have her children spend the summer there while she stayed with friends in Europe. Şehsuvar, who loved the children as his own, regarded their presence as normal, but I, although I was very fond of them, thought it peculiar that a bride of five months should have to play stepmother. Moreover, I found living in such close quarters uncomfortable and annoying. When we made love, we had to muffle our voices; once the little boy opened our shutters from the outside and caught us in the act.

What really spoiled the summer, though, was my second miscarriage. Like my American doctor, the Turkish gynaecologist did not ask for a blood test, and thus the reason for my miscarriage remained a mystery. Both Şehsuvar and I, who were looking forward eagerly to parenthood, were deeply disappointed.

Back at the flat that fall, what I enjoyed most about living in Istanbul was being able at any time of the day to drop in on the numerous members of my family – lunch at Father's, a cup of tea in Fureya's studio, a glass of yellow vodka in Aunt Aliye's wild home, or a whisky with darling Uncle Suat. To be able to share one's news, thoughts, joys and sorrows with one's loved ones without having to make appointments and consult calendars was a luxury I could never have had in the United States.

Soon I discovered that Şehsuvar was a jealous and possessive husband, so much so that when he went away on short business trips he did not allow me to go out at night, even with a group of friends. It seems incredible to me now that I put up with such restrictions and did not actually mind them. It was only in the summer of 1957, a year and a half after our marriage, when we moved into the big house with Şehsuvar's sister Reyan, her children and a staff of four, that trouble started brewing. That summer stands out in my memory as a nightmare in which everyone, myself most of all, acted impulsively, irrationally, stupidly and, in the end, destructively.

The house, instead of being built for two families with separate kitchens and entrances, had been designed as a big, one-family house with two separate bedroom wings for brother and sister. A hand-carved wooden walkway connected both wings across the cathedral-ceilinged living room. As Şehsuvar had not intended to marry, this arrangement suited his needs. His sister would run the house and be his hostess. Now, with me there, the problem soon arose as to who was going to be the mistress of the house. Instead of the three of us discussing the matter openly and logically beforehand, we let it become a bone of contention.

Even our Bolu cook was confused at receiving orders from both

Reyan and me. 'Who is the mistress here?' he shouted one day. 'Who am I supposed to take orders from? In our village we have a saying: "Two watermelons don't fit under one arm." '

Şehsuvar finally suggested I let Reyan run the house. 'Why do you want to bother your pretty head with household chores? Enjoy the summer and don't worry about anything,' he said. I liked running the house and going to the fruit and vegetable markets, but to keep the peace I acquiesced.

Peace, however, was the last thing I had that summer. The house and grounds were crowded continuously with Şehsuvar's and my family and friends, as well as Reyan's, Esra's and Mehmet's, who came to visit, swim or simply watch the moonlight on the Marmara. They stayed for lunch, tea, dinner and a nightcap. I quickly realized that if one has a house on the water in Istanbul, one never has a moment of privacy.

The household was loaded even more by the arrival in Istanbul of young King Faisal II of Iraq and my brother Raad, who was spending his holidays from Cambridge with his cousin. While Emir Zeid went from London to Baghdad to govern the nation once more as acting regent, King Faisal and his immediate family had decided to holiday in Istanbul. His 500-ton yacht *Aliye*, named after his late mother, was anchored in the Bosphorus, and there the royal family and Raad took up residence.

Shortly after their arrival, I invited Faisal and Raad to spend the day at our house. They came in a Chris-Craft followed by the king's guards and Turkish security forces in two other motorboats. We prepared a luncheon on the patio under the pine trees and invited some of Esra's girlfriends. It was one of those bright, blue, breezy June days. Faisal and Raad, both in their early twenties, enjoyed swimming and water-skiing from our dock, and also the company of the pretty Turkish girls in bathing suits. The day was a great success, and the young king had a wonderful time. To see this shy, retiring, sweet young man, who had suffered under the restrictions of his position ever since the age of four, relax and enjoy himself like any other young man pleased me no end.

As Faisal considered me family, he felt free to drop in without protocol at any time, and from then on did so almost every other day. It was easy for him to come, for he could jump into his Chris-Craft in a bathing suit and be there in fifteen minutes, and our house offered many attractions.

Another regular visitor that extraordinary summer was Bereket, grandson of the maharajah of Hyderabad. He was also spending the summer holiday from school in England with his brother and mother, the formidable, falcon-like Princess Dürrüşehvar, daughter of the last Ottoman sultan, Vahdettin. As he was a friend of King Faisal and also loved to water-ski, Bereket came to the house often, always bringing his girlfriend. Our niece Esra had already met him and had become infatuated with him; yet she graciously welcomed him and his girlfriend and encouraged their visits.

The already crowded household was overrun with all these young-sters, not to mention the guards and security people, and the kitchen had to be ready at all times to serve at least twenty extra mouths. However, my sister-in-law Reyan, who was flattered that the king chose to come to our house despite the many other invitations he was receiving, and seemed to be interested in her daughter Esra, did not mind the extra work at all.

Taller than Faisal, Esra had a lovely figure and long, shapely legs. Auburn hair which fell loosely to her shoulders framed a rather wide face with high cheekbones. Her warm, luminous smile was charming. What I found most attractive about her was her gentle and agreeable personality. She bent with the breezes like the willow tree on our terrace, and I could clearly see that Faisal was taken by her. Reyan was thrilled, and naturally hoped that he might marry her and make her queen of Iraq. Instead of letting her live out her fantasy and allowing events to take their course, I made the enormous mistake of discouraging her and warned her not to be hopeful. 'Faisal will never marry Esra,' I said.

I knew that King Faisal was expected to marry Princess Fazila of Egypt. She was the daughter of Prince Mehmet Ali and his much younger wife, the Ottoman Princess Hanzade, whom many people regarded as the most beautiful woman they had ever seen. Fazila and her family were expected to arrive in Istanbul at the end of the summer for the official announcement of her engagement to King Faisal.

Emir Abdullilah, who since Faisal's majority had been named crown prince, had hand-picked Fazila to be the queen of Iraq. Since King Ghazi's death, Emir Abdullilah had been Faisal's father figure and, especially since the loss to cancer of his mother, Queen Aliye, his only parent. Since he never failed to follow his uncle's advice, I doubted that the young king would marry Esra over the girl his uncle had picked.

Although I told Reyan all this, she still remained hopeful, for she believed that if the king loved Esra he would marry her. Perhaps she was right. Of course she expected me to encourage the union by praising Esra to the members of the royal family, with whom she knew I was very close. But as I did not share her hopes and illusions and showed no enthusiasm, she convinced herself that I did not want Esra to be queen. She went so far as to believe that I had spoken badly of Esra to the family, and she complained about this to Şehsuvar. Both Reyan and Esra began to regard me as their enemy, and the situation in the household became intolerable, full of Byzantine intrigue and accusations which I was unable to handle. Meanwhile, the eternal crowd scene continued with parties and moonlight dances on the terrace. I felt trapped.

Just about then Mother arrived from London and settled in a hotel on the Black Sea which was at least an hour and a half by car and ferry from my house. To the other strains of the summer were added her demands.

In her honour, on 14 July, Bastille Day, we gave a large luncheon in the garden, to which we invited the king and his aunts, Bereket, his mother Princess Dürrüşehvar, whom Mother knew well from London, Bereket's girlfriend, some of the Shakirs and many of Esra's young friends. Like all summer luncheons in Istanbul, it turned out to be an all-day affair.

If at that luncheon there had been a clairvoyant, he might have predicted some unbelievable events.

To me he would have said, 'A year from today, Shirin, you will be opening in a play at the Court Theater in Beloit, Wisconsin.' I would have replied, 'Impossible! I am married to a man I love; I have a beautiful home in Istanbul, and why should I be in Beloit? That is something of the past.'

He then would have turned to Mother and said, 'You, Nissa, will be living in your villa in Ischia.' 'Ischia!' Mother would have exclaimed. 'Where is that? How can I be living in a place I don't know exists?'

'And your husband, who is now acting regent in Baghdad, will never set foot on Iraqi soil again.' 'Ridiculous!' Mother would have retorted.

The soothsayer then would have whispered to Esra, 'Don't take

Bereket's attachment to his girlfriend seriously. It is *you* he will marry, and *you* will become maharani of Hyderabad,' and she would have said, 'How could that possibly be? At the end of the summer I'll return to Florence, and Bereket will go back to school in England. We will probably never see each other again.'

Then the mystic would point at my cousin Erdem and his fiancée Gökçen and say, 'Your next post, Erdem, will be secretary at the Turkish Embassy in London, and you, Gökçen, will be expecting a son whom you will name Ahmet.'

Finally the fortune-teller would have turned to King Faisal and, in a grave voice said, 'And you, young man, on this very day next year, will be mortally wounded.'

All these incredible events came to pass.

An absurd incident at Erdem's wedding on 26 July triggered a series of events which led to the dissolution of my marriage. Tipsy Aunt Aliye, whom Şehsuvar considered frumpy and daffy, reprimanded him in front of others for some minor discourtesy. Her tactless remarks infuriated him. That night after the wedding, in the privacy of our bedroom, Şehsuvar and I had a painful confrontation which had nothing to do with our personal relationship – we were still very much in love – but only with each other's families. As if we were their defence lawyers, we took stands and hurled insults and accusations at each other. When Şehsuvar charged me with trying to prevent Esra's marriage to King Faisal, I exploded.

Early the next morning I had the chauffeur drive me to Mother and told her that my nerves were shot and that I could not stand that nightmarish household any more. Seeing me so distraught, without considering the consequences, Mother decided immediately to change her plans and take me to the Italian Riviera for the rest of the summer so that I could get away from it all.

In such a situation most families try to appease, to reason, to compromise and work things out if possible. My family did the exact opposite. 'Why should Shirin put up with this?' they declared, and, without thinking of my best interests, applauded Mother's decision. Of course the wise thing for me to have done would have been not to go to Mother, certainly not Mother, who could not tolerate seeing someone she loved unhappy. I should have left the house quietly for a time, thought things over rationally and eventually returned for a reconciliation. Instead, our departure was like a declaration of war. The gossip columnists announced that I had walked out on Şehsuvar, that I had cancelled a dinner dance we were to give, that my mother, the princess, was taking me to Italy and that it looked as if a divorce was imminent.

Just before we left, to make matters worse, Mother told the king and Raad 'not to set foot in *that* house again'. Reyan and Esra were furious, and Şehsuvar was humiliated and angered at my abrupt public departure as well as the hurt I had inflicted on his family. What fools we all were; most of all, me, *mea culpa*!

When we left in early August, the Shakirs as usual saw us off. Mother and I arrived at the Iraqi Embassy in Rome, only to discover that all the good resorts on the Italian Riviera were booked up. We then remembered Uncle Suat's shouted advice as we boarded our plane: 'If you can't get rooms on the Riviera, go to Ischia. It's a lovely island near Capri.' After several telephone calls, we found rooms in a second-class hotel in Ischia. A short ferry ride from Naples took us there, and we were pleasantly surprised, for the island, with its turquoise bays, oleander-lined cobblestone streets and horse carriages, reminded us of Büyükada.

In my condition, however, I could not enjoy what the island had to offer. I was upset, regretful, overwhelmed at what I had done, and fearful for the future. Mother at times was so frustrated at my obvious misery – for I think she too felt that we had acted rashly and illogically – that one night she went into the bathroom, sat on the toilet and, while furiously snipping her hair, complained, 'If you loved your husband so much, why did you come running to me like a madwoman? What did you expect me to do? I did what I thought you wanted, to help you get away from that house. You are almost blaming me for having brought you to Italy.'

'I'm sorry, Mother. I'm terribly sorry,' I kept saying, shedding tears. Although our going to Ischia at that particular time wrecked my marriage, ironically, it saved Emir Zeid's life.

In late August, as expected, King Faisal and Princess Fazila were engaged in Istanbul. The wedding was planned to take place in Baghdad in about a year, pending the completion of a new palace where Faisal intended to live with his bride. Emir Abdullilah suggested that Fazila, the future queen, meanwhile attend a finishing school in London, and her mother duly enrolled her in one.

On my return from Ischia to Istanbul, I knew there could be no reconciliation. Although Şehsuvar and I still loved each other and neither of us wanted a divorce, there had been too much hurt inflicted on both sides, the arrow had left the bow, and we could not back down. When I went to the house to collect my personal belongings, I saw Şehsuvar for the last time. 'I am cutting off my arm by letting you go,' he said, as he stood in the door of our bedroom, tears spouting from his big black eyes. As I was going down the stairs, weeping, I wished I would fall and break a leg so that I could not leave.

Giving Şehsuvar power of attorney so that he could start divorce proceedings, I left for the Iraqi Embassy in London, where I was expected to live the life of an ambassador's daughter, going to parties and receptions and helping Mother entertain. All that winter, however, because my marriage had ended so abruptly and so unnecessarily, and because I still loved Şehsuvar, I was depressed and miserable. A godsend was the presence in London of Erdem and Gökçen, for Erdem had been appointed secretary to the Turkish Embassy. To them I poured out my heart, which I could not do to my mother, for when she saw me pining after Şehsuvar, she became overwrought. Unable to mourn my loss but, instead, having to put up a good front for Mother was very difficult. I regard that period as one of the unhappiest of my life.

Poor Mother tried unsuccessfully to divert me. One morning she announced that at the annual reception for the diplomatic corps at Buckingham Palace she would present me to the queen. She then had her couturière make me a strapless white slipper-satin gown with a train. White satin shoes and long white kid gloves were purchased, and Mother gave me a strand of her pearls to wear. I looked like a virginal debutante! At the reception, the different ambassadors, their families and selected staff members stood in clusters along one wall of the enormous room. Queen Elizabeth, followed by many members of the royal family, walked slowly past us, shaking hands and making polite conversation, while the visitors bowed or curtsied. When Mother introduced me to the Duke of Gloucester, he asked, 'But my dear princess, where have you been hiding your daughter?' (My parents had already been in London for eleven years.) Not knowing what to say, Mother laughed. 'Ha, ha, ha, she has been travelling.' (She could hardly have said, 'She has been getting married and divorced,' for divorced young women were not supposed to be presented at court.)

Later, when the line had broken up and we had moved into another reception hall, I saw Emir Zeid in one corner talking to the prime minister, Harold Macmillan. When he noticed me, he called me over. 'This is my American daughter,' he said to Macmillan, whose mother was American, 'and she is an expert at American accents. Come on, Shirin, do a few for the prime minister.' To his amusement, I repeated the same lines in Southern, Midwestern and New York accents. As I was doing so, I noticed, right behind Mr Macmillan, seated on a bench, Winston Churchill, who was joined in a few minutes by Clement Attlee. There I was, standing in the midst of three British prime ministers! 'Photographers, where are you?' I thought, wishing that one could have materialized and recorded the moment for posterity.

In London that autumn we had several guests. Princess Hanzade stayed at the embassy while she visited her queen-to-be daughter, Fazila, at finishing school. So did Emir Abdullilah, the crown prince, in order to attend some political meetings and to visit his Savile Row tailor. At the time he was married to his third wife, the attractive daughter of a prominent Iraqi sheikh, and I helped him shop for her and his sisters. The emir and I had remained devoted cousins.

One morning, as I was passing Emir Zeid's study on the main floor, I heard voices. To my utter astonishment Emir Zeid was reprimanding Emir Abdullilah in Turkish. His use of Turkish surprised me, for he normally spoke Arabic with his nephew. I had never heard my stepfather speak so forcefully; he was actually shouting. Stopping dead in the marble hall, I could not help listening.

'Why does the future queen of Iraq have to go to a British finishing school?' Emir Zeid asked in an irate voice. 'Our people won't like that.'

'As long as she is going to be queen, I feel she should learn the correct demeanour. Who else but the British, who have had so many queens and have one now, can advise her better?' Emir Abdullilah replied, trying to make light of the matter.

'You seem to be oblivious of the anti-British sentiment that is sweeping the Arab world,' Emir Zeid continued. 'Don't you hear Nasser blasting his vitriol from every radio in town and calling the Hashemites "imperialist stooges"?'

'Please, Uncle, don't talk to me about that demagogue,' Abdullilah said in an angry tone.

'I don't understand why you are pursuing such a pro-British policy,' added Zeid, and I could almost see him shaking his head incredulously. 'We don't need *them*; they need *us*. They need our oil.' Emir Abdullilah was silent, and Zeid continued, 'You have embarked on a collision course and, if you don't watch out, some army colonel, gun in hand, will confront you.'

'Come on, Uncle,' the prince scoffed in a cold, controlled voice, 'you are exaggerating. Besides, why make such a fuss over a girl's schooling?'

When I heard a chair scrape, I ran in fear of being caught eavesdropping.

As another diversion, Mother suggested that, for my thirty-second birthday, I give a party at the embassy, and I invited everyone who had entertained me in London. One of the guests was Princess Dürrüşehvar, who lived across the street from us in Hyderabad House. When she told me that Esra had left Florence and was now studying art history in London, which I had not known, and that her son Bereket was seeing her, I was happy for Esra. 'She got what she wanted,' I thought. 'Clever girl.' Esra eventually married Bereket and became the maharani of Hyderabad.

Discouraged at my continuous moping and the loss of my old *joie de vivre*, Mother finally decided that a trip to the States, where I could see my friends and visit my old haunts, would do me good and help me forget Şehsuvar. Accordingly, she gave me a mink stole and a plane ticket and sent me packing.

In New York, while I was staying with my dear old Turkish friends, the Korles (he later became chief of protocol at the UN), I received a phone-call from Kirk Denmark, the director of the Court Theater in Beloit, Wisconsin, where I had made my theatrical début seven years before. Denmark wanted me to be his leading lady in the summer season of 1958. I seized the opportunity, for I knew that work would be the best thing for me.

That spring, after my departure for the States, Mother returned to Ischia, with which she had been so charmed, and purchased a summer house which she named the Villa Fahrelnissa. Once back in London, 'Enough is enough!' she said to Emir Zeid. 'Every summer you go to Baghdad and work in that sweltering heat as acting regent while your nephews go on holiday. You have done more than necessary for your family. This summer bow out, and let us enjoy our new home together. Raad has promised to spend his summer holiday with us.' Emir Zeid acquiesced.

After giving a sumptuous reception at the embassy to celebrate King Faisal's twenty-third birthday, my parents and Raad left for their new villa in Ischia. They looked forward to a blue-skyed, sunny, Mediterranean summer. It turned out to be a bloody one.

21

The Show Must Go On

The morning of 14 July 1958, I was awakened by a rapping on my ground-floor window. Groggy, I heard the sharp knocks but could not bring myself fully awake. The dress rehearsal of Charles Morgan's *The River Line*, in which I played a French Resistance leader during World War II, had lasted until late the previous night, and I had collapsed into bed, exhausted from a full day and evening of rehearsals. When I finally managed to open my eyes and look out, I saw Mrs Gage, a trustee of the Court Theater, gesticulating and beckoning me to open the window. She looked alarmed. When I raised the sash, her words poured out.

'There has been a military coup in Iraq. The crown prince has been assassinated, and many members of the royal family have been killed. It was on the early-morning news.'

An excruciating pain pierced my chest as if someone had plunged a spear into it. I tried but could not utter a word. I fell back into my bed, curled up in a foetal position, and buried myself under the covers. Mrs Gage muttered a few more words, 'I am sorry to be the bearer of bad news, but I thought you should know . . .' and, realizing there was nothing she could do for me, left.

The news was not of a revolution in some far-away land and the killing of its leaders; it was about people I loved like brothers and sisters and aunts and uncles, the man with whom I had been in love as a young girl. My tears soaked the bed.

Suddenly I thought, 'Oh, my God, what has become of Faisal? Mrs Gage did not mention anything about the young king. I must find out,' and leapt out of bed. Hastily, I stepped into a pair of blue jeans and threw on a T-shirt. Since there was only a coin telephone in the hall of my building, I ran to the director's home to try to call Ischia. 'Thank Allah, Emir Zeid and Raad are not in Baghdad,' I thought as I ran down the path. 'They would have been killed too. How fortunate that Mother bought the villa in Ischia! Kismet!'

When I reached the director's house, he said, 'Come in. Come in. I've heard the terrible news. You must be very upset. Do you want me to excuse you from this morning's rehearsal? I can always work with the other actors.'

'How can you? I am in practically all the scenes. No, no. Let us hold the rehearsals as scheduled. Only loan me your transistor radio which I'll keep in the green room and listen to the news as it comes in during breaks. Just give me a few more breaks than usual,' I replied.

Then I immediately turned on his radio and heard the announcer say, '. . . his whereabouts are not known. There are rumours he is still alive. According to unofficial reports, soldiers wrapped his wounded body in a carpet and removed him from the scene of carnage.'

'That must be Faisal,' I thought. 'Please, please let him live!'

I picked up the receiver and asked the international operator to ring the Café Maria in the little village of Forio in Ischia. 'Damn,' I thought, 'why does Mother always have to be different? Why can't she have a phone like everyone else?' As in Büyükdere, she had decided not to have one in the villa so that people would not disturb her, particularly when she painted. In case of emergency, one called the café and had them dispatch a messenger to the villa.

Once the connection was established with the Café Maria, I managed in my non-existent Italian to make myself understood.

'Si, si, signora,' said the café owner, 'Principe Raad verra qui e lei lo telefonera tra un hora.' I hung up and waited for the hour to pass.

'Here, have a cup of coffee,' said Kirk, handing me a mug. 'Do you think this will affect your parents?' he asked innocently.

'How naive Americans are!' I thought to myself. 'How could he ask me such a question?'

'Of course,' I replied, nonplussed. 'Let alone the killing of the family, if the coup is successful, the army will take over and there will be no royal kingdom of Iraq. That means my stepfather will be a member of the royal family in exile – jobless, stateless and homeless. He will probably lose all his property in Iraq. It will all be seized by the new government.'

'That is very serious,' Kirk replied with concern. 'And what will you do when the season is over?'

'I don't know,' I replied. 'Yes, where will I go?' I thought. My room at the embassy flashed in front of my eyes. I probably would never see it again. I never did.

An hour had gone by. I picked up the receiver and called Ischia.

'*Si, si, signora, el Principe e qui,*' said the café owner and passed the receiver to Raad.

'Raad, my darling brother, how are you all?' I asked, my voice breaking with emotion. 'The radio just announced that Faisal may still be alive,' I added, knowing how much this meant to him.

'I doubt it,' he replied in a muffled voice, as if telling me a state secret. 'It is bad, *abla*, very bad!'

'How did you find out?' I asked.

'One of the neighbours came and told Father there had been a military coup in Iraq. At first he did not take it so seriously; there have been coups before. Then we turned on the radio and television and heard of the killings. Mother screamed and fainted and hasn't stopped crying since. She prays for Faisal to live. "You will live, Faisal," she says. "You *will* live." Father is like a zombie. He won't even talk. What a terrible, awful tragedy, *abla*! Why did they have to kill them? Why kill all those innocent people? They were on their way to Turkey. The plane was waiting. Why didn't they let them go?'

Tears poured from my eyes. I felt so deeply sorry for my family. I ached, hurt and bled for them. 'A mob out of control is worse than the wildest beast,' I said. 'Tell Mother I would have jumped on a plane and come to be with you, but I cannot leave. Perhaps she won't understand, but try to explain to her that the show must go on. Remember, our parents are in shock now, but once the magnitude of the tragedy sinks in they will be totally devastated. You are the only one there who can help them. Be strong!'

'I'll try, *abla*. I promise I'll try,' he said, his voice quivering.

'I love you, Raad. Take care. I will call again tomorrow at this time,' I added and hung up.

That afternoon, when we took a break during rehearsal, I heard on the radio that the body of Emir Abdullilah, the crown prince, had been mutilated, his arms and legs cut off, and that the mob had dragged his torso through the streets of Baghdad. At that I became violently ill and vomited all over the green room. Kirk ran in and said, 'Come on, Shirin, go home and rest. No more rehearsing for you,' and led me to the exit door.

A few hours later, my eyes bloodshot from crying, and my stomach aching from retching, we opened *The River Line*. But the drama we were performing was tame compared to the tragedies taking place on the streets of Baghdad.

Two days later it was reported that King Faisal II, aged twenty-three, had died of his wounds, although the mutinous soldiers had tried to save him at the last minute.

The leaders of the coup, Brigadier Kassim and Colonel Arif, established a new revolutionary government and declared Iraq a republic. Kassim became its first president and Arif his deputy. Soon, however, they disagreed, and in 1963 in another military coup Arif had Kassim assassinated and assumed the presidency himself. Not long after, Arif perished in a plane crash. Was that the will of Allah or the hand of man? We shall never know.

Soon after the coup, Emir Zeid received a caller in Ischia, the Iraqi ambassador in Rome, who told him to go to London to empty the embassy of all personal possessions. The new government would give him only twenty-four hours to accomplish the task. He immediately took the helicopter to Naples and from there the plane to London. Once at the embassy he hurriedly packed all our belongings into trunks and suitcases, while some members of the staff who had already pledged allegiance to the new 'republic of Iraq' (the king is dead, long live the king) watched him. They were making sure that he did not take anything that belonged to the government. It was a humiliating and demeaning experience. Each time I read the letter he wrote my mother after the packing was completed, I wince. 'Nissa,' he concludes, 'clearing your studio was some job! So many paints and brushes, books, papers and clippings, not to mention all the finished and unfinished canvases. I tried my best. The whole thing was a nightmare.'

When Mother and Raad returned to London, Emir Zeid leased a partly furnished flat in Oakwood Court. Mother bought linens and towels, pots and pans, and set up a new household as best she could. She felt so deeply sorry for Emir Zeid – a man who had fought for Arab independence only to have his family slaughtered and his country taken over by a military dictator – that, for the first time, she put his well-being ahead of her own. 'I am going to be a good wife and take care of Zeid,' she vowed. 'My priority is my husband,

and I am not going to paint any more.' Rising to the occasion, as always, in the dismal new apartment, she entered the kitchen and, at the age of fifty-seven, cooked her first meal.

In mid-December I bought a multitude of little gifts, wrapped them elaborately with lots of satin ribbons – Mother always loved ribbons – and set off for London. I knew that my first meeting with my parents after the Iraqi tragedy was going to be a difficult and emotional one.

When I arrived at the London airport late at night – of course, no car or chauffeur to meet me – I went by taxi to Oakwood Court. It was a huge, gloomy, Victorian, red-brick apartment complex, dark and very quiet, with no doorman or porter to help me with my luggage. Putting all my things in the lift, I pressed the button for the top floor. When I rang the doorbell of my parents' flat, no one answered. Nothing happened, in spite of frequent ringing and banging on the door. Mother had probably removed her hearing aid, and Emir Zeid was, no doubt, in a deep sleep. I returned to the ground floor in search of a porter or anybody who could call the flat, but there was no one there. I went back up and knocked once more. Nothing! What was I to do? Would I have to go to a hotel and come back the next morning? Where could I find a taxi that late at night? The main street was at some distance.

As I stood in front of the door trying to figure out what my next move would be, I noticed a window to my right that led to a fire escape. Opening it, I stepped out and walked as far as I could until I came to another window. There was Mother, asleep in bed with all the lights on. If I knocked, would she hear me? After I had stood there on the fire escape for some time, Mother suddenly turned and reached for a bottle of Vichy water on her bedside table and, by some miracle, saw me. I cannot begin to describe her expression. Jumping out of bed like a porpoise, she came to the window, gesticulating wildly and sending me kisses. She then signalled me to go back to the front door. When it finally opened, there in the small hall stood my mother in her nightdress and Emir Zeid in pyjamas. 'Oh, forgive us, your plane was so late we fell asleep waiting for you,' Mother said as she hugged me. We kissed and cried and held on to one another for a long time.

Next morning in the living room, an ordinary square room with ordinary furniture at the end of the longest and darkest corridor I ever saw, I gave them my gifts. As they opened them, Mother said,

'Oh, Shirin, Shirinaki, you arrived just like Santa Claus, and from the rooftop, too!'

We had lunch in the kitchen. Mother served me a Scotch roast with a marvellous port sauce, and I ate with pleasure the first meal she had ever cooked for me. It was delicious. After lunch Emir Zeid started to wash the dishes at the sink. When I jumped up to help him, Mother signalled me to sit down. Once the dishes were done, Emir Zeid took his pipe and newspaper and returned to his room. Mother then rewashed the dishes. 'He likes to feel he is helping, so I let him do it,' she said. It was touching to see how they had already settled into a retired couple's routine. While Mother did the cooking, Emir Zeid carried in her afternoon tea tray and her hot-water bottle and put out the rubbish.

Although at first they had hired cleaning women, Mother could not tolerate any of them, and they ended up with a gay boy, an aspiring opera singer, who became their devoted friend and servant. During this period my parents saw very few people. I don't quite know whether all their friends in the diplomatic and social circles 'evaporated' or whether they chose not to see anyone. All I know is that, during the month I was there, no one came except Erdem and his wife, bringing their baby Ahmet, for Emir Zeid loved the way the boy kicked. On weekends, of course, Raad came from Cambridge and, occasionally, so did Emir Hassan, now the crown prince of Jordan, from Harrow. On the whole they lived a quiet life, spending their evenings watching television.

At night I snuggled with Mother in her bed and we talked of the terrible events which had taken place in Iraq. What seemed to pain her most was the destiny of the young king.

'Imagine,' she would say, shaking her head incredulously, 'at the age of four he lost his father. At fourteen he lost his mother, and at twenty-three he was assassinated. What a destiny!'

Then it was my turn to moan. 'How could they do that to Emir Abdullilah? Like rabid dogs they went after his corpse. Every time I think of it, rage possesses me. And Mother,' I'd say, 'I feel so terrible, so disgusted, so sick! How are we ever going to forget?'

'We will never forget. We'll learn to live with it, and time will help,' she replied wisely and hugged me tightly. We lay in each other's arms until one of us fell asleep.

What I admired most about Mother at this time is that she never complained or sentimentalized about the past. 'If Zeid were still ambassador', 'If he had not lost his fortune', 'If Iraq were still a kingdom' – these were phrases she never used.

In a diary covering the period after the coup, I found a very revealing and, to me, touching entry written in English and dated 14 February 1959. The piece, which is entitled 'I Decided to Re-create my Happiness', shows how unhappy Mother really had been for those eight months and how she was trying consciously to remake herself into a happy person:

This morning at dawn I decided to become a happy human being. It was six o'clock in the morning, and I lay in bed afraid to open my eyes, afraid to face the new day and all the days to come. It was cold outside, and I felt warm and secure under my down comforter. I lay in the dark, racking my brain as to how to remake myself. How was I going to bring myself to go out? And why should I go out? I am afraid to leave my husband alone. Maybe it is because of this that I do not want to go out, for he would be alone. He has no occupation, no work, nobody to talk to, to be with. He has no country.

Then, in an abrupt shift, she continues:

And the cleaning lady left yesterday in a huff, without saying goodbye. Was I rude to her? Did I scold her too much? What if she doesn't return? Oh, she must and, when she does, I will be nice and charming to her. I will welcome her with a smile.

I got up and turned on all the lights in my room and in the long corridor. I then went to the kitchen and pulled open the curtains to let the morning light in. When Mrs Springle arrived, I threw my arms around her and kissed her.

'You seem to be quite chipper this morning, Ma'am,' she said sourly.

'Yes, Mrs Springle,' I replied smiling. 'I am quite awake and feel great.'

Reconfirming her decision, she then adds:

Well, after all, I have decided to be a happy person. Therefore, everything must be pleasant, peaceful and comfortable, and I will be grateful for everything, and I will smile. It is only eight o'clock, and Mrs Springle is pushing the Hoover. The vigorous sound in the corridor pleases me. I like the noise it makes. But then she pulled the plug and there is silence again. I must reconstruct myself, atom by atom, to be happy, happy, happy.

But scarcely does she allow herself to pen these lines when suddenly her handwriting changes and in bold, black underlined words she writes: '*Yes, my poor, beloved Faisal, this little darling king, KILLED, KILLED, KILLED, I tell you!*'

The pain that lay at the bottom of her being had spilled out like a monster rising from the bowels of the sea.

After the coup Emir Zeid was a broken man, for he had lost all faith and hope in the Arab world. One morning while reading his paper, when he saw me come into the room, he lifted his head and said bitterly, 'The Arabs will agree on one thing only, in *not* uniting. Think of the power they would have if they did. All they do is bicker and plot against each other.' Another morning I caught a glimpse of him sitting in an armchair, staring at the wall. He had such a pained expression! God only knows what thoughts were going through his mind. Raad and I believe that if Mother had not literally enveloped Emir Zeid with tender, loving care, he would never have survived.

At that time Raad was a roly-poly young man of twenty-two. He had taken after his father in every respect. Like Emir Zeid he was unambitious, modest and self-effacing, had absolutely no concept of money and gave material things no importance. All he wanted was to serve and do good. The killing of his aunts and cousins deeply affected him, particularly that of King Faisal, his childhood friend whom he had loved like a brother.

In addition to the loss of his family, he was desolate at no longer having a country. One day when we were alone, he said to me, '*Abla*, I have no country. I am stateless. What am I going to do?'

My heart went out to him. Yes, what was he going to do? At Cambridge he had not studied for a profession. Like all Arab princes who get a good English education, he had hoped to work for the government in some capacity.

'You have Turkey,' I said reassuringly. 'Regard it as your country. After all, your mother is Turkish, and so was Emir Zeid's mother. You can easily get a Turkish passport.'

'It is not a question of passports,' he replied, and I was sorry to have made the suggestion, for he had meant something that went much deeper than a document. Although Raad was three-quarters Turkish, he regarded himself as an Arab and, above all, a Hashemite and felt the weight of his position.

'*Abla*, all I wanted was to serve my people,' he added in a sad voice.

'Poor boy,' I thought, 'how will you ever be able to serve your people when you have none?'

As Mother continued to take care of Emir Zeid and to work in the kitchen, the chicken and turkey bones she handled, their different shapes and sizes, intrigued her, and she started to clean, polish and collect them. One day she picked up a brush and casually painted one and then another and another with china ink. Finally she immersed the painted bones in coloured plastics, creating small and large pieces of sculpture which she called 'paleochrystalos'. Some of these she mounted on revolving discs, and others she had back-lighted. They became her toys and her joy. Her need to create, which she had tried to suppress in order to be 'a good wife', had found its way out through the kitchen.

Eventually, Emir Zeid encouraged her to paint again and to go to Paris. Not wanting to leave him alone in the London flat, Nissa went rarely, but when she did, living in Paris and seeing her friends in the art world – the eminent art critic Charles Estienne and the gallery owner Dina Vierny – lifted her spirits. Dina Vierny, who had been the sculptor Aristide Maillol's model, lived in a farmhouse outside Paris, and Mother, who loved her, went there to visit. They would sit in Dina's marvellous country kitchen and talk of art. In 1955 Nissa had exhibited at the Vierny Gallery, and now Dina encouraged her to work hard to prepare for a bigger show.

What really saved my family after the Iraqi tragedy was the Ischia house. After their monotonous winters in the dark, gloomy London flat, the Mediterranean sun and ambience were a most salutary change. The Ischia villa, with its huge stone roof terraces, where one could simultaneously see the sun setting into the sea and the moon rising behind the mountain, had great charm. Mother hired a local couple from the village to do the housework. As the villa had comfortable guest quarters with private patios, my parents, who wanted and needed companionship, often had visitors. Over the next several years, all the Shakirs came for extended stays and took advantage of the mud baths which were a feature of the volcanic island. Even Zeid's old Oxford classmate, whom he had not seen for years, Israel Treiman, came from St Louis to visit. In an article in the *Los Angeles Times* after Zeid's death, entitled '*Shalom*, Zeid', he wrote at length about the idyllic week he had spent at the villa. Eventually Mother purchased a small dory with an outboard motor, and she and Emir Zeid went on excursions, poking into bays and caves and visiting the different villages of the island. For Raad they bought a Vespa, with which he sped around, ogling the pretty Italian girls. Sometimes when I visited I sat behind him, and we toured the island or went to those marvellous open-air night clubs where Italian crooners sang the most romantic songs.

Apparently the Italian *signorinas* Raad dated in Ischia had not seriously interested him, for one spring day in 1963 he announced to Mother that he intended to marry a Swedish girl he had met while she was taking a special English course at Cambridge. Mother was taken aback. How could Raad, her beloved son, marry some ordinary Swede? What about the lovely Hashemite cousin they expected him to marry? What about the beautiful Turkish girls of good family whom she knew and whom even I had lined up as prospective brides? Although Mother was terribly disappointed in Raad's choice, she consented, and Raad and Margareta Lind were married that summer in Sweden at her parents' home. Mother and Emir Zeid were unable to attend; at the time, going to Sweden from Ischia seemed too complicated to them.

So the newly-weds, instead of going on a honeymoon, came to Ischia, and Mother gave a party in their honour, the first since King Faisal's birthday party in London five years before. With her usual creativity, she decorated the villa, spreading Bukhara rugs on the tile floors of the balconies, where Japanese lanterns had been hung and where big pillows were strewn on the parapets of the low balcony walls for the guests to sit on while they enjoyed the views on all sides of the house. To this reception Mother invited everyone, from princes and counts to some of the butchers and bakers of the village of Forio, where the villa was located.

Since my return to Istanbul from London after the coup, I had been working as actress and director at the Istanbul City Theatres and was, by now, quite well-known. The summer of Raad's marriage I had been invited by the Greek government to observe the Epidaurus and Athens festivals. It was in Piraeus, therefore, that I boarded the

Italian cruise ship which carried me to Ischia to meet my new sister-in-law. When I arrived at the villa, I was delighted to see the bright yellow walls of the living room covered with Mother's latest abstract paintings, most of them in blue-green, turquoise shades inspired by the seas and grottos of the island. The room was like a jewelled box hit by a ray of sunlight. The Ischia paintings have turned out to be among her best.

When I met my sister-in-law, I gave her one of Şehsuvar's diamond and enamel butterflies as a wedding gift. She was overwhelmed. In fact Margareta, a petite, shy young girl, near-sighted and wearing glasses, with a fringe and buck teeth, seemed forever at a total loss, ill at ease and almost tongue-tied in the presence of both my mother and myself. We obviously intimidated her, and she probably looked on us as terrors. In the privacy of Mother's room late that night, we talked and wondered what Raad had seen in this insignificant girl. We were both wrong in our judgment. Margareta, who became Majda when she converted to Islam, turned out to be an extraordinary woman, a good wife, a perfect mother who gave Raad five children, a first-class housekeeper, a respectful and caring daughter-in-law (which was not easy) and a delightful sister-in-law. With a lot of effort she established and built a home for the crippled in Amman, which she runs with an iron hand, visiting at least once a day to make sure all is in order.

When Raad told me that his cousin King Hussein had invited the newly-weds to live in Jordan and become Jordanian citizens, I was overjoyed. Raad was going to have a new country and a new people to serve. And serve he has done! Loved by the people for his many charitable acts, he is now called the 'Wailing Wall of Jordan'.

22

The Wheels of Change

On Shakespeare's 400th anniversary in 1964, the five Istanbul City Theatres were going to produce five of his plays, and I was given *The Merchant of Venice* to direct. It had been a good season for me, and I had very much enjoyed performing Dolly Levy in *The Matchmaker*. Now I was looking forward to a four-month Rockefeller grant which would take me to ten countries to observe all kinds of theatre. I felt fulfilled, fortunate and grateful.

Mother had not been to Istanbul for five years, and it had been almost twenty years since she had exhibited her works there. In her recent letters from London I felt that she was depressed and was starting again to take to her bed, complaining of numerous ailments, as she had often done before. Wanting to do something really special for her to take her out of her slump, I decided to organize a big retrospective exhibition of her paintings at the Istanbul Academy of Fine Arts, as well as one at the Hittite Museum in Ankara. That spring I nearly went out of my mind, negotiating for the exhibitions, constantly having to report back to Mother, and having to tell Aunt Aliye everything that went on, for she always meddled in the arrangements, all the while acting and directing and planning for my trip.

When Mother arrived, she stayed in my flat. Of course, I gave her my room and slept on the couch in the living room. Getting the enormous crates full of her art out of customs was a major problem. Going personally to the pier, I screamed, I cried, I kicked, I threatened, for it became clear that the customs officers were looking for a pay-off. We have a saying in Turkish: 'No one gives milk to the baby who does not cry.' My efforts succeeded, and without paying a penny, I had the crates loaded on a truck. To set up the exhibition I asked help from set designers, electricians and carpenters with whom I had worked at the City Theatres. The electricians brought spotlights from the theatre to enhance the Academy's poor lighting. The set designer was particularly imaginative. On the long, narrow, marble terrace of the Academy, which was directly on the Bosphorus, against a scaffolding he constructed, he placed two ten-foot-high abstract canvases so that the viewers could see them through the glass doors against the blue water.

The opening was a social and cultural event, for a new generation was, for the first time, seeing a major Turkish painter's works. The Shakirs were there *en masse*. Raad and Majda came from Amman; so did Uncle Cevat from Izmir. William Saroyan, the renowned American writer whose Armenian ancestors were from Turkey, was also present. A few days before, he had come to dinner at my home, and Mother had made an excellent sketch of him, which was published the next day in the Armenian newspaper. At the opening, in the middle of the crowd, Saroyan seized my arm. 'Shirin,' he said, 'these paintings are fantastic. Your mother is a very great artist. What an honour it is for me to have met her.'

Mother was overjoyed and elated at her success, and it gave me great satisfaction to have been able to please her.

Soon it was time for me to leave for my first stop on the Rockefeller trip. As I was unable to accompany Mother to Ankara, my cousin Fureya did so. It was the first time the Turkish government had given over the entire Hittite Museum for a one-man show. From all reports, Mother's large abstract paintings were even better displayed in that beautiful museum than they had been at the Academy, and when I saw the photographs of the exhibition I realized that, of all her shows, that was her very best. She has had many since then, but it still is her best. Overwhelmed by her reception in Turkey, Mother returned in high spirits to London, and she and Emir Zeid then went on to Ischia for the rest of the summer.

The next few years they spent shuttling between their three homes – the London flat, the Paris studio and the Ischia villa – Mother as always having her ups and downs. What helped her a great deal during these years was her friendship with Katia Granoff, who owned several art galleries in France. Mme Granoff believed in Nissa's art and was convinced that she was as great a painter as any she had known. Granoff's continual support encouraged Nissa, who at times felt the international art world had not given her her due. In 1969, at Granoff's Place Conti gallery in Paris, Nissa exhibited a few of her latest abstract paintings and many 'paleochrystalos', those sculptures made of chicken and turkey bones set in plastic. These oddities caused a great deal of interest. One day Nissa took a turkey breast bone, painted with black china ink and wrapped in a green chiffon handkerchief, to Monsieur Malraux, the French minister of culture. 'This is art!' he declared and had it mounted on a stand which he kept on his desk. The French press was intrigued. 'What is this strange sculpture, which looks like a centipede, on Monsieur Malraux's desk?' asked one journalist and, showing a photograph of the turkey bone, went on to explain its origin.

As Emir Zeid had begun to have heart problems, it was getting harder for Nissa to go to Paris and leave him alone in London. Emir Zeid knew this; he also knew that for Nissa's well-being she needed to be in Paris. So, in an altruistic move, he decided to go to Paris to live with her in her studio-apartment. They gave up the London flat and disposed of most of their belongings. I have always wondered how Emir Zeid could sleep in a tiny dark bedroom cluttered with furniture, bric-à-brac and paintings. The few times I have stayed in that room I have had serious bouts of claustrophobia. Emir Zeid, however, was so undemanding that he would have been satisfied to live in a little pup tent. In Paris, living in such close quarters, Nissa and Zeid became even more attached to each other. When she was painting or entertaining her artist friends, he would disappear as needed. As he did not know French and was in poor health, he never ventured out alone, but instead quietly found a corner in which to sit, puff on his pipe and read, content that his move had given Nissa the chance to live in Paris, something she had wanted all her life.

In the spring of 1966 three consecutive events shattered the happiest, most exciting and productive period of my life, the eight years I spent in the Turkish theatre.

First, my father died of Alzheimer's disease. Always a lover of the theatre, during the last years of his life his greatest pleasure had been to see me perform. The last time he came to the City Theatre in Istanbul to see me play Serafina in *The Rose Tattoo*, he was quite ill and could not walk. I had the stagehands carry him in an armchair to a box. I don't know if he recognized me or understood anything, but I am sure he was happy just to be there.

Soon after Father's death, I underwent a gall-bladder operation which, due to post-operative complications, nearly killed me. Thirdly, my mentor, Muhsin Ertuğrul, the founder of modern Turkish theatre, was fired by the municipal council in a spate of dirty and petty city politics. I and three others resigned in protest. To leave the theatre which I so loved was a wrenching decision; yet I felt I could not live with myself if I did not protest the unfair and brutal dismissal of the great man.

After my resignation at the age of forty, disenchanted, I left Turkey to start a new career in the United States and spent the next four years teaching drama at Carnegie-Mellon University and acting and directing at the Stanford Repertory Theater.

In the autumn of 1970 Tunç Yalman, the artistic director of the Milwaukee Repertory Theater, invited me to play the title role in his opening production, *Medea*, and in his second play, *You Can't Take It With You*, the part of the Grand Duchess Olga. On my way to Milwaukee from Istanbul, where I had been for the summer holiday, I went to Ischia for a couple of weeks to visit my parents.

I found that Mother had put on a lot of weight. Extremely sensitive about her figure, she resented talk about food, dieting or exercise; so I skirted those subjects. However, she was in relatively good spirits, painting and enjoying Ischia, most of all its ravioli, spaghetti and calamari. In contrast, Emir Zeid seemed much more frail than before, with a drawn, haggard expression. He picked at his food like a bird, and all he seemed to want to do was to sit on his patio and look at the mountain.

When Mother saw me studying and fretting over my forthcoming part, Medea, she insisted I take a series of mud baths. 'It will do you good,' she said. 'It will relax you.' She was right, for I found the baths very soothing. As my parents rarely went out, I spent most of my time in the villa. In the evenings, always joined by Anna, the cook, and her husband, we watched Italian television, which I did not understand. At times I felt like charging out of the villa to the moonlit beach across the street and throwing myself into the Mediterranean, or going to the village square and joining the throngs of people sitting in cafés and enjoying the evening air. However, I clenched my teeth and sat in the dark room opposite the TV screen. On the whole, it was a very quiet visit.

The morning of my departure, while Mother remained in bed, Emir Zeid, though not well, arose early to see me off at the heliport.

As he knew I was worried about my part, when I kissed him goodbye on his pate, he patted my back and said, "Don't worry, Shirin. You will be great as Medea. I know you will.' Then, placing his hand on my shoulder, he added, 'You are a good girl, Shirin. You have been a fine daughter.' He had never said such things to me before. Perhaps he knew he would never see me again.

Standing above the stage on a small rounded platform which represented a chariot in the sky, looking down at Jason as I uttered the last lines of the play *Medea*, I felt a swaying of the theatre below. My knees seemed to give way, and I had to use every bit of willpower not to fall on to the stage. Once I had delivered my last line, I turned with a sweep and made my exit down a narrow winding staircase. As I stepped on the floor backstage, I collapsed, sobbing hysterically. Expecting me to take my curtain call, the audience kept applauding, but I could not move.

As soon as the house lights went on, the stage manager ran backstage to see what had happened to me, and when she saw me lying prostrate on the floor she had me carried to her car and drove me to Columbia Hospital. I was still wearing my Grecian costume, elaborate wig and heavy make-up. When the young intern in charge of the emergency room saw this oddity, in the middle of the night, grab his hand and, in a foreign accent, babble agitatedly between sobs, 'I have killed my sons, but my nephews are dead,' he put me in a bed with iron grilles on all sides, like a crib; I think they use those beds for mad people. They rolled me to another room for a test to make sure I did not have concussion, and then the doctor injected me with a sedative. I felt myself sinking into the depths of the cool blue sea, where I ended up lying blissfully on its sandy bottom, oblivious of the world.

Playing Medea eight times a week is a *tour de force* for any actress, but my backstage collapse had little to do with the rigours of the part. It was more the result of something happening almost halfway around the world.

Following the 1967 war between Israel and the Arab nations, most of the defeated Palestinians had gone to Jordan. Armed and militant, they became almost a state within a state and threatened the legal authorities of the country. Their aim was to overthrow the monarchy and take over Jordan. Although King Hussein hesitated for months to take action against them, he was finally persuaded by his Bedouin troops and his chief of staff that the situation had become intolerable. In mid-September he ordered his army to put down the militant Palestinians. It was full civil war, with shooting and tanks all over Amman. Syria invaded Jordan, and it was feared that Iraq as well would come to the aid of the Palestinian guerrillas. Never had Jordan been so threatened; it looked as if Hussein would lose his kingdom. At the height of the civil war, the situation became so critical that the king ordered all women and children of the family to take refuge in Aqaba, a port on the Red Sea, and, leaving my brother Raad in Amman, my sister-in-law Majda went there with her two little sons, aged six and seven. In *Medea*, as I hugged the two sons that I would later kill, I had thought of my little nephews. The anxiety I felt for my beloved brother and his family consumed me. After all, the situation was '*déjà vu*'. Twelve years before, while I was performing in another play in another theatre in another city, again in the state of Wisconsin, the slaughter of the Iraqi royal family had occurred. Now, fearing that the same would happen in Jordan, I was tormented by visions of murder and assassination and spent restless and sleepless nights.

The morning after my collapse, I heard a familiar voice. 'Shirin, Shirinaki, wake up,' said Tunç Yalman, standing at the foot of my hospital bed, his voice full of concern.

'What time is it?' I asked. 'Eleven,' he replied. 'It is seven p.m. in Jordan,' I thought. 'Another day of fighting has gone by.'

'Did you listen to the morning news?' I asked Tunç. 'Are there any new developments?'

'No, there is nothing new. They are still fighting. However, please forget about Jordan; you have two performances today,' he said, sounding desperate.

'Oh God,' I thought, 'it would be Wednesday.' I pulled myself together and, of course, performed. How, I shall never know. One just does.

With his 55,000-man army fiercely loyal to him, King Hussein overcame the dissident elements. By 23 September the Syrians had withdrawn, and the king could concentrate on the situation in Amman. On 27 September, at a conference in Cairo at which the heads of all the Arab states were present, a peace was brokered between Yasser Arafat and King Hussein which put an end to the civil war. Arafat and the guerrillas left for Lebanon, life in Jordan returned to normal, and I could finally relax.

When I called my parents in Paris for the sixth time since the crisis had started, Mother told me that the anxiety Zeid had felt for Jordan, Raad and his family had aggravated his heart condition so that he had been taken to a hospital for treatment. She herself was absolutely exhausted from the strain of the last few weeks. 'Thank God it is all over without any major tragedies,' she said. 'Let us bless our stars. It could have been another Iraq.' How wonderful of her always to see the good side of things!

A week after my call, on a Monday, our Equity day off, one of the local ladies, who was a member of the chorus in *Medea*, had invited all the actresses of the company to lunch. After the stress of the past weeks, I was looking forward to the hen party. On my way to the luncheon I stopped at the theatre to pick up my mail. Tunç Yalman must have had his spies out, for the moment I stepped into the building he flew out of his office and, in a serious voice, said, 'Shirin, please come into my room. I have to talk to you.' My heart skipped a beat. Had things flared up in Jordan again? Tunç picked up a newspaper from his desk and asked, 'Have you seen the morning paper?'

'No,' I replied.

On the front page of the Milwaukee *Sentinel* I read the caption: 'Uncle of King Hussein Dies in Paris'. I was shocked. The death of Emir Zeid was a terrible blow for I had loved him dearly. 'Poor man,' I thought. 'All the events of the last weeks were too much for his ailing heart, and it just broke.'

Leaving Tunç's office, I ran to my little apartment and called Paris. Mother was surprised that I had already heard the sad news. Since we could hardly talk, for our tears were choking us, Mother passed the telephone to Raad, who had just arrived from Amman in a private plane which King Hussein had sent to pick up Emir Zeid's body. The king was to give Zeid a state funeral and have him buried in the royal cemetery next to his brother King Abdullah, Hussein's grandfather. That pleased me, for I remembered how, after the Iraqi coup in 1958, Zeid had said, 'If I die, where will I be buried? I no longer have a country.' I shall always be grateful to the king for his noble and loving gesture.

Early in December, at my request, the Milwaukee Rep. replaced me for the last two weeks of *You Can't Take It With You*, and I flew to Paris to be with Mother on her birthday. She, of course, was happy to see me and grateful that I had come; however, there seemed little I could do. Traumatized as she was by Emir Zeid's death, nothing I said or did seemed to console her. Time was her only ally.

After losing Emir Zeid, Mother felt so bereft and lonely that, instead of painting abstract works alone in her studio, she began to paint people. 'I need the warmth and the presence of a human being,' she told me. In large, stylized portraits she made, giving her subjects enormous eyes, she tried to capture the soul of the person more than the likeness. These portraits added a new and important phase to her art.

At the beginning of January it was time for me to return to Carnegie-Mellon University, from which I had taken leave of absence, to resume my teaching for the second semester. As I packed, Mother watched me. 'Shirinaki, you really hate to return to Pittsburgh, don't you? You were so happy acting and directing in Istanbul. You had everything you wanted. I wish you had not given it all up by resigning from the theatre as a matter of principle,' she said, frustrated that I had made the wrong decision.

'I had to, Mother,' I replied, annoyed. 'You know I had to.'

After all the emotional stress of the past months, once back in Pittsburgh I felt drained, lonely and homesick. Teaching in the late 1960s in American universities, with student riots and sit-ins, was trying and unpleasant. I knew I needed to return to Turkey. So at the end of the school year I packed up and left for Istanbul, not knowing what I would do next. I was fortunate, for soon after my arrival Mücap Ofluoğlu, my ex-third husband, who ran a small private theatre invited me to play opposite him in the French comedy *Four in the Garden*. I had married Mücap in the early 1960s, when we were both working at the Istanbul Municipal Theatres. Although our impulsive marriage had lasted only two months, we had remained colleagues and friends. I re-rented my old apartment which, as luck had it, happened to be available, took my furniture out of storage and resettled in the city I so love among family and friends. My Armenian maid even returned and washed me in the tub, as she had done before. The wheels of change had spun again, this time for the better.

23

The Grand Tour

Four Shakir women were to have four openings during four consecutive months in 1972. In late April Fureya was to show her ceramics in Ankara; in May Aunt Aliye was preparing to exhibit her etchings in Istanbul; in June a vernissage of Mother's latest paintings was to be held at the Katia Granoff Gallery at the Place Beauveau in Paris; and I was scheduled to open in *The Play is the Thing* at the Playhouse in the Park in Cincinnati, Ohio.

Before any of these events, because Istanbul was having an exceptionally cold spring, I went south to Side, where my Uncle Suat and Aunt Mizou then lived, to find the sun and to relax.

In the early 1960s, while on a cruise to southern Turkey, Suat and Mizou had discovered Side, an enchanting village surrounded on three sides by the blue Mediterranean and brimming with Graeco-Roman ruins. Having fallen in love with it, they decided to retire there and make a living by running a gourmet restaurant. Mizou cut her long, manicured nails, entered the kitchen and put to use the culinary talent she had inherited from her French mother.

To Uncle Suat's and Aunt Mizou's restaurant, which was called *Pamphylia* after Side's ancient name, in a garden in front of a Roman arch overlooking the Mediterranean, archaeologists, writers, journalists, diplomats and even hippies from all over the world came for its culinary delights and its charming, entertaining host. Uncle Suat's table became an international meeting place. With his wit, personality and story-telling ability, Suat put Side on the map as his older brother Cevat had done, some years before, for Bodrum. Uncle Suat and Aunt Mizou remained in Side until the end of their lives and now lie in the village cemetery.

From Side I made my way to Izmir to visit my Uncle Cevat, who was suffering from bone cancer. Even though he was still called 'The

Fisherman of Halicarnassus', in the early 1940s, in order to further the education of his children, he had moved to Izmir. There he provided additional income for his family by becoming a guide, the first official guide in Turkey – passionate, informed, sensitive, fluent in many languages – the paragon of a lowly trade. When the government had official visitors, it usually asked Cevat to escort them to Ephesus, the greatest Graeco-Roman site in the world, close to Izmir, where Cevat re-created the ancient city in words and stories which put life into the marbles. Sometimes when he was inspired, he became Zeus, Poseidon or other characters of Greek mythology and recited to his eminent tourists in Greek and Latin. He particularly enjoyed meeting Lord Kinross, the historian, the Belgian prime minister Henry Spaak, and Georges Pompidou, the president of France who, after a tour of the Aegean coast with Cevat, remarked, 'I have finally met Homer.'

Although Cevat was an indulgent father, and nothing his children did could anger him, on political and philosophical matters he was completely intolerant and given to fits of rage. Once when he was very ill, a dear old friend called on him, and in the course of their conversation admitted that he had shifted political parties. When he began to condemn leftist intellectuals, Cevat bellowed, 'So what? I'm a leftist, too. Does that make me a bad man? Get out of this house,' and kicked him out.

One evening in an Izmir bar, where he had had too much to drink and was pontificating as usual on numerous subjects to the locals gathered around him, the question arose of the origin of the Turkish flag (white crescent moon and star on a bright red background). A romantic legend holds that one of the sultans came to a battlefield strewn with corpses. A star was visible in the hollow of the crescent moon, and both were reflected in a pool of blood. 'Let this be our flag,' the sultan said. Cevat described this legend as 'Hogwash! Those symbols have nothing to do with our Turkish heritage. We did not even take the crescent and star from the Arabs as a symbol of Islam. They originated with the Romans, on many of whose monuments one may see them. Just go to the theatre in Side; you will see a huge slab of marble lying there with the most beautiful crescent and star carved on it.'

So vehemently did he discourse on this and who knows what other sensitive subjects that he was arrested for 'insulting' the flag and Ismet Inönü, the president of the republic. Although he was held in prison without trial for the next nine months, by then he was such a colourful and famous personality that he was well treated, surrounded constantly by admiring fellow inmates and the jailers themselves, whom he regaled with mythology and his other favourite subjects. Finally a group of law students visited the prison to study the criminal system in place and were shocked to find the beloved 'Fisherman of Halicarnassus' there. Their protests having led immediately to a trial, Cevat was declared innocent and released.

His reputation as an outspoken critic of the government earned him constant harassment from the authorities. My cousin Sina says, 'His writings were closely censored, and many of them disappeared during the frequent searches of his home. The police never left him alone. They always followed him. Sometimes, when he saw them standing at the bottom of the hill and Father was in a joking mood, he would say, "Come on, let's play drunk and lie on the ground," and the police would have to carry us home.'

Cevat's aversion to the government lasted all his life. When he heard shortly before his death that they had named Bodrum's main street after him, he lamented, 'Ai! Now the donkeys and camels will be doing on to me what the government has done all my life.'

That last time in Izmir, when I saw my Uncle Cevat suffering in bed, to cheer him up I read him some of his short stories, for he loved my dramatic expression. I also recited passages from plays in which I had acted.

'Haven't you performed in any of Shaw's plays?' he asked.

'No, Uncle. Unfortunately I have not,' I replied.

'What a pity! He is the greatest dramatist of our century. Now you see to it that you act in his plays. You'd be good as Candida. By the way,' he added, 'I am glad you have decided to return to Turkey. Last summer I felt a sadness in you. You are a Mediterranean, and once a Mediterranean, always a Mediterranean. In those far-away places you will shrivel up and die.'

'Don't worry, Uncle,' I said. 'I have moved back, settled again in Istanbul, and all is well.'

As I kissed him goodbye, I knew it was for the last time, for the old lion lay prone, unable to roar any more. A year later he died, famous and beloved by his country. His funeral was a remarkable epitaph to a man who had killed his father and served three terms in his country's jails. Cevat's American son-in-law John Noonan, my sweet cousin Ismet's husband, in a letter to Alfred Friendly, the ex-editor of the *Washington Post*, who knew our family well, wrote:

> On Monday the most incredible experience of my life took place . . . We took Cevat Bey to his beloved Bodrum in convoy . . . As we drove into town on the Cevat Şakir Caddesi [Cevat Shakir Avenue] virtually everybody turned out to line the streets – a wholesale communal showing of love – schoolchildren spaced out with flowers, hundreds upon hundreds of peasants and fishermen. His coffin was put on a boat for a final ride upon his deep-blue sea; when it was taken off at the port, it was carried by thousands of lifted arms to the crest of the rocky hill overlooking the Aegean. A truly magnificent site for a truly magnificent human being.

Uncle Cevat has become a national hero. A film has been made about him with Hanna Schygulla as one of the women in his life. Only recently I received a letter from Turkey, and to my surprise, next to an Atatürk stamp, there was a stamp showing Uncle Cevat's face, his beret cocked to one side, smiling up at me. I could almost hear him saying, 'And now the whole nation will lick me.'

From Izmir I flew to Ankara to attend Fureya's opening and stayed with my cousin Erdem and his wife, who were in the throes of packing for his first ambassadorial post – Pakistan. At the time his mother, Aunt Ayşe, was visiting there too. Uncle Ahmet had died the previous year of heart trouble, and Aunt Ayşe continued to live in Istanbul, thanks to Ahmet's business acumen, with a sizeable income, a car and chauffeur. Once a week she played poker, and, still hoping to give a concert, she continued to take piano lessons. A year later Erdem saw to it that at the age of seventy-five she gave a piano recital in Islamabad.

All of us went to Fureya's opening. She was by now the leading ceramist of Turkey. With her murals adorning many buildings, her ceramic tables in many homes and hotels, and her celadon-like plates on many walls, the output of her studio was in great demand. Her exhibition was well received, and she sold many of her works.

As Aunt Aliye was anxiously waiting for me to help her with her show, after Fureya's opening I hurried back to Istanbul. When I returned to my apartment, I found several messages from Aliye tucked under my door. One said: 'The moment you return from Ankara, call me.' Another said: 'Please come immediately. I need you.' So, without bothering to unpack, I went directly to Aunt Aliye, who was still living and working in the old Charles Berger apartment. When she opened the door, she cried, 'Finally you're here, Shirinaki. Come in. Come in. I've been waiting for you,' and, pulling out a large black cardboard folder from under a pile of clothes, she added, 'Please help me pick out the etchings for my exhibition.'

We spread a series of coloured etchings printed on coarse butcher paper over the floor and, by a process of elimination, chose the ones we felt were the best. I very well knew that each person who dropped in would be asked to do the same and that the final result would be totally different. My task accomplished, I started to leave. Aunt Aliye hugged me tightly. 'Please, Shirinaki,' she said, 'come again tomorrow and make the price list; as usual, you will be in charge of sales. You're so good at it.' As I left, I thought to myself, 'Why is she so worked up? She's had so many shows!'

Aunt Aliye's exhibition at the Taksim Gallery that spring was an event in Istanbul. Hordes of people attended it, and, as if they knew this was going to be her last show, they bought up all her etchings. I was in charge of sales, and I could not write the bills fast enough. Aliye's show did, indeed, turn out to be her last, for she died of emphysema two years later in Aunt Ayşe's home in Büyükada, where she was brought by motor launch at the very last moment. She now lies in the little cemetery on the hill. Her etchings have become collectors' items.

Before I left for Paris, I called on my stepmother Fatma, who lived among my father's books and possessions. As she had taken such good care of my father during his long illness, I felt a deep debt of gratitude toward her. She was very frail, and her only wish seemed to be to die as soon as possible so that she could join the man she had so loved. Soon she got her wish.

At the Katia Granoff Gallery in Paris, my mother was showing for the first time a series of portraits she had painted, including one of Madame Granoff herself with enormous black eyes and purple ropes of hair piled on top of her head. The opening was a crowded affair attended by the Paris art scene, journalists, diplomats, personal friends and family, including my brother Raad and his wife, Majda.

My older brother Nejad was notably absent, for Mother and he were estranged. Over the years, both temperamental artists, they had constantly clashed, and finally Mother had cut him off completely. One day I tried to pin her down and find out why she had acted so decisively. 'After all,' I said, 'Grandmother forgave her son Cevat, who killed her husband. What is it about Nejad you cannot forgive?'

I could never before have asked her such a question; it was only when she was in her late eighties and had mellowed that I dared to do so. Previously, the mere mention of Nejad's name would have brought on an avalanche of angry words. Once in Istanbul Mother and Fureya were dining as guests of a friend at a waterside restaurant. During the conversation the friend politely asked, 'How is your son Nejad?' Immediately with a sudden contemptuous gesture, Mother swept everything on the table – plates, glasses, food and cutlery – into the Bosphorus. 'Don't you ever mention his name to me again!' she said, livid. The friend was stunned.

In answer to my question, Mother gave me several reasons for her animosity toward Nejad, but none really justified her total rejection of him. She had simply acted in self-defence, for he exasperated her and drove her to distraction. Although Nejad and I were raised together and were very close during our childhood, over the years he and I have also become estranged. I love his work, however, and some of his best paintings, which hang in my home, give me great joy.

After having made a name in the 1950s as a member of the Ecole de Paris, Nejad, easel in hand, wandered all over the world, even travelling to China as a guest of Mao. Inspired by his journeys, he held many shows in all the capitals of Europe, including one in New York. He finally settled in Poland with his second wife, a Pole like the first, who gave him two more daughters and a son. One daughter, alas, died tragically in her early twenties. In spite of having become one of Turkey's leading painters, Nejad has, on the whole, had a difficult and unhappy life.

Leaving Mother in high spirits, I flew to Cincinnati to start rehearsals for Molnar's *The Play is the Thing*, where I was to play Ilona, the glamorous Viennese actress. Although the play is a drawing-room comedy, the director, Mr Word Baker, effectively using the spacious thrust stage of the lovely Cincinnati Playhouse, had the entire action take place on the terrace of a villa in Italy with tile floor, real bouganvillaea bushes and a swimming pool. Sandor, the leading man, and I played an early-morning scene in which he swam laps while I sat on the edge of the pool splashing my feet and talking on the phone.

One night after the performance, while I was resting a sprained ankle and relaxing in my actor's digs with a can of beer in hand, the telephone rang. That telephone call changed my life. A lady I had met in Milwaukee was inviting me to spend a weekend with her when the show closed. She had an ulterior motive.

The night I arrived in Milwaukee, the Ogdens gave a little dinner party, to which they invited Robert Trainer, whom I had met once before at a luncheon while I had been performing in *Medea*. Tall and good-looking, a charming New Yorker, a Harvard Law graduate who worked for the Jos. Schlitz Brewing Company, he had been widowed about a year and half before. Our meeting was electric.

During our conversation Bob said, 'I have been to Turkey, for we were planning to build a brewery there, but I have never visited Troy. I would love to see it.'

'Please do come,' I replied, delighted. 'I will be glad to show you the sights.'

A month later Bob arrived in Istanbul. Mother was also there, having come by boat from Naples. After her successful exhibition in Paris, she had spent two months in Ischia, and now, visiting her family again, she was in the best of spirits. Both she and Bob stayed at the art deco Park Hotel opposite the Hayırlı and Park apartments where Nissa and Zeid had once courted. During his visit Bob never got to see one stone of Troy, but he met my relatives and friends and saw me in my habitat, and a week after his arrival he proposed. I was thunderstruck. Although I knew he had fallen in love with me, I did not expect a proposal so quickly from such a reserved and laid-back Anglo-Saxon.

'I would like to ask your mother's permission,' he said correctly.

That afternoon Mother was at Fureya's studio, for, as she was returning to her home in Paris, Fureya had planned a farewell party for her. When I called Mother and told her that Bob had proposed and wanted formally to ask for my hand in marriage, Fureya reported to me later that Mother had nearly fainted.

'Give me a cognac,' she had cried. 'I am not used to such things. I won't know what to say. Each time Shirin got married, I did not meet the man until after the wedding. "Mother, this is my husband," Shirin would say, and that was that. Much easier that way.'

When we arrived at Fureya's that evening, most of the guests were already there. Mother, Bob and I went into a little alcove, where Bob formally asked Mother for my 'hand in marriage'. Not knowing what to say or do, she turned to me, who was shedding tears of joy, and said, 'Why are you crying, Shirin? This is a happy occasion. Don't cry. Stop it. Please stop,' and her own eyes filled with tears.

Fureya's farewell party for Mother, attended by many friends and my aunts Aliye and Ayşe (Aunt Hakiye had died of a stroke the previous year), turned into an engagement celebration. Ercüment Karacan, the owner of the popular daily newspaper *Milliyet*, and his columnist, Zeynep Oral, were at the party! They summoned a photographer, and the next day's paper featured on the front page a large photo of Bob and me embracing, over the headline, 'Jet Engagement'.

When I asked Bob, who wanted me to leave with him, 'What am I to do with my flat and all my possessions? I only moved in eight months ago,' he simply replied, 'Just close the door and come.'

A couple of days after Mother's departure, we left for Paris, because I wanted my mother, for once, to be present at my marriage. We were married in a brief civil ceremony in the Turkish Embassy in Paris and celebrated with a dinner in the restaurant of the charming L'Hotel on the Rue des Beaux-Arts. Our guests included two Turkish ambassadors, a cabinet minister and some friends who happened to be in Paris at the time. To please Mother, we served only Dom Perignon throughout the meal. After our guests had left, Bob and I walked, holding hands, through the narrow streets to our little hotel opposite the church on the Boulevard St Germain. It was an Indian summer night; the air was like velvet. No two people could have been happier.

The next day we flew to New York and on to Milwaukee, and Mother went to Rome to attend a meeting of women painters at the Vatican.

In mid-December, anxious to meet my new family, see my new home and what 'this Milwaukee' was like, Mother arrived from Paris, laden with gifts, to spend the Christmas holidays with us. As she knew only of San Francisco because of her sister-in-law Syida, of Chicago because of its reputation, and of New York, which she had visited in 1949, she thought the rest of America was a vast wasteland and that she was going to the 'provinces'. When she saw the beer barons' mansions on the lake, she exclaimed, impressed, 'But my dear Shirin, what beautiful houses these people live in! The one which belongs to Mrs Uihlein [Bob's ex-mother-in-law] is like the Iraqi Embassy in London – the same mouldings, same style, Georgian, I believe.'

But what she loved most was the cosiness of our lake house, with its beamed ceilings, early American furniture and big stone fireplace. I had decorated the house for Christmas, and a huge Christmas tree stood in the living room, surrounded by piles of gifts. When Mother met Bob's three sons and their wives, she said, 'All your life you wanted children, and after each miscarriage you were devastated. Now Allah has given you a ready-made family. You see? In life one must never, never despair.'

Inspired by the company and the ambience, Mother brought out her pens and ink and sketched everything and everyone – the lake, the trees, the house, the people, even the dog.

When she saw me scurrying around the house and working all the time, for we had no help, she took pity on me and announced, 'I will cook the Christmas turkey.' On Christmas morning she descended into the kitchen, put on an apron and started giving orders like a master chef. She wanted to create a 'very special' stuffing, for which she had Bob and me shell and peel pistachios, one of the sons pit prunes, and another boil, shell and mash chestnuts. The daughters-in-law were put in charge of the vegetables and the salad. When she demanded port, and Bob said he had none, she had the third son run around the neighbourhood to find some, for, 'Without the port,' she declared, 'I cannot cook.' Having finally roasted the turkey to perfection, Mother decorated it by wrapping its legs in fringed paper leggings which she cut out and on which she wrote in red ink, 'Merry Christmas'. Seated around a long pine refectory table with a new family, we were both reminded of the 'togetherness' we had had at the Büyükada table.

Mother looked at me, nodded and smiled.

24

Amman, A Birthday Party – 1987

For her eighty-sixth birthday Mother threw one of her extraordinary parties in her home in Amman, for which I flew from Manhattan where we had moved after Bob's retirement from the Schlitz brewery.

Twelve years before, feeling the onset of old age and lonely, Nissa had sold her Rue de Grenelle apartment and moved to Amman to be close to Raad, who was by then chamberlain. When she had abruptly made the decision, Fureya and I had been extremely apprehensive. How could a woman who had lived in London and Paris most of her life be satisfied with the limited life of Amman? However, we were thrilled to learn that, by moving to Amman, Nissa started the most creative, productive and rewarding period of her life.

Once she had settled into a small stone villa close to Raad's home, she decided to teach art. All her life she had wanted to teach, and in Amman the occasion arose. Every week she held classes in her home for about fifteen young women. Not only did she teach them the techniques of painting, but she also helped develop their personalities. Her sessions covered the history of art, philosophy, her views on life and art, the ways of the world and human relations. She was more than a teacher. She became a mentor to these students, who were totally devoted to her and gave her the six 'A's – attention, appreciation, affection, admiration, adoration and adulation – on which she thrived. But most of all she derived satisfaction from passing on to them her creative passion. Holding mixed exhibitions with her students, she encouraged them to exhibit also on their own, which they did all over the world.

King Hussein decorated her with the 'Star of Jordan' for her contribution to art in his country, and the French government made her 'Commandeur des Arts et des Lettres' for her continuous contributions to art in general. Her house was named the 'Royal National

Fine Arts Institute Fahrelnissa Zeid', and many visiting dignitaries were brought to see it as if it were a private museum.

When one entered her institute, one was immersed in a magical world of colour, eclectic to the point of being fantastic. All the walls and ceilings, including the bathrooms and the kitchen, were covered with Nissa's art – watercolours, china ink and gouache drawings, lithographs, small and large oils she had painted over a period of seventy years – some figurative, others impressionist, and many abstract. Her latest stylized portraits were to be seen everywhere.

The floor of the long living room was entirely covered by two priceless Bukhara rugs from Sherif Hussein's time, now badly worn and full of holes. Along the walls and on stands and shelves were displayed her paleochrystalos, some backlit and others rotating with a whirring sound. In different corners of the room were mounds of stones, small and large, which Nissa had carried from the beaches of Brittany to those of Aqaba, and painted. Photographs of kings, queens and presidents dedicated to her were crowded with masses of bric-à-brac on all the tables. Prominently displayed were two large pictures of Cevat Pasha and Shakir Pasha in full military uniform, chests covered with medals. Nissa wanted to be sure that all Arab royalty who visited her would be aware of her illustrious Ottoman heritage.

The household consisted of Jebril, an ex-policeman who was her chauffeur, majordomo and confidant, and Abu Mohammed, a Bedouin Arab who had once been Raad's gardener and now was Nissa's cook, butler, launderer, tailor and nurse. A sentry assigned to her by the army, who stood guard at her door, completed her male triumvirate. When Nissa was sick, which was often, for she suffered from diabetes and heart trouble, Raad had hired various nurses so that the men would not have to deal with her intimate needs, but each time she had found a reason to fire the women. She was perfectly happy with her male servants, who put up with her temper and her endless demands, for she was generous to them and their families.

The day before the birthday party, hoping to help with the last-minute preparations, I walked over from Raad's house nearby. I need not have done so. As always, Mother had had everything prepared days in advance. Four round tables, all places set, were lined up in front of her eighteen-foot painting, My Hell, considered her master-piece, soon to be hung in the new Eczacıbaşı Museum of Modern

Art in Istanbul. Along a second wall, in front of an unfinished portrait of Queen Noor, stood a table covered with balloons and noisemakers for the guests' children.

As soon as I arrived that morning, Mother, holding on to Abu Mohammed, descended from her bedroom, wearing a black trouser-suit and the Chanel necklace and earrings I had just brought her from New York. We kissed, and Mother fell into one of the throne-like gilded armchairs from the Büyükada house that had followed her from Istanbul to Berlin to Baghdad, back to Istanbul, then on to London, Paris and finally to Amman.

Surveying the tables with an eagle eye, she noticed that there were not enough spoons. 'Spoons are missing,' she called out, banging a table with her fist. 'Abu Mohammed, bring spoons, more spoons, spoons, spoons. Quick, quick!' Like a frightened impala, Abu Mohammed leaped into the kitchen and bumped into the chauffeur Jebril, who was just then coming out.

'Where have you been, Jebril?' she scolded. 'Come here. I need you.'

'I was putting film into the camera,' he replied, holding out the latest model Polaroid.

Everything had to be instantaneous, even her pictures. 'Mother has become so impatient,' I thought to myself. 'Like a spoiled child, she demands immediate gratification. Attending to her needs can be tiresome and exasperating; yet she is so irresistible that everyone indulges her.' How many times Majda has told me, 'If your mother were not the great artist she is, and did not have such a colourful and interesting personality, I would never have put up with her.'

'Jebril,' she cried, 'we need more chairs. I want more chairs. One never knows how many people will show up. People come and go, and besides we need chairs for the musicians. Quick, Jebril, call Raad's home, tell them to send over chairs.'

'OK, *Sitti*,' Jebril said, jumping up and running to the phone.

Just then six large cardboard boxes, piled one on the other like a pyramid, filled with a variety of salty and sweet wafers, arrived from the pastry shop. Mother instructed me to put them into the various little silver dishes on the tables and scattered all over the room. Once my task was completed, I found that two full boxes remained.

'What am I to do with these?' I asked.

'I like to order much, much,' Mother replied. 'Abundance. Give the leftovers to Abu Mohammed. He'll distribute them to the chauffeurs and guards. This is nothing. Wait until you see all the desserts that will arrive this afternoon. The Moroccan ambassador's wife promised a very special one.'

Then, with an impish smile, she added, 'My birthday cake this year will be in the shape of a tennis racquet.'

'A tennis racquet,' I exclaimed incredulously. What did a tennis racquet have to do with Mother? The last time I remembered seeing her holding one was at least fifty years ago.

'Why are you surprised?' she asked innocently. 'A tennis racquet, because Zeid courted me while we played tennis.'

Just then through the door came a tall Swedish lady, the wife of a Jordanian doctor, carrying two beautifully wrapped packages.

'Oh,' the lady said, dismayed. 'I thought the party was today.'

'Come in. Come in,' called Mother. 'You'll come tomorrow too, and this way we will see you twice. How fortunate for us!' Then she introduced me. 'This is my daughter Shirin, the great actress' – to her I was always great – 'who just came from New York for the party,' and started to open the gifts the lady had given her.

Taking a satin bow off the package and holding it on top of her head, she exclaimed, 'Oh, what a pretty pink bow!' and read the card: ' "Look for a rainbow on a rainy day." Charming thought,' she added. 'Charming! What would we do without a rainbow?'

The first package contained a large rhinestone-studded black bottle of perfume. 'What a chic bottle!' she commented and sprayed perfume all over her hair and in the room. 'It smells so good!'

As she started to open the next package, she called to me, 'Come on, Shirinaki, recite something. Some Shakespeare. Let us enjoy ourselves.' While I went around the room filling little dishes with pistachios, I recited Kate's last speech from *The Taming of the Shrew.*

'I love that line – "Thy husband is thy lord, thy life, thy king, thy sovereign",' said Mother. Knowing that she had never believed a word of it, I smiled.

Once the Swedish lady left, Mother turned to me and asked if I had brought the dress which I intended to wear to the party. 'Yes, Mother,' I replied, 'I brought two outfits for you to choose from. They are hanging on the old Japanese screen over there.' This was one of the Büyükada relics.

'Put them on. Put them on,' said Mother, clapping her hands. 'Model for us. Let us see which is most becoming.'

As I went into the little anteroom and started to undress, I could hear Mother talking to her portrait of Emir Zeid, an extraordinary piece of art which museum director Joseph Kelleher had compared to Faun paintings.

'Zeid, my love. Thank you,' she said in a warm voice. 'You are making all this happen. You are here with me. I am happy, Zeid. Thank you. Thank you.'

I entered wearing a Valentino brocade suit and modelled it, walking and turning as I had done so many years before as a professional model on Seventh Avenue.

'I don't like the pattern. It is too busy,' cried Mother, waving a hand. 'Take it off. Take it off. Put on the brown satin.'

'The brown satin is strapless. I think it is too dressy for the morning,' I replied.

'There is *no* morning!' declared Mother imperiously. 'I want you to look your best. You can wear the brown satin dress with its velvet bolero.'

I modelled the brown outfit. She turned to Jebril and Abu Mohammed, who were watching me, and asked, 'Which outfit do you think she should wear?'

'The brown, *Sitti*,' said Jebril, and Abu Mohammed shook his head in obedient agreement.

'You see,' Mother said, 'they too like to give their opinion. These men amuse me so. They love me, you know!' And when she noticed my dubious expression, she added, 'As a mother, of course.'

Mother truly believed that all men in her periphery were in love with her. During one of my last interviews, I mustered up courage to ask her, 'Why do you think that every man in the world, including the street cleaner, is in love with you?' In my youth I would never have dared to talk to her like that, for she would have been enraged and thrown something at me.

'Because they are,' she declared positively.

'Oh, Mother,' I said. 'We are too old for these games. I really would like to know what makes you believe in these fantasies. Please tell me, for it's important for me to understand you.'

Wanting to give me an intelligent explanation, Mother paused for a long moment and then said, 'I love being in love. The notion of being in love pleases me, makes me happy. If I think somebody is in love with me, it makes all encounters meaningful and exciting. It heightens life.'

To such a logical explanation, all I could say was, 'As long as it makes you happy, go ahead.' Then, patting her hand, I asked, 'Who is the lucky man now?'

Her face lit up, and she replied, 'Oh, the new Turkish ambassador. What a charming, refined man! I adore him. I just painted his portrait. Wait until you see it.'

Party preparations complete and brown dress chosen, I started to return to Raad's house for lunch. As I was leaving, a huge, four-foot-round birthday cake arrived from the Marriot Hotel as a gift from the manager. How many cakes were we going to have?

As Mother tired in the afternoon, the party was scheduled to begin at ten a.m. and last until after lunch. When Raad, Majda, their children and I arrived, all dressed up at nine forty-five a.m., we found Mother seated in the large gilded armchair, wearing a long beige lace dress. She was coiffed and bejewelled, ready to receive her guests. Soon a four-piece Polish band came from the Marriot Hotel; Abu Mohammed seated them and served them champagne. 'To the Princess,' they toasted.

At ten o'clock sharp, guests bearing elaborate gifts started to arrive. Princess Saliha, Mother's ninety-seven-year-old sister-in-law, the one who had sent her the *abayeh* in Mosul fifty years ago, was among the first to come. She was followed by the Chinese, French, Moroccan and Turkish ambassadors' wives. Mrs Mufti, the first woman minister of Jordan, came accompanied by a woman journalist. Present also were the museum director, Mr Bisharat, and his wife. To please Mother the guests were all dressed as if they were going to an evening party.

As Mother never charged for her lessons, her students came with valuable gifts as a token of their appreciation. Souha, one of her most devoted students, presented her with a magnificent turquoise necklace lying on a silk pillow, and another, Hind, gave her a gold ring. Mother was enchanted. All morning bouquets of flowers kept coming, including huge ones from Crown Prince Hassan and his wife and King Hussein and Queen Noor.

The band played continuously. Its repertoire varied from 'Jingle Bells' to 'The Saints Come Marching In' to the Greek 'Siratiki' to the Can-Can and Arab songs. Everyone danced – the ladies, the children and the several husbands who had dropped in during their lunch hour. At one point we all formed a conga line and snaked around the room, and the children showered us with confetti. One of Mother's beautiful Arab students, dressed in an elaborately embroidered kaftan, got up and danced seductively to a catchy Arab tune. When Abu Mohammed joined her, wiggling his hips, lifting his arms and snapping his fingers, everyone clapped wildly. 'Happy Birthday' was played and sung, to the best of my count, thirty-two times.

With great feeling I recited a poem I had composed on the plane, celebrating Mother's life, and, when I said, 'Here you are at eighty-six, full of wisdom and many tricks,' I got a big hand and a bravo from the group.

The guests helped themselves to the salmon and caviar canapés, the sweet and salty wafers and pistachios, and drank everything from tea, coffee, Coca-Cola and orange pop to whisky and champagne. At one o'clock sharp, a full luncheon was served – grilled lamb with mounds of rice pilav, an array of various vegetables and salads, and an Arab dessert of clotted cream and honey. There was no room left for the birthday cakes!

Mother, overjoyed with the profusion of love, appreciation and attention she was getting, rose, raised her arms to the sky and said, 'Thank you. Thank you all. I am so happy. So happy! I am not here any more. I am up there with the stars, and you are all with me. So we are all together rotating with the stars.'

Mother died on 5 September 1991, three months before her ninetieth birthday, the last of her generation. The year before she had held two large retrospective exhibitions, one in Aachen, Germany, at the Peter Ludwig Museum, and the other in Paris at the Institut du Monde Arabe, both of which she attended in a wheelchair. King Hussein gave her a state funeral, and she is buried next to Emir Zeid in the little mausoleum in the royal cemetery where the birds twitter continuously.

Epilogue

Although I live and work in the United States, I return as often as I can to Istanbul, which now is a big, bustling metropolis of some 11 million people as a result of the constant influx from the countryside, a far cry from the half-million residents at the time of my birth. I return to have a cup of tea under an elm tree at a waterfront café, to purchase a *simit* from a street vendor and sink my teeth into its crisp, sesame-seeded crust, and to see the sunset over the Golden Horn that sets ablaze the windows of the houses on the Asiatic shore.

Of course, each time I visit Büyükada, which one can now reach by *motorscaffe* in twenty minutes. The Shakir Pasha property has been developed into two-storey condominiums and our big house cut up into tiny, crooked flats. Cousins Nermidil and Erdem have built two small adjoining homes on the site of Aunt Ayşe's old house, which was directly on the water and where we used to swim off her dock. But as public policy now decrees that the seashore belongs to the people, the waterfront has been filled in, and a little park and a road separate the houses from the sea. It does not really matter, for the Marmara Sea is so polluted that one can rarely swim in it any more. The mainland opposite Büyükada used to be pitch-dark at night. Now its hills are covered with a million lights from the thousands of houses built for the burgeoning population.

I never fail to take a tour of the island by carriage. Thank God, that is one thing that has not changed; motor vehicles are still prohibited. As the horses clip-clop, clip-clop along the road, through the dancing tassels of the awning I catch glimpses of familiar vistas, the pine groves, the turquoise bays and the blue Marmara. And now I can ride on a street which has been named after my grandfather.

Normally I climb up to the little cemetery on the hill, which has now become a forest of helter-skelter, overcrowded tombstones, one nestled against the other. As I look for my family's graves half enmeshed in the tangled foliage, the loss I feel is so poignant that tears come. On the graves of Grandfather, Grandmother and her brothers, Uncle Emin and Aunt Hakiye, Uncle Ahmet and Aunt Ayşe, Uncle Charles and Aunt Aliye I place roses and recall with longing the togetherness we once enjoyed many years ago in the house on the island.

I throw a handful of jasmines into the sky and walk toward the iron gate.